Improving the Psychological Wellbeing
of Children and Young People

of related interest

A Multidisciplinary Handbook of Child and Adolescent Mental
Health for Front-line Professionals, Third Edition
Nisha Dogra, Andrew Parkin, Fiona Warner-Gale and Clay Frake
ISBN 978 1 78592 052 3
eISBN 978 1 78450 309 3

DBT Therapeutic Activity Ideas for Working with Teens
Skills and Exercises for Working with Clients with Borderline Personality
Disorder, Depression, Anxiety, and Other Emotional Sensitivities
Carol Lozier
ISBN 978 1 78592 785 0
eISBN 978 1 78450 718 3

Supporting Toddlers' Wellbeing in Early Years Settings
Strategies and Tools for Practitioners and Teachers
Edited by Helen Sutherland and Yasmin Mukadam
ISBN 978 1 78592 262 6
eISBN 978 1 78450 552 3

Supporting the Mental Health of Children in Care
Evidence-Based Practice
Edited by Jeune Guishard-Pine OBE, Gail Coleman-Oluwabusola and Suzanne McCall
Foreword by Jenny Pearce OBE
ISBN 978 1 84905 668 7
eISBN 978 1 78450 172 3

Promoting Child and Parent Wellbeing
How to Use Evidence- and Strengths-Based Strategies in Practice
Carole Sutton
ISBN 978 1 84905 572 7
eISBN 978 1 78450 015 3

Improving the Psychological Wellbeing of Children and Young People

Effective Prevention and Early Intervention Across Health, Education and Social Care

Edited by JULIA FAULCONBRIDGE, KATIE HUNT AND AMANDA LAFFAN

Foreword by Sarah Brennan

Jessica Kingsley *Publishers*
London and Philadelphia

First published in 2019
by Jessica Kingsley Publishers
73 Collier Street
London N1 9BE, UK
and
400 Market Street, Suite 400
Philadelphia, PA 19106, USA

www.jkp.com

Library of Congress Cataloging in Publication Data
A CIP catalog record for this book is available from the Library of Congress

British Library Cataloguing in Publication Data
A CIP catalogue record for this book is available from the British Library

ISBN 978 1 78592 219 0
eISBN 978 1 78450 496 0

Printed and bound in Great Britain

MIX
Paper from
responsible sources
FSC
www.fsc.org   FSC® C013056

*To our families and colleagues for their support;
and the children, young people and families we have
worked with and from whom we have learned so much.*

Contents

Tables and figures

Foreword

The authors here have achieved a scope and breadth in this book that is to be applauded. It is both ground breaking and refreshing. The book brings together research and practice to positively construct a comprehensive vision for children and young people's mental health and psychological wellbeing by placing it clearly within the framework of family, community and the social and economic factors that affect them. The authors have taken the research and applied it to their own experience and practice to create a very practical and thorough exploration of how we can create a society which truly grows psychologically healthy and resilient children, young people and thus adults in future.

Importantly they define frequently used terms which, too often, mean different things to different people. So misunderstandings are clarified; confusion is brushed away. Thus concepts like 'resilience', 'ecological', 'holistic', 'systems approach' are defined and then the evidence is explored to appreciate how they may help in the creation of a new mind set and approach where everyone knows what their crucial contribution is.

Locating mental health clearly within the ecological system of healthy development from before birth enables us to think and plan about mental health in its literal sense of 'health', rather than the assumption of 'illness'. Health promotion is widely accepted in physical health but is still nascent in mental health.

There is no doubt that embedding the development and management of our mental health and psychological wellbeing into the way society operates is a huge challenge – that's why this book is brilliant. For the first time, we have here some ideas and practical examples of how we might achieve this. Treatment is part of the holistic approach, but again the authors place treatment within the ecology of the system around the child, and argue convincingly that by understanding and working in this way we will properly begin to address the mental health issues of our young people today.

By recognising that we all have a responsibility to understand better how to support the healthy development of psychological wellbeing of our children, and how we support those most directly involved like parents and families we will address the crisis we are currently facing for children and young people.

Providing practice examples makes this a very readable book that anyone can relate to, and enables the reader to see how the research and ideas can play out in practice.

From my work at YoungMinds, I know only too well how those people around a child or young person in mental distress most often feel guilty and desperate – whether they are parents, other family members, teachers, friends – and they don't know what to do to help. They too need to be able to understand and be supported. So, here there is an opportunity to understand better. Each aspect of the ecological system is explored in detail, along with the inter-relationships and practice examples to give us encouragement and a path for future improvement.

Sarah Brennan
Freelance consultant and former
Chief Executive of Young Minds Trust

About this book

This book aims to stimulate debate about what it would mean to have a model of child services that truly pays attention to helping the next generation to grow up to have greater psychological wellbeing and be more resilient, rather than directing the majority of resources to trying to help after things have gone wrong. We are not just looking to prevent mental health problems, but at what would promote positive child development. It is not a handbook on child rearing but about the necessary conditions in our society that would enable more families to be able to care well for their children. Following a broad introduction to the field, there are a set of chapters looking at the research and practice-based evidence for primary prevention, mental health promotion and early intervention across all the key areas of work with children, young people and families. All the chapters include case histories and a wealth of practical information. The final chapter lays out some principles for the development of holistic, integrated and effective models of child services.

Note on language

There is debate around how best to describe some of the experiences discussed in this book. The use of diagnostic and medical language is often considered problematic in psychological services, and we have tried to use non-medical language in as much of this publication as possible. There are some instances, however, when we have used medical language (such as when discussing other published work which has used a medical framework). Using these terms does not mean that we support medical explanations of mental health difficulties in children and young people. For further information, please see:

British Psychological Society (BPS), Division of Clinical Psychology (2013) *Classification of Behaviour and Experience in Relation to Functional Psychiatric Diagnoses: Time for a Paradigm Shift.* Leicester: BPS.

British Psychological Society (BPS), Division of Clinical Psychology (2015) *Guidelines on Language in Relation to Functional Psychiatric Diagnosis.* Leicester: BPS.

Chapter 1

Risk factors, protective factors and resilience

How we can nurture psychological wellbeing in children and young people

JULIA FAULCONBRIDGE, KATIE HUNT, AMANDA LAFFAN,
IYABO FATIMILEHIN AND DUNCAN LAW

We have learned a great deal, over recent decades, about what is harmful to the psychological wellbeing of children and young people, and have a better understanding of what affects their mental and physical health. We are also learning more about the positive factors which enable children to grow up well, to cope and sometimes even flourish, despite significant adversity. The challenge is to use this knowledge to develop ways to both prevent children from suffering serious harm and harness the protective factors that contribute to resilience. There are positive examples of such interventions, based on the research evidence and with proven efficacy, but this field of applied psychological intervention remains underdeveloped and is fertile ground for new approaches.

In this chapter, we endeavour to look at child mental health and psychological wellbeing from the opposite perspective to that often employed. Rather than focus on what to do when serious problems arise, we will consider what we can do, as a society, to raise children to be psychologically healthy and resilient people, able to enjoy productive lives and manage the difficulties and challenges which will inevitably occur.

Prevalence of mental health problems
in children and young people

There are many difficulties in assessing the levels of psychological distress in children and young people. Large-scale population studies are expensive and inevitably 'broad brush' in their approach, lacking detail at the level of the individual. More focused approaches tend to be snapshots in time and lose the insights gained from longitudinal studies of the same children over time. The majority also use psychiatric diagnostic criteria to identify subjects, thus missing large numbers of children whose difficulties do not fit a label (see Hagel and Maughan 2017).

The last systematic study of the prevalence of mental health problems in the UK (Green *et al.* 2005) estimated that at any given time point, at least 10 per cent of children aged between 5 and 16 years have a diagnosable mental health condition. A report on a similar study is due to be published in 2018. The figures are significantly higher in some groups of children:

- Children in the social care and criminal justice systems.

- Children with chronic or serious physical health problems and disabilities.

- Children who have neurodevelopmental or learning difficulties.

- Children living in poverty.

A report for the Centre for Mental Health by Gutman *et al.* (2015), *Children of the New Century: Mental Health Findings from the Millennium Cohort Study*, looked at the mental health of 11-year-olds in the UK. This study has been following the same cohort of children since 2000, using the Strengths and Difficulties Questionnaire (SDQ; Goodman 1997). The headline findings were as follows:

- Approximately 10 per cent of parents and 8 per cent of teachers rated children as having significant problems.

- The overall incidence was similar to the surveys in 1999 and 2004.

- Children from families with the lowest incomes were four times more likely to have psychological difficulties than those from higher earning backgrounds.

- Those not living with natural parents were at higher risk of problems.

- There were geographical differences; children in Scotland were significantly less likely to have problems with hyperactivity or their peer group.

- At age 11, boys were twice as likely to be showing problems as girls, particularly with behaviour.

Murphy and Fonagy (2012) report that around 50 per cent of lifelong mental health problems develop before 14 years, and 75 per cent before 25 years. Other studies, such as The Children's Society (2008), indicate that only 25–40 per cent of children with mental health problems receive any specialist help, despite evidence for interventions that are both clinically and cost effective.

Other researchers have looked at children's subjective accounts from a wellbeing perspective. The Children's Society has pioneered this approach in the UK using its Good Childhood Index. The *Good Childhood Report* (2017), which studied 8000 children aged 14–15 years, highlighted a decrease in children's reported happiness with friends and with life in general between 2009 and 2015, in contrast to steady improvement from 2000 to 2008. There was a gradual increase in happiness in the area of schoolwork. Girls were less happy than boys in general, specifically in the fields of friends, appearance and their lives. Boys were less happy in the field of schoolwork.

The report considers the impact of disadvantage on children's wellbeing. It looked at 23 potential areas of disadvantage, grouped into:

- parent–child relationship, for example neglect

- family/household, for example domestic violence, parental illness

- material, for example overcrowding, homelessness

- neighbourhood, for example safety.

The study found that 84 per cent had at least one, 53 per cent had three or more, and 18 per cent had more than seven areas of disadvantage in their lives, with a cumulative negative effect on wellbeing with increasing experiences of disadvantage.

Both the United Nations Children's Fund (UNICEF) and the Organisation for Economic Co-operation and Development (OECD) have developed comprehensive measures of childhood wellbeing and have ranked countries on these measures over recent years. The UK rarely comes above the midpoint of such international comparison tables and is frequently found in the lowest third on a range of measures. As an example, the OECD Child Wellbeing Data Portal for 2017 shows the UK in the top third of countries on only two measures out of 23 (adolescents talking to parents before or after school, and those having books for schoolwork at home) and in the bottom third on 12 measures, including adolescent subjective wellbeing. The Varkey Foundation, in a report, *Generation Z: Global Citizenship Survey* (2017), ranked the UK next to bottom of 20 countries for wellbeing. The Children's Commissioner's report on vulnerability (2017) similarly discusses how a large number of children are in vulnerable situations, such as living with adults who require treatment for alcohol or drug misuse, being involved in gangs, and being victims of slavery. Compared with many countries in the developed world, we are not doing well.

Raising psychologically healthy children

There are many descriptions of what a psychologically healthy child is. An authoritative example comes from the World Health Organization (WHO 2005) which states that good mental health in children and young people:

> includes a sense of identity and self-worth; sound family and peer relationships; an ability to be productive and to learn; and a capacity to use developmental challenges and cultural resources to maximize development… Good mental health in childhood is a prerequisite for optimal psychological development, productive social relationships, effective learning, an ability to care for self, good physical health and effective economic participation as adults. (p.7)

The question that needs to be addressed is: how do children and young people get to be like that? Most people accept that we need to look at a child's development and potential in relation to the context in which they are born and are raised, an approach usually referred to as 'ecological'. Perhaps the most significant early proponent of this idea was Bronfenbrenner in his 1979 book, *The Ecology of Human Development: Experiments by Nature and Design.*

Bronfenbrenner described child development as occurring within a set of nested systems, usually represented diagrammatically as a set of concentric circles, starting at the individual child and moving outwards into the wider society:

- The *microsystem* refers to the institutions and groups that most immediately and directly impact on the child's development including family, school, peers, religious institutions, neighbourhood and health services.

- The *mesosystem* consists of the interconnections between the microsystems, for example the interactions between the family and teachers.

- The *exosystem* describes the wider social factors in which the child does not have an active role (such as mass media, local politics and industry, and social services) but which influence the child's immediate context. An example of this would be a parent working long, stressful hours and therefore being relatively unavailable to their child.

- The *macrosystem* describes the culture and the wider society in which the child and their family live.

Bronfenbrenner later refined his theory to include the *chronosystem,* which describes change over time.

Like many later theorists, Bronfenbrenner saw the inner ring, the microsystem, as having the strongest influence on a child's development, with decreasing influence going out through the rings. A criticism of the model is that it fails to recognise how all parts of the child's ecological system are influenced by the outermost rings: the society and political culture in which they live. Proximal factors, like family and friends, are close to us and therefore more visible. The social and economic factors in society are distal factors which act on us through others, and their influence is often hidden. We can say good parenting is a positive influence on a child, but what enables a parent to be a good one? David Smail discussed this way of understanding the social space and the impact on psychological wellbeing and mental health in detail in his book, *Power, Interest and Psychology – Elements of a Social Materialist Understanding of Distress* (2005).

We can use poverty as an example. Many studies have demonstrated the correlation between living in relative poverty in a given society and poorer mental health in both adults and children. Gershoff, Aber and Raver (2003) identified three pathways by which poverty exerts this impact on children:

- Parental investment – how poverty affects the quality of the home environment that parents can provide, the activities they can afford for their children, and so on.

- Parental behaviour and stress – how the stress of living in poverty leads to parents having insufficient psychological resources to care for their children through high levels of depression and parental conflict.

- The impoverished local communities in which families are living, with lack of facilities and opportunities.

Gershoff *et al.* (2007) developed this further and looked at the effects of material hardship as well as low family income. Their research indicates that family income is most strongly correlated with cognitive development and academic achievement in children. They argue that improving academic performance is best achieved by increasing family income and, thus, parental investment. However, it was material hardship that was more strongly correlated with impaired social and emotional development and consequent behaviour problems. They argue that ameliorating hardship and, in turn, parental stress, would have the greatest impact on behaviour.

Cornerstones of raising psychologically healthy children

Within this discussion there must be recognition of the individual challenges posed for some children and families due to health problems, disabilities, etc. These require additional measures as they alter the developmental trajectory of the child and create different demands for their families. The aim is to enable the child to develop as well as possible, given their individual circumstances.

In order to understand what enables children to grow up to be psychologically healthy, we need to consider what is happening at a number of levels.

At a societal level, child and family friendly policies which address:

- levels of poverty and social inequality
- employment, including hours of work, security and pay levels
- benefits
- housing
- education and early years provision
- discrimination and human rights
- health provision
- social care provision.

At a community level:

- schools which support personal and social development, as well as learning
- opportunities for outdoor play and exploration
- safe streets
- freedom from threat of crime and violence
- affordable, accessible facilities like libraries, play areas, leisure, arts and sports venues
- cohesive, supportive communities
- support for parents who may struggle at times to provide good quality parenting.

At an interpersonal/social environment level:

- development of positive peer group relationships
- development of good relationships with adults outside the family, including teachers
- protection from bullying, victimisation and exploitation
- enabling of the development of positive self-esteem, and a sense of self-efficacy.

At a family level, providing an environment in which a child can:

- develop positive, secure attachments to adult caregivers

- thrive, even with constraints that may be imposed by physical health, neurodevelopmental conditions, and so on.

- feel safe and secure

- develop autonomy appropriate for their age and developmental level

- feel loved and accepted for who they are.

These issues will be explored in greater depth throughout this book.

'Attachment' is an important concept and is discussed throughout this book. It describes a certain quality of the relationship between two people, usually a child and caregiver. Different attachment styles lead to different behaviours, emotions, and ways of relating to other people, as well as to the development of views about the self, the world and others. Attachment Theory originated with the work of Bowlby in the 1950s (Bowlby 1969, 1973, 1980), and typically categorises people as having one of four attachment styles:

- Secure – a child feels loved and protected by their caregiver(s), they know they can depend on them, even when left for a period of time.

- Anxious-ambivalent – a child feels very anxious when left by their caregiver(s), and does not feel safe or reassured when they return.

- Anxious-avoidant – a child finds it difficult to rely on their caregiver(s) and avoids interacting with them.

- Disorganised – a child feels fearful and is not sure how they can get their needs met by their caregiver(s), so their behaviour can seem inconsistent, for example seeking closeness but then pulling away.

A child's attachment style develops over time in response to the nature and quality of their experiences with their caregiver(s). If, for example, a child experiences consistent, sensitive responses from their caregiver(s), they are more likely to develop a secure attachment. Secure attachments support mental processes that enable the child to regulate emotions, reduce fear, attune to others, have self-understanding and insight, empathy for others and appropriate moral reasoning (Bowlby called these mental representations 'the internal working model'). Insecure attachments can have unfortunate consequences. If a child cannot rely on an adult to respond to their needs in times of stress, they are unable to learn how to soothe themselves, manage their emotions and engage in reciprocal relationships.

Discussions of the importance of secure attachments are to be found throughout the book but the more detailed information is to be found in Chapters 2 and 3. For further reading on attachment see Gerhardt (2004) and Music (2011).

Risk factors for psychological difficulties

In discussing risk factors, it is essential to note that these operate at a population level and are not deterministic of an individual's development. The research shows that the presence of a risk factor increases the likelihood of a child having psychological difficulties, but not whether they will have these and, if so, what sort of difficulties.

The World Health Organization (2012) outlines a number of risk factors which may contribute to the development of psychological difficulties, grouped into three broad areas:

- Environmental factors: like injustice, discrimination and exposure to trauma.

- Social factors: like loneliness, bereavement and neglect.

- Individual factors: like cognitive/emotional immaturity and medical illness.

Examples of environmental risk factors
Poverty and social inequality

Townsend (1979) defined child poverty as 'lacking the resources to obtain the types of diets, participate in the activities and have the living conditions and amenities that are customary – in the societies to which they belong' (p.31). It is important to note that this is not just about meeting a child's basic needs, but about them being able to participate in the community and with their peers.

Relative income poverty is formally defined as living at 60 per cent below the household median, and in 2014–15, 28 per cent of children were deemed to be living in poverty in the UK – 3.9 million children. Research evidence brings these figures to life:

- The Department of Health published research in 1999 showing that children in the poorest households had three times more mental health problems than those in the best-off households.

- The National Child Development Study data gathered between 1958 and 2008 found that children from the poorest families were four times more likely to show psychological problems than those in the richest (Centre for Longitudinal Studies 2015).

It is often assumed that it is externalising problems like anti-social behaviour that are higher in poorer areas, but the figures were the same for internalising problems like anxiety and depression (Centre for Longitudinal Studies 2015). This is obviously of concern given the impact of austerity and benefit cuts since 2008, which have significantly increased the numbers of children living in poverty in the UK.

The ways that poverty impacts on the physical health of a population have been well documented. Michael Marmot has been an influential figure in the research in this area in the UK and documents a personal view of the history of the topic (Marmot 2001). Marmot and his team produced a broad-ranging report in 2010, *Fair Society, Healthy Lives*. They found average life expectancy in the poorest communities was seven times lower than in the wealthiest, and disability-free life expectancy was 17 years lower. The report argues that:

Reducing health inequalities will require action on six policy objectives:

- Give every child the best start in life

- Enable all children young people and adults to maximise their capabilities and have control over their lives

- Create fair employment and good work for all

- Ensure healthy standard of living for all

- Create and develop healthy and sustainable places and communities

- Strengthen the role and impact of ill health prevention.

(Marmot Review 2010, p.15)

The complexities of the relationships between health outcomes and social conditions are illustrated by the report on the 'Glasgow Effect' (Walsh *et al.* 2016). Scotland, and particularly Glasgow, experiences high levels of 'excess' mortality compared with other major UK cities with similar levels of deprivation and de-industrialisation. The causes of death are wide ranging, impact across all social classes (though most on the poorest) and are highest in those of younger working age. They are particularly influenced by death rates from alcohol, drugs and suicide – all significant indicators of mental health problems. The research has highlighted a number of contributory contextual factors:

- Historically high levels of deprivation.

- Large post-war slum clearances, poor quality council house estates, more high-rise developments, low investment in repairs and maintenance.

- Relocation of industry and the more skilled workers and their families to new towns.

- Inner city gentrification and commercial development, exacerbating damaging impacts on an already vulnerable population.

- Inadequate measurement of poverty and deprivation that failed to recognise the impact of a negative physical environment and low educational attainment.

A report by David Ayre for The Children's Society (Ayre 2016), which combined both a literature review and new research, discusses the following in terms of their negative impact on the mental and physical health of parents and children:

- lack of work and poorly paid work

- benefits

- household debt

- poor housing

- disadvantaged communities.

The Children's Society also established a Children's Commission on Poverty, which enabled a group of young people to investigate and report on the impact poverty was having, particularly on their education. The report, *At What Cost: Exposing the Impact of Poverty on School Life* (The Children's Society 2014), describes the impact from the viewpoint of the young people with personal stories about how it feels to grow up in a poor household, with recommendations about what needs to be done.

Research evidence strongly indicates that reducing levels of child poverty would have a significant positive impact on the psychological wellbeing and the risks of mental health problems in children and their families. It can be done: UK government figures show that child poverty reduced dramatically between 1998/99 and 2011/12 when 800,000 children were lifted out of poverty. However, that trend has since been reversed and, as a direct result of tax and benefit decisions since 2010, the Institute of Fiscal Studies projects that the numbers of children growing up in poverty will rise from 2.3 to 3.6 million by 2020.

Discrimination and racism

The Equality Act (2010) sets out definitions of discrimination, with direct discrimination referring to people being treated less favourably than others, while indirect discrimination is related to putting rules or arrangements in place that apply to everyone but put someone with a protected characteristic (e.g., race, sexuality, gender) at an unfair disadvantage. This is also consistent with the process of institutional racism, which is:

> The collective failure of an organisation to provide an appropriate and professional service to people because of their colour, culture or ethnic origin. It can be seen or detected in processes, attitudes and behaviour which amount to discrimination through unwitting prejudice, ignorance, thoughtlessness and racist stereotyping which disadvantage minority ethnic people. (MacPherson 1999, p.369)

International data and research findings over several decades provide strong evidence that discrimination (both direct and indirect) is experienced by many black and minority ethnic (BME) people on the basis of their race and/or ethnicity, and this has a significant and detrimental impact on their emotional wellbeing (Alleyne 2009; Carter 2007; Malek 2004; Patel and Fatimilehin 1999; Priest *et al.* 2014). Direct discrimination includes racial harassment and violence, as well as being treated unfairly or disrespectfully on the basis of one's race or ethnicity (e.g., by shopkeepers, receptionists).

- Between 2013/14 and 2014/15, the number of racially motivated hate crimes increased by 15 per cent to 42,930 offences and the number of religious hate crimes increased by 43 per cent (EHRC 2016).

- Racist bullying in schools increased by 69 per cent between 2012/13 and 2014 in the UK, and is a particular risk for black and minority ethnic pupils (EHRC 2016).

Priest *et al.* (2013) published a systematic review of 121 studies of young people from a range of BME backgrounds, and found statistically significant associations between racial discrimination and mental health outcomes (e.g., depression, anxiety, psychological distress). A growing body of research evidence is demonstrating strong associations between maternal experiences of direct racial discrimination, maternal perinatal mental health and adverse children's outcomes (Becares and Atatoa-Carr 2016; Kelly, Becares and Nazroo 2012). More specifically, mothers' experiences of interpersonal racism and levels of racism in the residential area were associated with social and emotional difficulties in children (measured using the Strengths and Difficulties Questionnaire), spatial ability and non-verbal ability (measured using the British Ability Scales). Thus, the impact of direct racial discrimination is not limited to the immediate victim but influences their relationships with others and has a detrimental impact on parental sensitivity and parenting practices (Kelly *et al.* 2012; Kim *et al.* 2018).

Research and statistical data over several decades has consistently demonstrated the impact of indirect discrimination and institutional racism in areas such as education, employment, mental health services, social care and the criminal justice system. Deprivation and poverty disproportionately affect people from some racial and ethnic groups:

- People from Bangladeshi and Pakistani ethnic groups are more likely to live in deprived neighbourhoods than any other ethnic group (Department for Work and Pensions 2015).

- Seventy per cent of Bangladeshi pupils and almost 60 per cent of Pakistani and Black African pupils live in the 20 per cent most deprived postcode areas compared with 20 per cent of White British pupils (DfES 2006).

The research into education also shows disparities such that people from some ethnic groups are less likely to achieve in the education system than others:

- In England and Wales, Gypsy/Roma, Irish Travellers and Black Caribbean pupils have the lowest attainment in schools (EHRC 2016).

- Black Caribbean and Mixed White/Caribbean children have rates of exclusion from school that are about three times higher than those for all pupils (EHRC 2016).

- A Black Caribbean boy is 37 times more likely to be excluded from school than a girl of Indian origin (Sunak and Rajeswaran 2014).

Similar patterns are found in employment:

- Men from all minority ethnic groups are less likely to be employed than White men, and full-time employment of White men is 72 per cent compared with 35 per cent for Bangladeshi men (Department for Work and Pensions 2015).

However, patterns of employment are not necessarily linked to educational attainment as people from some minority ethnic groups (e.g., Chinese, Indian, Black African) are more likely than White British people to have degree level qualifications. Gender and socio-economic status (SES) are also important variables to consider because research has shown that low SES White British boys and girls, and low SES Black Caribbean boys are the lowest achieving groups (Strand 2014a, 2014b). Furthermore, high SES Black Caribbean boys underachieve in comparison with average and high SES White British boys (Strand 2014a, 2014b). Thus, the links between ethnicity, discrimination and poverty are complex, with some ethnic groups being more likely to experience marginalisation than others.

Discrimination is also evident in the provision of mental health and social care services and in the criminal justice system:

- People who identify themselves as Black (or Black British) are almost three times as likely to be arrested as White people (Ministry of Justice 2015).

- The most common outcome for White and Mixed ethnic group offenders is a community sentence; the most common sentence for Black, Asian and Chinese offenders is immediate custody (Ministry of Justice 2013).

- Over 60 per cent of inpatients from Mixed White and Black African, Caribbean, and Any Other Black backgrounds are subject to detention under the Mental Health Act compared with less than 40 per cent of White British inpatients (Thompson 2013).

- Children from Black, Black British and Mixed ethnic groups are over-represented in the looked-after population and comprise 16 per cent compared with approximately 9 per cent of the population of England (Zayed and Harker 2015).

However, research has consistently shown that people from minority ethnic groups are under-represented in primary care and early intervention services and over-represented in more coercive forms of intervention.

Bronfenbrenner's ecological systems theory is a useful approach to conceptualising the influence of direct and indirect discrimination on the emotional and psychological wellbeing of children (Bronfenbrenner 1994). At the levels of the micro- and mesosystem, there is the influence of direct discrimination from peers and adults that the child is in contact with; whether this is at home, in their school or in the community that they live in. The exosystem can influence the child's development indirectly by impacting on the people that the child lives with, and the macrosystem influences the overarching culture, customs and beliefs. Discrimination and racism do not just affect individuals; the impact is on whole communities and the contexts in which children develop. Furthermore, the experience of discrimination is not episodic but cumulative and undermines emotional health through feelings of anger, depression and a sense of powerlessness due to a limited ability to control external realities (Carter 2007; Priest *et al.* 2013, 2014). The ability to realise a positive sense of identity can also be undermined and lead to internalised racism and a belief in the inferiority of people from one's own ethnic background (Fatimilehin 1999; Patel and Fatimilehin 1999).

Intersectionality

Kimberlé Crenshaw first used the term 'intersectionality' in a paper in 1989 in which she described how discrimination against women and black people are two powerful, separate but interconnecting axes of impact in the US legal system. The concept is grounded in feminist theory and has become widely used in analyses of the overlapping systems of oppression and discrimination that women face, based not just on gender but on ethnicity, sexuality, economic background and a number of other axes. It is, of course, also applicable to men as it is attempting to describe how these elements are not separate but interwoven in a complex manner in the creation of personal identity and social and economic circumstances. For further discussion see the TED talk given by Crenshaw and Dobson in 2014.

Trauma and maltreatment

There is an ever-growing evidence base exploring the impact of trauma and maltreatment on child development, psychological wellbeing and the incidence of mental health problems, often of the most serious kind. Much is gathered together under a heading of 'adverse childhood experiences' (ACEs), where child maltreatment and related experiences are considered as a set of exposures that have broad implications for human development and health problems (Anda *et al.* 2010). The original research was based on a large US study (Felitti *et al.* 1998), and initial studies defined ACEs in terms of childhood abuse (emotional, physical, sexual), neglect (physical and emotional) and household challenges (substance abuse, mental illness, domestic violence, parental separation, family member in prison). More recent research has been extended to include more diverse groups and cultures and includes forced marriage, witnessing criminal and collective community violence (Lee, Larkin and Esaki 2017) and early conscription, and includes ACEs due to other children (e.g., bullying, peer-to-peer violence, sibling physical and emotional violence) (Anda *et al.* 2010).

The thrust of the research on ACEs strongly suggests that adverse childhood experiences have wide-ranging effects on a child's emotional, psychological, behavioural and interpersonal functioning and are linked to a large number of negative health outcomes, including:

- post-traumatic stress

- early death

- increased use of psychotropic medication

- suicide attempts

- substance misuse

- autoimmune disease

- cancer

- smoking

- obesity

- adult depression

- sleep disturbance

- risky sexual behaviour

- teenage pregnancy and foetal death

- involvement in violent crime (Crooks *et al.* 2007; Elklit 2002; Thornberry *et al.* 2010).

Despite the methodological difficulties inherent in research that relies on retrospective reports of events many years in the past (Colman *et al.* 2016; Reuben *et al.* 2016), the findings of studies that have looked at the effect of ACEs on later life are undeniably powerful.

It may be that it is the way in which a child's environment differs from what is expected (e.g., *inadequate input* such as neglect and deprivation, as opposed to *harmful input* such as threat, abuse and exposure to violence) that leads us to a better understanding of the mechanisms of risk in relation to future functioning (Humphreys and Zeanah 2015; McLaughlin, Sheridan and Lambert 2014). The advantage of this kind of approach is that it may lead to more tailored prevention and intervention for children living in less than optimal environments.

Trauma can be due to a single unforeseen incident, like being in a road traffic accident or being caught up in a terrorist incident. However, there are significant groups of children and young people for whom the experience of trauma and maltreatment has been the norm. These would include:

- looked-after children

- refugees and asylum-seekers

- trafficked young people

- victims of child sexual exploitation.

Examples of social risk factors
Family relationships
Everyone who works with children in difficulty will be aware of the importance of relationships within the family to a child's psychological development and wellbeing, and work with families is a key area of child mental health services. The research evidence presented throughout this book also illustrates this, but one example is the BELLA study, the mental health module of KiGGS, the German National Health Interview and Examination Survey among Children and Adolescents, commissioned by the Federal Ministry of Health, where mental health problems and their assumed determinants were examined in a representative sub-sample of 2863 families with children and adolescents aged 7–17. It was found that adverse family climate stood out particularly as a negative contributor to children's mental health (Wille *et al.* 2008).

Parental conflict
Harold *et al.* (2016) reviewed the evidence for the impact of parental conflict on children and young people and the effectiveness of interventions. They argue that the quality of the interparental relationship, specifically how parents communicate and relate to each other, is a *primary* influence on effective parenting practices and children's long-term mental health and future life chances, and that the couple relationship is an important site for early intervention.

This has implications for a wide range of policy areas, from effective approaches to child mental health to managing child behaviours. In particular, it is important that policy makers and commissioners consider interventions and support for both the couple and the parenting relationships. Just targeting the parent–child relationship in the context of ongoing interparental conflict does not lead to sustained positive outcomes for children.

Social isolation and bullying

Despite significant steps in increasing awareness of the impact of bullying in schools and models to help reduce it, it is still a common experience and out-of-school bullying is even harder to deal with. As an example of the frequency of these experiences, the Department for Education's Longitudinal Study of Young People in England in 2014 found that among Year 10 pupils:

- 22 per cent had suffered name-calling

- 15 per cent had suffered social exclusion

- 10 per cent had been victims of violence and 14 per cent had been threatened with violence.

Girls, young people from ethnic minorities and those with special educational needs or disabilities were all more likely to experience bullying, although the survey was able to report an overall reduction since 2005 (Lasher and Baker 2015).

Lesbian, gay, bi and trans (LGBT) young people are also at higher risk of being bullied. *School Report*, produced in 2017 by Stonewall and the University of Cambridge Centre for Family Research, was a study of over 3,700 LGBT pupils across Britain. Whilst they found that the number being bullied because of their sexual orientation had fallen by almost a third since 2007, overall nearly half of LGBT young people were still bullied at school for being LGBT. This was even more prevalent in some groups like trans pupils and those receiving free school meals (Bradlow et al 2017).

Children who feel rejected by their peers can be left feeling isolated and lonely, and may experience a range of mental health difficulties (Asher, Hymel and Renshaw 1984; Lereya *et al.* 2015). Being socially isolated also means that a young person cannot turn to those around them for advice and support, and so has fewer resources to help them deal with difficulties in their lives.

Being bullied, including online bullying, is correlated with a range of negative effects, including:

- symptoms of post traumatic stress (Nielsen *et al.* 2015)

- suicidal thoughts or behaviours (Kim and Levanthal 2008)

- self-harming behaviours (Arseneault, Bowes and Shakoor 2010)

- 'psychotic' experiences (Thornberry *et al.* 2010; Van Dam *et al.* 2012).

This is discussed in more detail in Chapter 5.

Bereavement and loss

Bereavement is an experience that many children face, whether it's of family, peers or pets. Feelings of loss and grief are natural reactions to losing someone and, usually, these ease over time and with the support of friends and family. However, for some children these feelings can be overwhelming for a lengthy period of time, leading to difficulties in moving on with their lives. For example, the death of parent has been found to be a significant risk factor for later depression in a number of studies, and the death of a parent or sibling was found in one study (Stikkelbroek *et al.* 2015) to lead to mental health difficulties in around 25 per cent of bereaved children.

Examples of individual risk factors

Learning disabilities

Learning disabilities relate to intellectual abilities at a certain level below the mean (average) and associated impairment in social and everyday functioning, with an onset early in life. For some children, there is a known reason for their intellectual difficulties, including different genetic conditions which may be recognised soon after birth (such as Down syndrome) whereas for other children, the recognition of difficulties may come later when a child does not meet typical developmental milestones. We increasingly understand that children with learning disabilities may be at increased risk of developing emotional and behavioural difficulties, but this is seen as being more related to exposure to social exclusion and poverty rather than as a feature of having learning disabilities per se (Emerson and Hatton 2007).

Neurodevelopmental difficulties

Neurodevelopmental difficulties are thought to have their origins very early in life. They are associated with factors including genetics, the gestational and perinatal environment and experiences, family factors, wider environmental factors, as well as events that may have happened in a child's brain (Bishop and Rutter 2004; Pennington 2009). Neurodevelopmental difficulties include the following: autism, attention deficit disorders, foetal alcohol spectrum disorders, Tourette's syndrome, and dyspraxia. For children with neurodevelopmental difficulties or differences it is important to note that even children who might share a diagnostic label may have different areas of difficulty and different underlying risk factors. Children who have been exposed to significant environmental challenges, including maternal alcohol and drug misuse, may be at particular risk. Evidence suggests that children with neurodevelopmental difficulties are at increased risk of psychological difficulties, predominantly anxiety (e.g., Bellini 2004; de Bruin *et al.* 2007).

Children born prematurely and children who experience significant birth difficulties

Survival rates for children born prematurely are improving and these children have an increased risk of lifelong difficulties with, for example, cognition, vision, and medical complications (e.g., Lundequist, Bohm and Smedler 2013). For other children, following medical complications around the time of birth there is an increased risk of difficulties which only fully evolve many years later; for both of these groups of children there can be significant impacts on cognitive, educational and psychological functioning (Anderson *et al.* 2005; Marlow *et al.* 2005).

Children with acquired brain injury (ABI)

This includes brain injury from falls and accidents as well as damage resulting from brain tumours, stroke and other medical conditions. ABI in children is complicated and serious because the injury occurs to a dynamically developing system. This means that things can look

'OK' once the initial physical injury is no longer obvious, but the long-term effects of damage only start to be seen many years later when certain brain functions come 'on stream' and this can result in a very different trajectory of development for many children. We increasingly understand that the earlier in life a child suffers a brain injury, the more significant are its effects later in life on cognition (including attention and memory skills), development and social and emotional functioning (e.g., Anderson *et al.* 2005).

How risk factors operate

Psychological health is influenced by a range of factors and the interactions between them. The relationship between risk factors and psychological difficulties is complex, and the impact of exposure to the risk will vary from child to child – but all children exposed to potential causes of psychological harm have an increased chance of developing mental health difficulties either in childhood or later in life. As such, biological, (individual) psychological, social and environmental difficulties and, most importantly, the interplay between them can all contribute to mental health difficulties.

The research on the mechanisms by which adverse childhood experiences lead to adverse effects in adults many years later is pointing to a cumulative risk model – adverse outcomes are better predicted by the total number of environmental risk exposures, rather than the nature of those exposures, although we are yet to fully understand how these mechanisms work (Fox, Levitt and Nelson 2010; Rutter *et al.* 2004).

Impact on attachment and social relationships

Adverse experiences in their own childhood or later will impact on how a parent is able to care for their child and decrease the chances of a secure attachment developing with their child. This is discussed in detail in Chapters 2 and 3.

Attachment in infancy is a significant factor in how the child understands other people and forms relationships with them. As an example, an anxious-avoidant child who finds it difficult to rely on their caregiver and avoids interacting with them is likely to relate to other people in the same way with consequent relationship difficulties developing into a negative spiral as others respond negatively to them as a result.

Children who do not form secure attachments with their caregivers are more likely to experience mental health difficulties, as they:

- may not have had the opportunity to develop resilience, or to learn how to manage their emotions, which can then seem overwhelming and lead to a range of difficulties when they are faced with difficult situations (Svanberg 1998)

- may not have had the opportunity to learn how to relate well to others, and so may have difficulties forming healthy relationships as they grow up (Fryer 1998)

- are more likely to engage in self-harming behaviours and have poorer problem-solving skills (Cromby, Harper and Reavey 2013).

Epistemic trust

Fonagy *et al.* (2015) have theorised about the mechanisms by which attachment relationships regulate the acquisition of knowledge in children and ultimately their ability to learn. They argue that secure attachment facilitates a child's ability to trust the adults around them and enables them to learn from them the necessary skills to function well in society. They have labelled this 'epistemic trust', and claim it brings significant 'cognitive advantage' to children who experience this kind of trusting relationship in which cultural learning is accelerated.

Adversity and trauma, and particularly maltreatment by a caregiver, lead to breakdown in epistemic trust so a child learns not to trust the caregiver and not to trust the information they may impart to them. In these cases, the child becomes 'hypervigilant' to taking on new knowledge from others, their ability to learn from others is shut down, leading to significant cognitive disadvantage. This state of mistrust or 'epistemic hypervigilance' means the child tends to protect themselves against further damage from the breakdown in trust of communications from adults. This often leads to them misinterpreting social cues and communication as threat, leading to social and emotional withdrawal, which in turn leads to significant social disadvantage. Such cognitive and social disadvantages impact on their ability to form social relationships, their ability to engage with education and their ability to engage in help-seeking activity, and has a long-lasting and profound negative impact on a child's ability to function and therefore thrive in the world.

Impact on brain and nervous system development

Babies' brains develop in a relatively predetermined way from conception through to birth: tissue is formed, connections made and cells move to their correct places. These processes also continue after birth, with different neural systems developing to maturity at different points. We have a developing understanding that there are critical and sensory periods in a child's development (Weiss and Wagner 1998). Things that go wrong in this period do not get rectified later and there is the potential for early prevention and intervention to have enormous benefit to children and their families. A detailed discussion is beyond the scope of this book, but Bick and Nelson (2016) provide a useful and accessible review.

There are numerous things that can impact on brain development in this early developmental period. Postnatally we know that it is experience that shapes development. Repeated exposure to particular experiences will lead to the development of particular synaptic connections but it is also the case that not having certain experiences, such as in the case of neglect, can deprive the child of experiences necessary for the brain's development.

An emerging area of research suggests that maltreatment can be associated with global changes in brain structure, the prefrontal cortex and brain connectivity, and appears to be related to changes in threat processing, reward processing, emotion regulation and executive control (McCrory *et al.* 2017). This is a complex area of research with numerous methodological issues, but it appears that there is a link between child maltreatment and brain development, and that these changes can pose a latent risk for later mental health problems (see, e.g., McCrory *et al.* (2017) for a review).

Shonkoff *et al.* (2012) propose a model of 'toxic stress' to link early adversity to later physical and mental health difficulties and suggest that it may be more helpful to view many adult diseases as developmental disorders with origins early in life. Toxic stress is seen as resulting from strong, frequent or prolonged activation of the stress response system in the absence of a supportive adult relationship (Shonkoff *et al.* 2012).

Impact on physical health

Disease processes may arise:

- as the consequences of different coping devices like overeating, smoking, drug use, and promiscuity (Felitti 2009). These types of behaviour are often seen as examples of personal inadequacy or failure, but can be seen instead as responses to various forms of adversity or threat that enable the person to cope. They tend to persist even when the immediate difficulties are over so that in adulthood, their origins are obscured

- due to the biological effects of chronic stress and trauma which are widespread and damaging across all bodily systems including musculoskeletal, respiratory, cardiovascular, endocrine, gastrointestinal, nervous, and reproductive systems (Middlebrooks and Audage 2008). Franke (2014) summarises how toxic stress is understood to impact on all bodily functions as well as on the brain and nervous system

- due to the impact of poor nutrition, low levels of exercise and other factors linked to poverty, poor housing, lack of employment and social isolation that often accompany mental health problems.

Impact on education

The combination of the family, social and biological impacts of adversity have a major effect on how a child copes in school. Research has shown that positive school experiences and a good relationship with an adult are both protective factors for children in adverse circumstances; however, these become harder to achieve for a child at risk. Researchers like Commodari (2013) and Geddes (2006) have found significant links between secure attachment in young children and their school readiness and school success.

Many children who have suffered adversity and trauma will show their distress through their behaviour at school, often getting into trouble as a result. For others, increased levels of anxiety, low mood or poor self-esteem and self-confidence will impact on their peer group relationships and ability to focus on learning in lessons. As an example, the impact of living in an atmosphere of family conflict or domestic violence means the child will often be fearful and preoccupied with thoughts about home and struggle to concentrate in lessons.

This is discussed in more detail in Chapter 5.

Developmental cascades

This is a term which tries to describe the way that these problems interact and escalate in a child's life as they develop (Masten and Cicchetti 2010). As an example, a child may have had a disrupted and neglectful early childhood with the result that they are insecurely attached to a carer and are lacking in the experiences necessary to render them 'school ready'. On starting school, the child may struggle with the behavioural expectations in the school environment and with forming cooperative peer group relationships. They are likely to have difficulties with academic expectations and with forming a relationship with their teacher. Faced with this range of adaptive difficulties, the child may become disruptive in lessons and start to fight with other children as ways of coping, and this leads to worsening relationships with their teacher and peers. It is not uncommon for children like this to be excluded from nursery and primary schools and they are therefore deprived of both the educational and social opportunities that could help them overcome the earlier adversity. The pressure that this puts onto their families also further diminishes their ability to care for their child. Unless support is quickly in place to support the child, the family and the school, the cascade will continue with ever more damaging results as the child grows.

Examples of models of intervention based on risk factors/ACEs

So, what can we do to intervene to minimise the effects of adverse childhood experiences in later life?

Yates and Masten (2004) identify three types of approach to intervention – risk focused, asset focused and process focused – and argue that the most effective interventions use all, or a combination, of these. Examples of approaches include:

- Trying to reduce the incidence of risk factors, for example supporting positive parenting. Most practitioners suggest that parenting skills are the crucial point of intervention across a number of different problems (Felitti 2009) and are perhaps the single most important strategy in the field of primary prevention. This can range from universal programmes through to very intense levels of work. A review by Barlow *et al.* (2016) looked at the effectiveness of interventions aimed at improving attachment and attachment-related outcomes on a universal, targeted or indicated basis. This led to some being incorporated into the UK Healthy Child Programme, a government initiative to monitor, evaluate and protect the health of children from birth to age 19 years. At the more intense level, Pause's 'Preventing Repeat Removals' project has demonstrated a range of positive outcomes working with mothers who have repeatedly had children taken into care (McCracken *et al.* 2017).

- Building support for those identified with risk factors, for example support following bereavement. While we cannot usually prevent a child from experiencing bereavement, we can try to make sure that they and their family get the information and support they need to reduce the risks of longer-term psychological difficulties arising. In part, this requires us to pay attention to the support which the adults around them need, especially as they may also have suffered the bereavement. A number of voluntary organisations working in this way including Cruse Bereavement Care, Child Bereavement UK, Winston's Wish and Macmillan Cancer Support.

- Working with communities to build their capacity to impact positively on their environment, for example to improve play facilities and increase safety. There is detailed discussion of this in Chapter 8.

- Working with policy makers and commissioners to change environmental risks such as homelessness and child poverty.

- Working to increase the awareness of the evidence base on risk factors in all those who work with children and families, including parents. This can be done directly through the provision of training and consultation as discussed in the later chapters, but also though online information such as that developed by MindEd (www.minded.org.uk).

Protective factors in child development

Protective factors in child mental health are defined as those which can protect a child who is suffering adversity in some form. The early studies indicating that there may be protective factors looked at children growing up in high-risk situations who did not appear to develop problems, such as the children of parents diagnosed with schizophrenia (Garmezy 1971). The seminal Isle of Wight studies (Rutter *et al.* 1976) demonstrated that while there were risk factors in a population which correlated with higher levels of psychological difficulties in children, there were children who experienced the risks but did not develop problems. Study of those less affected children gave indications of what helped to protect them; for example, positive school experiences and a good relationship with an adult, like a teacher, were found to be protective experiences. This has developed into the field of study often referred to as developmental psychopathology (Cicchetti 1989; Rutter 2013a) which looks at how psychological problems develop over time through the complex interaction of risk and protective factors across different areas of a child's life.

There are individual, family and social factors found to be correlated with lower levels of psychological problems in population studies. Some factors may be variable over time, like family income, or relatively fixed, like ethnicity. There are protective factors, often for specific problems, which have been found to reduce the impact of a particular risk factor, while others are widespread in their impact across a range of difficulties. However, Rutter (1987), in his paper on psychosocial resilience and protective mechanisms, argues that protective factors must not just be the opposite or absence of risk, as their apparent impact may just be that a child has a lower burden of risk. A protective factor that is associated with mental health problems in general, irrespective of adverse circumstances, would not fit his definition although it would be considered a factor which promotes mental health. He stresses the importance of establishing evidence that a specific factor 'buffers' against specific risk factors in determining whether it is actually protective.

Wille *et al.* (2008) reported on a large study in Germany, the BELLA study, in which they sought to determine the frequencies and distributions of potential risk and protective factors and analyse their effects on children's mental health in order to begin to elucidate the theoretical basis on which protective factors were operating. They argue that, in order to meet Rutter's definition, a protective factor must either be associated with lower rates of mental health problems only in children in adverse circumstances or be linked to lower levels of problems in all children but more effective in children exposed to risk factors.

A report on the BELLA study (Klasen *et al.* 2015) discussed the findings in relation to depression. Parental reports of their own mental health problems predicted depressive symptoms in the self-reports of their children as well as the development of these symptoms over time. Child-reported protective factors of self-efficacy, positive family climate and social support were associated with less depressive symptoms at baseline, and positive changes in protective factors were associated with the development of less depressive symptoms over time so it can be argued that family climate and social support moderated the detrimental influence of parental mental health problems on the child's depressive symptoms.

Although there have been increasing levels of research, this is a relatively young field, with many studies still being cross-sectional and correlational rather than longitudinal and developmental.

How protective factors operate

Rutter (1987, 2013b) has described a number of ways in which a protective factor can work:

- Altering the experience of risk factors, for example by coping strategies.

- Altering exposure to risk factors, for example parental monitoring of involvement with anti-social peers.

- Averting negative chain reactions, for example harsh parenting leading to oppositional behaviour leading to increased conflict.

- Strengthening protective factors, for example self-esteem, problem solving.

- Turning points which change context and provide new opportunities, for example moving from institutional care, moving school.

Grant *et al.* (2006) conducted a literature review of studies looking for examples of how protective factors could moderate the effect of risk factors and mediate in the process by which the risk factor leads to psychological problems. The moderator effects were often not the major focus of the research in the studies and there was variability in the constructs examined and the outcome measures used. Not surprisingly, they found significant variability in findings for both fixed factors like age and ethnicity, and more malleable factors like family relationships. They concluded that the research to that date lent only limited support to the hypothesis of moderation, with the exception of research in depression.

In contrast, they considered that the studies testing the hypothesis that mediators explain the relationship between stressors and developmental psychopathology did provide support for the hypothesis. Most of these studies set out to test the hypothesis and were theory driven, in contrast to the moderation research. The most consistent finding was that family-based variables, like the quality of the parent–child relationship and parenting, were the mediators, and this suggested that stressors exert their negative impact on children and young people by disrupting important interpersonal relationships and interactions.

All children exposed to potential causes of psychological harm have an increased chance of developing mental health difficulties either in childhood or later in life. Biological, psychological, social and environmental difficulties and, most importantly, the interplay between them all, contribute to the outcome for any individual child. This can be illustrated with a risk that directly impacts on brain development, often considered to be a relatively clear-cut example of the impact of biological factors on psychological and cognitive development. Some children are born with, or develop, conditions known to carry a higher risk of psychological difficulties. These difficulties are not, however, inevitable and will come into play to a greater or lesser extent depending on the family's ability to adapt to the child's needs (which, crucially, may depend on their knowledge and the support available), on education provision, and the resources available in the community and wider society.

An illustrative case example: children who have been exposed to adverse levels of alcohol prenatally

Not all women who drink alcohol in pregnancy expose their developing baby to harmful effects because it depends how much they drink and the stage of foetal development, but there is a risk of conditions such as foetal alcohol spectrum disorder (FASD). The 'spectrum' is important as there is not a direct link between the degree of foetal exposure to alcohol and FASD.

- FASD affects around 1 in 100 people and impacts on areas as diverse as motor skills, cognition, language, academic achievement, memory, attention, executive functioning, impulsivity and social communication, as well as resulting in characteristic facial features.

- FASD is also associated with an increased risk of mental health difficulties (Pei *et al.* 2011), social isolation, and involvement with the criminal justice system.

FASD is, however, a good example illustrating that risk factors do not necessarily lead to a predetermined outcome, since although FASD is associated with a known cause and has a characteristic pattern of impairment, outcome varies. FASD is also associated with positive features in some children, including taking pride in doing activities individually, participating in family activities, accepting household routines and accepting help.

Streissguth *et al.* (2004) looked at over 400 young people with FASD, over 80 per cent of whom were not living with their biological mother. The study found that children with FASD grew up to have more difficulties with disrupted school experiences, contact with the criminal justice system, and inappropriate sexual behaviours, but the children's outcome was positively affected by a number of factors. The most important of these was being diagnosed at an early age (often difficult for the children not raised by their biological mother, since confirmation of significant alcohol use in pregnancy is a core part of the assessment) and spending a larger percentage of their life in a stable nurturing environment. Streissguth *et al.* noted that:

an early diagnosis allows capable caring families to effectively advocate for their children's needs… These findings are congruent with clinical experience, where we find that stable, nurturing families with a child diagnosed early, are better able to plan effectively for the transition from adolescence to adulthood, and to maintain as close a relationship with their child in young adulthood as seems necessary. (pp.234–235)

Assets and promotive factors

While protective factors are defined as those particularly important for positive adaptation for children in high-risk situations, factors associated with better outcomes at all levels of risk or none are often referred to as assets or promotive factors.

Evidence is starting to emerge that the factors which promote positive psychological wellbeing are not necessarily those which are the opposite of risk factors. In a detailed analysis of 11-year-olds in the UK Millennium Study, Patalay and Fitzsimons (2016) found, for example, that enjoying school and spending time outside school with friends were associated with higher wellbeing scores, but did not have a strong impact on symptom scores on the Strengths and Difficulties Questionnaire.

Studies consistently find that good family relationships are a key asset in child development. A securely attached infant will experience a consistent, warm, attentive and responsive caregiver so they develop confidence that their needs will be met, learn how to relate positively to others, become able to regulate their emotions, and feel themselves to be worthy and valued.

Some features of schools will be positive to all children. These include good pupil–teacher relationships, good classroom management, opportunities to find things they are good at, and good social opportunities. They may be of even greater importance to children experiencing adversity elsewhere in their lives (Verschueren and Koomen 2012).

It is outside the scope of this book to detail the range of ways in which positive child development can be supported across the field of child rearing, but Figure 1.1 gives an indication of the breadth of these. For further reading see Zimmerman *et al.* (2013).

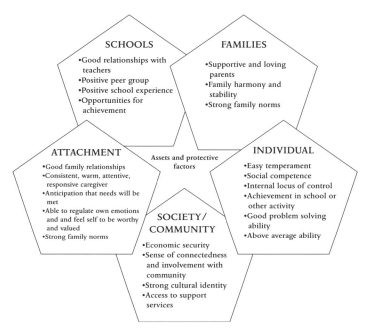

Figure 1.1: Assets and promotive factors

Examples of interventions based on protective and promotive factors

Impact of parental depression

Beardslee *et al.* (2003) conducted a study which looked at resilience in the children of depressed parents who are typically found to be three to four times more likely to become depressed than children of non-depressed parents. They found several factors in the children themselves. The non-depressed children had the capacity to accomplish age-appropriate developmental tasks, be deeply engaged in relationships and be self-reflective and self-understanding. They shared an understanding that the parents had a problem for which they were not to blame or responsible, and that they could get on with their own lives. The question, of course, is what enabled those children to be ab2le to function in those ways? Very significantly, the study found that the parents of the more resilient children were both committed to and *able to* parent despite their own depression. This, and the 2015 findings from the BELLA study discussed earlier (Klasen *et al.* 2015), indicates that significant intervention strategies should be directed at parents and not just at the children.

While there are programmes trialled in schools for children and young people considered at risk of becoming depressed that have shown some promise (discussed in more detail in Chapter 5), this research points to the importance of working with parents with mental health problems to support them in parenting, rather than just working on their own problems.

Parenting support

There is widespread advocacy for the provision of parenting support to help to reduce the risk factors of insecure attachments, problematic child-rearing practices, and so on, particularly among families judged to be 'at risk' or vulnerable, and a number of well-validated models of delivering such support are discussed at length in later chapters, particularly Chapters 2 and 3.

Developing strategies to enhance parenting across larger populations is a more recent development, pioneered by Sanders *et al.* (2008) in Australia. The Midlands Area Parenting Partnership in the Republic of Ireland delivered a range of Triple P parenting programmes (Sanders, Turner and Markie-Dadds 2002) of differing intensity, provided free to all parents of children aged 7 and younger in Counties Longford and Westmeath between 2010 and 2013 and evaluated independently (Fives *et al.* 2014). The programmes were delivered by a partnership of voluntary, statutory and community agencies to around 4500 parents. The evaluation compared results in the two Triple P counties with families in a larger county not using Triple P. The aim of such a population approach is not just to improve outcomes for the parents who attend, but to change the ecological context for parenting in the area. They used four modes of delivery:

- A media strategy targeting the whole population to promote positive parenting.

- Triple P seminars open to all parents, designed to help the management of discrete behaviour problems.

- Workshop Triple P: a series of four workshops targeted at parents whose children were showing mild to moderate behaviour problems.

- Group Triple P: an eight-week programme for parents whose children were showing more severe behaviour problems.

The detailed results of the implementation and evaluation can be found in the report *Parenting Support for Every Parent* (Fives *et al.* 2014). The headlines, however, were that in the families who were actually involved in the various interventions, there was a 37.5 per cent reduction in the numbers of children with clinically elevated social, emotional and behavioural problems, and a 30 per cent reduction in parental reporting of psychological distress and stress. This is in keeping with other studies of the effectiveness of Triple P. What is, perhaps, of greater interest, is that there was a ripple effect across the whole community. The data show a number of significant and positive effects for the intervention areas compared with the comparison areas on:

- child behavioural and emotional problems

- parental psychological distress

- reporting a good relationship with the index child

- appropriate parenting strategies

- satisfaction with parenting information available

- satisfaction with parenting services

- likelihood of participation in future parenting programmes.

The results are similar to those reported by Sanders *et al.* (2008) in Australia. Both studies found no significant impact on hyperactivity, conduct problems and peer group relationships, and have hypothesised that more intense interventions are needed to create change in these areas.

Resilience

Resilience is a much studied and more widely debated concept (Masten 2015; Rutter 2012; Windle 2011). Interest in resilience has been driven as much by politics and philosophy as it has by academic research. This has inevitably led to a range of differing approaches to resilience as an idea and as unit of study. As a consequence of this ongoing debate, the concept still lacks a unifying definition (Hart *et al.* 2016). However, most definitions vary on the themes suggested by Rutter (2006): seeing resilience as reduced vulnerability to environmental risk, the overcoming of stress or adversity, or a relatively good outcome despite risk experiences.

Studies have demonstrated very wide-ranging variations in individual responses to adverse events and environments. The variability of response meant that vulnerability could not be seen as a summative concept of risk and protective factors. These observations led to interest in the factors that determine an individual's ability to manage, or even flourish, in the face of adversity – described by Rutter (2012) as a view of a fixed, internal 'invulnerability'. Until relatively recently, the focus of interest remained at an individual level – assuming that an unexpected and relatively positive response to childhood adversity could be understood by looking for internal, individual characteristics. These early studies took an interest in 'extraordinary individuals' who 'triumphed over adversity' and focused on the internal characteristics of the child (e.g., Garmezy 1985). This early conceptualisation and subsequent research led to the development of narrow thinking around resilience, that has proved irresistible to many and, despite more recent conceptualisation and research into resilience, has shown remarkable longevity: ideas such as 'grit' (Duckworth *et al.* 2007).

Masten (2015), however, suggests resilience is not the preserve of 'extraordinary people' with 'extraordinary internal resources' ('grit'), but rather is built on more ordinary things: '...a healthy human brain in good working order; close relationships with competent caring adults; committed families; effective schools and communities; opportunities to succeed; and beliefs in the self, nurtured by positive interactions with the world' (p.8).

This moves the idea of resilience from being something located *within* the individual to a concept that also includes the environmental factors *around* them (Hart *et al.* 2016). Friedli and Carlin (2009) suggest we need to consider not just resilient people but also *resilient places* and *resilient communities*. They argue this translates into policy interventions that can help build resilience across communities, places and individuals including:

1.   those that strengthen social relationships and opportunities for community connection for individuals and families, e.g. parents

2.   those that build and enable social support, social networks and social capital within and between communities, e.g. reducing

material inequalities, tackling discrimination and improving the physical environment, especially for children and young people

3. those that strengthen and/or repair relationships between communities and health and social care agencies, e.g. enhancing community control through co-production

4. those that improve the quality of the social relationships of care between individuals and professionals, e.g. practice that avoids social disparagement.

(Adapted from Friedli and Carlin 2009)

Recent longitudinal studies have strengthened Friedli's views. Rutter (2012) describes how longitudinal studies have shown resilience to be a *dynamic* process that can only be understood in terms of the individual *and* their environment, *and* as fluid interaction between the two *over time*. Hart *et al.* (2016) argue that the individual is not just a passive recipient of their environment but a (though often limited) shaper of it. As Ungar (2011) puts it: '...resilience is less an individual trait and more a quality of the child's social and physical ecology' (p.1).

If we adopt the wider, evidence-informed view that resilience is a dynamic interaction between an individual and their ecology, over time, it opens up new, exciting and perhaps more helpful concepts of what a psychological intervention is and how we conceptualise mental health services. These broad approaches to promote and strengthen resilience are under-researched, but much of the approach fits with that of the Community Psychology movement (Smail 1994) and discussed in detail in Chapter 8. At a 'microsystem' level there is a growing body of literature on whole-school-based approaches to resilience (Hart *et al.* 2016), discussed in more detail in Chapter 5.

Returning to Bronfenbrenner's ecological model with this new understanding of resilience mechanisms, Bronfenbrenner saw the impact of the macrosystem on the individual, but perhaps underestimated the degree of impact between the different parts of the system. We know that environmental processes impact down to genetic level – genes are 'switched' on and off as a result of environmental interactions (discussed in Rutter 2012). This leads to a more radical shift in our understanding of the impact of the macro, not only on the child as a whole person, but also on the genetic level. Genes, switched on by environmental factors, will in turn impact on the child as a person, so they in turn will impact differently on their environment and change it, and the ripples will spread out and back across the system from the macro to the genetic and back again. We can now see how, for example, world economic policy will have an impact at a genetic level and these genetic changes will impact on the child's physical and mental wellbeing. If we are to make this shift, it raises questions about the level in the system where the focus of psychological 'treatment' should take place. Hart *et al.* (2016) argue that we need to hold a 'social justice' lens to resilience, and adopt a set of principles and practices to research and intervention that take this wider ecological view into account. They suggest the adoption of a set of principles to:

> ...challenge our own practice and those of others, we might ask questions such as whether interventions (a) promote psychopolitical literacy; (b) educate participants on the timing, components, targets, and dynamics of strategies to overcome oppression; (c) empower participants to take action to address political inequities and social injustice within their relationships, settings, communities, or even internationally; (d) promote solidarity and strategic alliances and coalitions with groups facing similar issues; and (e) account for the subjectivity and psychological limitations of agents of change (p.7).

These are an ambitious set of measures but some projects are beginning to live up to them in real-world settings. This approach is described in more detail in Chapter 8. MAC-UK, for example, works with marginalised groups of young people in inner city London – their philosophy fits closely with that of radical resilience-building models. They aim to work at all levels of the system – from working with individuals to campaigning to change government policy – and co-production is central to everything they do. They have shown it is possible to do this at a small local level. The next challenge is to apply these principles in the mainstream and at scale (Durcan, Zlotowitz and Stubbs 2017).

Taking this wide view of the causes and protective factors of children's psychological wellbeing and distress, and looking at the whole system as dynamic and interactive, opens the doors to new and exciting possibilities in what we understand as psychological, or even clinical, interventions, both as prevention as well as cure.

Chapter 2

Working psychologically with infants, parents and families in the perinatal period

RUTH BUTTERWORTH, RUTH O'SHAUGHNESSY
AND MICHAEL GALBRAITH

Introduction

'Probably the most important period in everyone's life is the one that they cannot remember.'

(Balbernie 2008, p.1)

It is now well recognised that the first '1001 critical days' of a child's life lay the foundations of wellbeing for their future (Leadsom *et al.* 2013). The WAVE Trust's 2015 *Building Great Britons* report summarised a wealth of evidence demonstrating a child's need for reflective and responsive relationships with their primary carers during infancy, describing how this environment:

> allows the child to develop in the most optimal way, with emotional wellbeing, capacity to form and maintain relationships, healthy brain and language development leading onto cognitive development, school readiness and lifelong learning. Such children contribute to the establishment of a caring, nurturing, proactive and creative society. (Wave Trust 2015, p.6)

In parallel with the growing recognition of the importance of infant mental health, the UK has also seen the growth of a powerful campaign led by the Maternal Mental Health Alliance, recognising the importance of mothers' (and increasingly fathers') perinatal mental health. Evidence suggests that between 10 and 20 per cent of women will report perinatal mental health difficulties, though there is also evidence that a huge number go unreported (Bauer *et al.* 2014). The MBRRACE-UK (mothers and babies: reducing risk through audits and confidential enquiries across the UK) report also highlighted that almost a quarter of mothers who died between six weeks and one year postnatally did so due to mental health related causes (Knight *et al.* 2015). Although there is less evidence available on fathers' mental health, a study by the National Childbirth Trust suggested that up to 38 per cent of new fathers are concerned about their own mental health (National Childbirth Trust 2015), with approximately 10 per cent experiencing clinical levels of depression (Paulson and Bazemore 2010).

In response to this evidence, additional government funding has been provided to develop specialist mental health services specifically for new mothers (NHS England 2016). The majority of these services also offer some intervention with the mother–infant relationship, although National Institute for Clinical Excellence (NICE) guidelines still indicate that where these needs are complex, infants should be referred to an Infant Mental Health Service (National Institute for Clinical Excellence 2014). While a small number of specialist infant mental health services exist in both the statutory and voluntary sectors, service delivery is patchy and inequitable. Furthermore, it is our contention that there is a risk inherent in seeing parental and infant mental health as separate entities. Jones (2010) discusses the significance of keeping both the baby and the parent in mind, suggesting that 'often a child's symptoms are a healthy plea to indicate that all is not well in their parent' (p.11). Parents in the perinatal period in particular are often more motivated to face their own troubles – it is a window of opportunity to prevent adverse experiences from the parent's past repeating with the new generation (Jones 2010). The infant's supreme vulnerability means that their mental health might be seen as situated primarily within the parent–infant relationship itself – meaning that it is more difficult to disentangle where one ends and the other begins.

This chapter will outline the importance of seeing infant, parent and family emotional wellbeing in context, where the circles of influence around the family are inextricably linked (Bronfenbrenner 1994). There is a need for intervention to transcend traditional service boundaries in order to respond sensitively to families' needs and maximise the potential for positive change.

Psychological development in the perinatal period – key messages from research

Since Bowlby first explored the importance of attachment relationships in the 1950s (Bowlby 1969, 1973, 1980), the majority of research literature has focused on the importance of the dyadic relationship between a parent (usually the mother) and their infant. We know that the development of a secure attachment relationship is hugely influential in terms of the child's social, emotional, physical and relational development and that this is predictive of significantly more positive outcomes over time.

A matrix of factors has been shown to contribute to the formation of a secure attachment, including constructs such as:

- sensitive responsiveness (Ainsworth, Bell and Stayton 1974), the ability of the parent to consistently pick up on their infant's cues and respond appropriately

- mind-mindedness (Meins 2004), where parents are able to see their infant as having a mind and intentions of his or her own (thereby making a sensitive response more likely)

- reflective functioning or mentalisation (e.g., Fonagy et al. 1991a), where the parent understands that infant behaviour can be driven by psychological and emotional factors. Reflective parents are able to reflect on both their own feelings and those of the baby, and effectively integrate these experiences to allow them to be responsive to the infant's needs.

Where this type of attuned parenting is available to the child, the child is significantly more likely to experience emotional wellbeing both in infancy and in later life (Sroufe et al. 2005). For example, the number of mind-minded comments to an infant at six months old predicts attachment security at age 1 (Bernier and Dozier 2003) and mentalising skills at age 4 (Meins et al. 2002), both associated with positive mental health in later life. Early attachment patterns can last a lifetime and be transmitted to the next generation. For example, children of mothers who were rated as securely attached during pregnancy were, at age 11, better able to manage complex emotions in themselves and understand feeling states in others (Steele and Steele 2005).

Attuned parenting and attachment security impact not only on the child's social and emotional outcomes but at a more fundamental level on their neurological development. The infant brain undertakes a rapid period of growth in the first two years of life, and there is increasingly robust evidence that it is 'experience dependent' (Siegel 1999), developing in response to the infant's interpersonal environment. Crucially, stress and hormone regulation systems develop in the context of the attachment relationship and have a long-term mediating impact on child mental health (Schore 1994; Newman *et al.* 2016).

There is also increasing evidence that it is not only the postnatal, but also the foetal, environment that can have a long-term impact on infant brain development (Gluckman, Hanson and Mitchell 2010). Newman *et al.* (2016) propose an interactive model whereby maternal anxiety, for example, contributes to a compromised environment within the uterus and potential epigenetic changes in the foetus, which are then compounded by the parent's difficulty in responding sensitively and in particular being able to support the infant's ability to regulate his or her physical and emotional states. In turn, these experiences are linked to attachment insecurity and longer-term difficulties with self-regulation and physical and emotional wellbeing.

However, a parent's ability to provide responsive parenting for their child is of course itself a product of their experience, with multiple historical factors interacting with their current circumstances. For example, parents' own exposure to adverse childhood experiences (ACEs) such as poverty, violence, neglect or abuse, and their experience of being cared for both as a child and as an adult will have a profound impact on their expectations of the world, their own mental health and their ability to tune into their baby's needs (Felitti, Anda and Nordenberg 1998). All parents will have had experience, for better or worse, of having been parented themselves, which will have impacted not only on their own neurological and psychological development, but also on the more explicit parenting roles that they might have learned. Winnicott (1965) emphasised the importance of 'good enough' parenting (i.e. imperfect parenting that allows infants to learn how to tolerate frustration as ruptures and repairs to the parent–infant relationship take place). However, an individual's sense of what constitutes 'good enough' parenting reflects an interaction between their own experience and their cultural context – and as such will vary considerably across individuals and communities.

Developmental tasks during the perinatal period – what helps and what hinders?

In this section, the challenges and barriers to optimal psychological growth during the perinatal period (from conception to age 1) will be considered to illustrate key messages from the research outlined above. At each stage of development in the perinatal period there are different tasks and goals. This section considers these goals and potential barriers to achieving them.

Growing and containing (pregnancy)

Pregnancy and its associated risks mean that the physical aspects of pregnancy tend to trump the psychological tasks. However, the foetus is its own 'person', profoundly influenced by its psychological and physiological environment. For example, the foetus responds to pain by turning away (Goodlin and Schmidt 1972); and responds to musical signals, moving in synchrony with a rhythm (Sallenbach 1993). The mother's state of mind can also influence the foetus, for example studies have shown that foetal movement is higher when a mother is depressed (Field, Diego and Hernandez-Reif 2006). Increasingly, research shows that many aspects of life before birth can be thought about from a psychological or social perspective, and not as purely physiological processes (Music 2011).

Mixed feelings about pregnancy are common for both mum and dad. Parents often report excitement at the prospect of new life, and fear of the responsibility that accompanies the task of bringing the baby safely into the world. Pregnancy can be full of hopefulness that life will be different for the baby, particularly when the parents' relationships with their own parents lacked vital emotional nourishment. Pregnancy signals a time for individuals and couples to 'take stock', with expectant parents remembering experiences from their own childhoods to help them work out how to be a 'mum' or a 'dad' (Daws and de Rementeria 2015).

Pregnancy can also bring a range of anxieties, including anxiety related to prospective parents' own experiences of loss. For example, fear of miscarriage can be particularly potent if a person has already experienced a miscarriage, or an ectopic or aborted pregnancy. Women may also worry about their changing body shape, the size of their 'bump' (too big/small), and whether their baby is growing optimally. Couples may worry about the changing boundaries of their relationship and the possibility of relationship breakdown, as they negotiate how to make room for a third person in the relationship.

Preparing for a baby can powerfully trigger previously excluded memories based on our early emotional experiences (e.g., Fraiberg, Adelson and Shapiro 1975). For those whose early experiences make it difficult to relinquish control (e.g., those who have experienced abuse or trauma), the experience of maternity care and the prospect of birth can further exacerbate a sense of being overwhelmed and can increase anxiety. For some women, anxiety or other mental health difficulties can become severe during pregnancy, placing both mother and baby at risk of harm (Knight *et al.* 2015).

Birth, meeting and greeting

The physical tasks of birth and the first few days postnatally are for the baby to be delivered, and mother and baby to achieve a fair degree of physical stability (breathing, temperature, food and fluid intake and excretion). Psychologically, this is the chance for the baby to meet his or her mother and other close caregivers, and for caregivers to meet and greet the baby with joy and pleasure. This may not happen in the moments after birth but grow over the first few days of the baby's life.

However, there are a number of factors that can get in the way of this connecting process, particularly to do with the baby's identity (parentage, appearance and health), the pregnancy and birth experience, and the simultaneous birth of motherhood (and fatherhood) for the parents. For example, when mums (or other primary caregivers) look at their newborn infant they may not see the child in front of them, but 'see' people and experiences that are associated with the child: the father of the child, the experience of the pregnancy or the birth and/or their own childhood/babyhood (e.g., Fonagy, Steele and Steele. 1991b; Gergely and Watson 1996). Babies born prematurely or with a congenital condition or who are unwell or injured in the birth process often do not look the way that parents expect them to look. Mums and other caregivers may find it unappealing, or even feel averse, to look at baby as the associations that they have are so troubling. Babies are born with an instinct to look at human faces (Tronick and Brazelton 1980) and babies who are not looked at or who are regarded with anger, disgust or fear have an early (primary) experience of emotional rejection or criticism.

For babies born unwell or physically fragile, the experience of being on a neonatal unit can be 'overwhelmingly invasive' from a sensory, pain and emotional standpoint (Browne, Martinez and Talmi 2016, p.275) for both infant and parents. When parents are told, or perceive, that their child might not survive, they may hold back from connecting with the baby and use a coping strategy of 'wait and see'. This holding back may be quite explicit or more subtle; parents may avoid visiting the baby on the neonatal ward, or may spend time with and provide good physical care for the baby but avoid eye-contact or making an emotional investment in the child. Some parents report feeling that they were caring for their baby as though he or she were someone else's; as though they were a part of the staff team (Ellis, Butterworth and Law 2017).

What counts as a traumatic birth may differ significantly between mums (or birth partners) and professionals, with physical trauma often having a less significant emotional impact than the psychological experience of care (Ayers 2014). Where mothers have a history of trauma, the experience of being exposed and vulnerable, having things 'done to' them and feeling invalidated can be re-traumatising, making it difficult to connect to the baby because of the association with the birth. It is not uncommon for birth partners to have an independent traumatic response to the birth process, perhaps having feared for the life of their partner and/or child, and often having felt excluded and powerless (Etheridge and Slade 2017).

It is harder to assess when the baby has experienced a birth as traumatic, but this remains an important consideration, as does the experience of being separated from the mother for health reasons, or where she is under general anaesthetic. As well as the association mentioned between the birth and the baby for the mother, there may be physical reasons why the mum is less able to be present for baby in the first hours and days post-birth, including tiredness, effects of medication, illness and being physically separated from the baby – and it can be easy in a busy maternity system for a healthy baby to be left in a cot for long periods where the mother is unable, physically or emotionally, to hold them.

Birth produces a new person and a multitude of new relationships. For the baby, this may also include relationships with siblings.

Some studies report developmental advantages to having older siblings, specifically better theory of mind (the ability to accurately intuit what others might be thinking or feeling) and executive functioning skills (the ability to plan, organise and complete tasks) (McAlister and Peterson 2007). For parents, a newborn baby is almost certainly the most physically, emotionally and financially dependent and intense relationship they will have been in since they were a child and on the other side of the parenting equation. The scariness and unexpectedness of 'ghosts in the nursery' – the stirring up of feelings, embodied experiences and core beliefs from one's own infancy and childhood (Fraiberg *et al.* 1975) – catches many parents by surprise. If the most important experiences in life are the ones that happen before we can (consciously) remember them, then to be confronted with difficult, painful and unresolved experiences when we have a baby can be shocking. Parents will have developed coping strategies, layers of identity and social-cultural status between their own babyhood and becoming a parent, so to be thrown back into emotional states that aren't mediated by conscious thought can be disorientating.

Responding and containing (0–6 months)

As newborn people adjust to life outside the womb and move out of the 'fourth trimester' (Brink 2013), their sensory abilities have developed, vision has become binocular and there is less kinaesthesia (mixing of sensory modalities). This allows longer and more nuanced kinds of conversations to take place. Babies in this stage are both 'scientists', learning 'cause and effect' rules between their actions and others' responses; and dynamically systemic, sensing their place in the social-emotional environment around them.

Babies at all stages want and need sensitive responsiveness (e.g., Ainsworth *et al.* 1974) and this is especially true in this period when they are ready and looking for physical and emotional interaction with their caregivers. It therefore follows that anything that dampens a primary caregiver's response to their baby is going to have an effect on their relationship and on the baby's development. Low mood and preoccupation with ideas in the parent's head interrupt playful and spontaneous conversation with babies. The 'still face experiment' – a procedure where a mother faces her baby, and is asked to hold a 'still face' and not react to the baby's behaviours (Tronick *et al.* 1975) –

demonstrates how distressing and disorienting it is for them to have an unresponsive parent. Some parents may believe (hope) that other kinds of visual stimulation (such as screen time) can fill in the gaps in what they are able to provide, perhaps unaware of the need for the contingency, i.e. that what the baby senses is closely paired to the baby's behaviour.

Parental mood may be disturbed by factors mentioned previously about remembrance of things past, but it is also affected by present circumstances. Parents living in the shadow of domestic control and abuse, struggling to survive economically, with the threat of racism or other forms of oppression, uncertainty about their nationality or residency status, and those living in war zones, have less mental and emotional space to be enraptured and entranced by their baby's bids for attention and comfort (Public Health England 2017).

Play, stimulation and separation (6–12 months)

Around 6 months of age many babies start to be able to sit up. This allows more options for interaction, not only with other people but also with things. Manual dexterity is usually good enough to grasp hand-sized objects, and the associations between how things look, feel, sound, smell, taste, move and fit with other things is mind-blowing, or perhaps more accurately, mind-expanding.

The social-cultural messages about what makes children of this and other ages happy, and what counts as 'good parenting' are pervasive and sometimes perverse. In some ways, it is totally consistent that a materialist-capitalist society such as ours recruits the next generation as soon as possible, and feeds on parental insecurities about getting it wrong. There is an interesting contrast between the policy of providing all parents with a cardboard box for the baby to sleep in and the marketing of cribs with wheels and awnings, or the custom of carrying (wearing) babies and the development of integrated infant transport systems that allow the baby to go from house to car to pram without being touched.

As babies move into toddlerhood their range expands – as they start to crawl and then walk, their physical domain and their social world grow. Babies who can move around can choose what and who to approach and what to retreat from. Those showing secure attachment patterns can explore from the safe base of their parent/carer into new areas, activities and relationships. Those showing a more avoidant pattern will also explore but with less inner security that any distress will be 'mopped up' by their parent. Children showing an ambivalent pattern are less likely to explore freely, sensing that they (and their carer) need to keep each other close.

Socially speaking, parents who are living or have lived with threat and abuse have good reason to worry about their child branching out. The recurring exposure in the media of abuse, especially in childhood but also in adulthood, and often to women/mums, reflects how unsafe society is for many people. And disturbingly one adverse childhood experience makes others more likely (Felitti *et al.* 1998), traumatising people further and setting up cycles of abuse whereby they go on to inhabit familiar roles of abused-abuser.

Case study

Jeannie is a 22-year-old pregnant woman. She and her partner, Sean (the baby's dad), have been together on and off for three years but describe their relationship as 'complicated'. Although Jeannie is unsure whether she and Sean will stay together to parent their baby, she is adamant that she wants to keep the baby (whom they have named Molly) and that she will give it a different experience of family life from the one that she has had.

Jeannie recently moved out of the home that she shared with her mum and two younger siblings. She describes finding it difficult to rely on her mum who has struggled with low mood and alcohol dependence throughout Jeannie's life, suggesting that they are close but argue a lot. She has not had contact with her dad since she was a little girl. Jeannie spent some time in local authority care during her mid-teens having been in a physically and sexually abusive relationship with a 25-year-old man. She became pregnant at the age of 13 but miscarried at 19 weeks following a serious physical assault. While in care, Jeannie frequently self-harmed and drank to excess and had a brief period of psychological therapy in CAMHS before disengaging. Since meeting Sean, she has been able to moderate her drinking and has not self-harmed regularly for several years, but she recognises that her mood can be up and down and she finds it difficult to trust other people.

Table 2.1: Jeannie

	'Care as usual'	What could be different
Pre-conception	Stigma and shame are ever present in political messages, social and other media in relation to parents with mental health difficulties, young parents, and relationship instability. Jeannie is left feeling that she does not deserve to have a baby and that she will inevitably fail as a mum.	Normalising messages about perinatal and infant mental health in public consciousness. Children's centres sit at the heart of communities and all staff have an understanding of attachment and trauma-informed care, including knowledge of perinatal therapeutic support available via local agencies. Therapeutic support is available to explore previous trauma and think about impact on future parenthood.
Antenatal	May have different midwife at every visit, making it hard to form a trusting relationship. Questions about emotional wellbeing are not asked, or asked without time to explore. Antenatal education is focused on pain management during labour and basic baby care.	Continuity of midwife means that trust can be built over time. Training and supervision are available for midwives to facilitate them to respond to individual psychological needs. Children's centres, midwives and health visitors have knowledge of perinatal therapeutic support available locally and are able to provide choices to Jeannie. Universal access to parent support groups for new mums (and dads) helps to build circles of support in the local community. 'Baby steps' antenatal group is available to strengthen relationship between Jeannie and Sean in preparation for their relationship with the baby. Parent–infant therapy is available if ready to understand and support this new relationship in the context of Jeannie's history.
Birth	Jeannie feels that things will be 'done to' her and she is scared, both of which mimic her experiences as a teenager. Birth stalls because of her anxiety and so intervention escalates, increasing her anxiety and lack of experienced agency. Sean feels pushed out and distanced from both Jeannie and Molly.	A tailored birth plan is on the hospital file and all staff have been trained to respond appropriately to Jeannie's needs. Jeannie and Sean both feel listened to, cared for and involved in decision making. Physical examinations are kept to a minimum and managed sensitively.

	'Care as usual'	What could be different
Postnatal	Jeannie feels too ashamed to admit that she is struggling to bond with Molly. She can't bear to breastfeed but feels criticised for making this decision.	Jeannie and her midwife, health visitor or children's centre worker discuss her feelings towards Molly in an early visit and monitor this together. Options for therapeutic support available locally are discussed with Jeannie (child/adult, voluntary/statutory, universal/specialist).
	Jeannie is worried about Molly crying so won't go out to visit friends or go to the children's centre. She feels more and more distant from Molly and from Sean.	Parent–infant therapy is one option offered at the earliest opportunity to support Jeannie and Molly to grow together and build Jeannie's confidence to respond sensitively to Molly's needs, with Sean able to join this work if they wish.
	Eventually, Jeannie tells her GP. She is offered antidepressant medication which somewhat lifts her mood but her relationship with Molly remains distant and challenging.	Jeannie is supported to recognise the barriers to breastfeeding and to make the decision that is right for her.
		The children's centre offers outreach to encourage Jeannie and Sean into the centre where they meet other families and receive practical and emotional support.

Structuring community resources to intervene early

It is clear that there is huge potential to influence a child's future psychological wellbeing by offering effective support across the systems of their early life. The earlier in the life of the child that potential struggles are identified and mitigated, the greater the capacity for parents (and the supportive systems that surround them) to promote healthy outcomes for both the child and the whole family.

We will outline a tiered model (Figure 2.1) that draws both on Bronfenbrenner's ecological systems theory and on a similar model presented by Ventevogel *et al.* (2013) to demonstrate the importance of intervening holistically. This model has three tiers:

1. Influencing the social and political landscape through wider health promotion and challenging stigma.

2. Providing trauma-informed, integrated and responsive care across services.

3. Delivering specialist psychotherapeutic support where needed, cutting across the artificial boundary of adult and child services.

Nelson and Mann (2011) highlight the potential role of psychologists to be 'credible experts who can be a voice for babies in public policy discussions' (p.137) at all of these tiers, including building a knowledge base for policy decisions, promoting public awareness of the importance of this period, contributing mental health expertise to community partnerships, and supporting efforts to improve access to specialist intervention where this is needed. We will attempt to outline what each of these tiers might look like in optimal circumstances, and the role that clinical psychologists and other psychological practitioners might play in supporting each of the tiers.

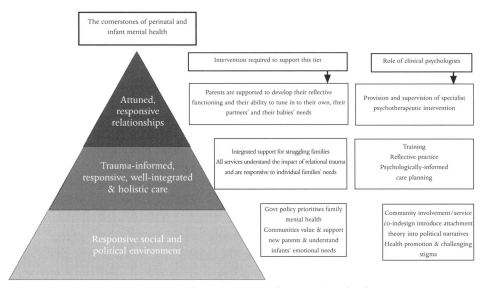

Figure 2.1: The cornerstones of perinatal and infant mental health and how these can be supported

1 Influencing the social and political landscape through wider health promotion and challenging stigma

There have been huge steps forward in recent years in terms of both politicians and the public recognising the importance of the first 1001 critical days. There is still, however, a long way to go in ensuring that this awareness translates into a shift in our attitudes, priorities and spending at both a societal and political level. Parenting is rarely given equivalent status to paid work, and political policy aimed at improving infants' life chances frequently focuses on the provision of out-of-home care rather than supporting parents to meet their child's needs. The stigma around perinatal mental health difficulties is reflected in a number of research studies which have shown that parents fear that they will be judged negatively, or their child will be removed, if they acknowledge struggling emotionally in this period (Hogg 2013).

Nelson and Mann (2011) identify a range of reasons why policy decisions do not always reflect the evidence base for the importance of intervening early in children's lives. These include the difficulty in 'swinging the pendulum' of funding from crisis care to early intervention; the complexity and interactive nature of difficulties and needs in this period, and policy makers' associated lack of confidence to make decisions; and the way in which funding is generally provided in silos, meaning that effective integration of child, parent and family needs can be difficult to achieve.

As a means of countering these difficulties, and capitalising on the current societal discourse around perinatal mental health and the '1001 critical days', in the UK the WAVE Trust has called for the development of 'pioneer communities' for perinatal and infant mental health, whose primary focus would be on channelling some of the money currently spent on child protection and other fire-fighting interventions, into developing a preventive approach focusing on the first 1001 days (Hosking and Kelly 2014, p.45). This model supports individual communities to see the emotional needs of both infants and their parents as important, and the role of the wider family and community as valuable in providing emotional support, containment and nurture to the whole family system.

2 Providing trauma-informed, integrated and responsive care across services

For many women and families, the perinatal period is the first time in their adult lives that they will have come into regular contact with primary care services, and they are dependent on these professional systems to help them navigate the transition to parenthood. Receiving perinatal care within a trauma-informed context (Seng and Taylor 2015) where there is a recognition that all care should be delivered with compassion and dignity and be responsive to individual need, might be expected to go some way towards healing previous trauma and framing this new journey in a more positive light. Trauma-informed care also requires staff in frontline services to be aware of the ways in which parents' histories, particularly of abuse and relational trauma, can influence care-seeking and wider interpersonal dynamics. Staff should also be supported to respond sensitively to these communications – helping parents to develop new narratives about relationships which might underpin more responsive relationships with their infants.

At a more specific level, McKenzie-McHarg and colleagues (2015) have demonstrated that training midwives and providing specialist maternity care plans for psychologically vulnerable women both improves parents' experiences of maternity care and reduces referrals to specialist therapy for birth trauma – suggesting that to develop services in this way not only improves outcomes for families but can potentially also reduce costs.

The principle of responsive care is also reflected in the UK Maternal Mental Health Alliance's philosophy of perinatal mental health being 'everyone's business'– where rather than specialist services being the only support structures available, wider service and community systems are encouraged to take responsibility for recognising when parents are struggling and offer screening, assessment, support or intervention at the earliest possible stage. Providing effective support at this tier is primarily based on putting into operation a set of core values. This might include prioritising the development of trust by providing continuity of care (Noonan *et al.* 2017), reducing stigma by ensuring that antenatal care is consistent and non-judgemental (WAVE Trust 2015), or committing to culturally responsive care by providing effective staff training and support (Noonan *et al.* 2017). The latter requires an awareness of the variation in attachment and parenting practices across cultures, and a willingness to acknowledge, reflect and respond when there is a difficult relationship emerging between the beliefs and expectations of the family and of the services who are aiming to support them.

The development of local communities of practice (Wenger 1998) with a shared interest in perinatal and infant mental health can help to maintain a shared value base and offer ways to address anxieties, create collaborative and fluid service systems and build on individual good practice. In an ideal world, there would be comprehensive training to all those coming into contact with infants and their parents across all services – in health or social care, the statutory or voluntary sector –

or who themselves may be focused on either adult or infant needs. This training should be co-produced by parents who have experienced difficulties during the perinatal period, but should also ensure that it continues to effectively balance the needs of mothers, fathers and infants in its focus, and that the voice of the child is not lost.

Nelson and Mann (2011) suggest that integrating psychological consultation into local provision can help to underpin these core values and the reflective capacity needed to sustain them. Joint working is another way of sharing good practice as well as developing the skills and confidence of frontline staff – for example, Chitty (2015) suggests a collaborative approach to screening between frontline health professionals (such as health visitors) and more specialist services. While effective screening is the first step to providing responsive services, there is also a need to ensure that parents do not ultimately feel undermined by perceived surveillance but instead that a respectful, collaborative approach is emphasised (Aston 2008).

Within specific perinatal systems, there have been increasing efforts to develop methods of working that promote infant mental health at all levels. Browne *et al.* (2016) describe the role of infant mental health providers (IMHPs) on neonatal units, who are able to offer support in a multitude of ways. This includes supporting parents to meet the wider practical and physical needs that can impede their time with their baby, to learn to pick up on their infant's cues and respond to these, to develop their skills in co-regulation of the infant's physiological and emotional states, and to explore some of the psychological barriers that can make it difficult to form a close bond with their baby. At the same time, the IMHPs are able to offer training and reflective practice for staff to understand the needs of both infants and their parents, to provide regular two-way feedback to build relationships between staff and parents, and to help staff reflect on structural aspects of the environment or procedures that may impact on family wellbeing.

As babies arrive home and families begin their lives together, it is imperative that the professional systems supporting them do so in a holistic and integrated manner. The 'toxic trio' of parental mental health difficulties, substance misuse and domestic violence are well known to have a significant impact on infant mental health and on the risk of abuse and neglect, but many families presenting with complex needs experience fragmented and often repetitive service involvement, further compounding their early experience of receiving insensitive and mis-attuned care. In response to this, the Think Family model (Diggins 2011) emphasises the need for services to implement 'family' threshold criteria, meaning that the needs of parent and child are seen as a unit and that creative means are employed to ensure that the whole family's needs are identified and addressed as a unit rather than individual parts. The emphasis here is again on seeing the infant at the centre of the work, with attuned parenting as a goal in itself rather than the emphasis being solely on a series of parent-focused interventions that may or may not improve the experience of the child.

3 Delivering specialist psychotherapeutic support where needed, cutting across the artificial boundary of adult and child services

The hope is that by providing the setting conditions for good infant mental health, as described above, there is a decreased need for families to access specialist therapeutic intervention. Nonetheless, it is unrealistic to expect that these efforts will remove the need for specialist support altogether, and many families who have experienced multiple ACEs are likely to require additional support if the intergenerational cycle of disadvantage is to be broken.

The University of Warwick Infant Mental Health Pathway (2013) provides an overview of many of the direct interventions at a universal, targeted and specialist level that have been demonstrated to promote good parent–infant mental health outcomes, developing in intensity in relation to level of need.

At a *universal level*, there is a range of antenatal programmes that can support parents to prepare emotionally for the experience of becoming a family. These include the Solihull Approach (Douglas 2016) and Mellow Bumps antenatal groups (Puckering 2013), which each have a particular focus on infant mental health rather than the primarily physical focus of many other group programmes. Health visitors can also use the antenatal promotional guides (Purra *et al.* 2005) to support parents to develop a sense of their baby as having its own mind, and to consider their own relationship with the baby at the early stage.

After the birth, and in the first year, frontline staff are encouraged to screen the relationship between infant and parent and to promote skin-to-skin contact and the concept of the social baby, using materials such as the 'Getting to know your baby' app (https://web.bestbeginnings.org.uk/web/videos/caring-for-my-baby/getting-to-know-your-baby). They are encouraged to model reflective functioning and to promote bonding activities such as infant massage, where parents will be supported to tune into their baby's cues.

For parents who are more vulnerable, targeted antenatal groups such as the National Society for the Prevention of Cruelty to Children's 'Baby Steps' programme (focusing on the couple relationship and their relationship with the baby) (Coster, Brookes and Sanger 2015) and Peep's Nurturing Parents programme (which focuses on developing reflective functioning) (Evangelou and Sylva 2003) may be more effective at starting to mitigate some of the potential intergenerational transmission of insecurity. The Family Nurse Partnership approach (Barnes *et al.* 2011) is another way of intervening early; in this case by giving parents who are vulnerable by virtue of their young age a family nurse who can provide integrated support for the psychological and physiological aspects of maternity and infant care. For more discussion of this approach see Chapter 4.

Where parents are experiencing significant difficulties with their mental health and/or within their relationship with their baby, a range of more specialist interventions might be offered to explore these needs. These might helpfully take a more individual focus for the parent (using individual models appropriate to his or her experiences and priorities), but there is evidence that offering effective intervention for the parent's own mental health may not automatically improve the relationship with the infant. Practitioners must therefore also be able to assess and intervene at a relational level. For example, parents might take part in a specialist group such as the Mellow Babies (Puckering *et al.* 2010) or Circle of Security (Cassidy *et al.* 2011) programme, developing their capacity for sensitive responsiveness and play in the context of the parent's own emotional wellbeing. Specialist parent–infant psychotherapy (e.g., 'Watch, Wait, Wonder'; Cohen *et al.* 1999) allows parents to explore the 'ghosts in the nursery' which might be impacting both on their own emotional wellbeing and their ability to relate to their baby. Interventions such as Video Interaction Guidance (Kennedy, Ball and Barlow 2017) have demonstrated good outcomes for promoting attuned and responsive parenting and, in parents with complex mental health needs, might be used as part of a wider intervention which allows them to integrate their experience of being a parent with the opportunity to develop their own emotional resilience (Kenny *et al.* 2013).

Whatever the specific model of intervention offered, the likelihood of success is increased hugely by the context in which it is provided – where the community and political landscape are supportive and where service provision is effectively integrated, holistically driven and responsive to the relational needs of both parent and infant.

Example of an emerging service model

There has been a long-standing commitment to early intervention within Liverpool, but the political and service contexts have fluctuated significantly in the last decade. Many pockets of excellent practice have fallen victim to cuts to both health and social care services, creating gaps through which families have fallen.

In 2013 LivPIP (Liverpool Parent Infant Partnership, connected to national organisation PIP-UK) was commissioned to offer support to some of the most vulnerable families during the first 1001 critical days. LivPIP offers parent–infant and systemic psychotherapy to families from conception to the age of two, as well as training and consultation in infant mental health to frontline staff.

In parallel, the Child and Adolescent Mental Health Service at Alder Hey Children's NHS Foundation Trust has developed a model of training, consultation and referral, based within Liverpool's Children's Centres, that aims to break down some of the traditional barriers to very young children accessing specialist mental health support. This model of offering training and consultation to both frontline providers and specialist CAMHS staff, as well as specialist therapeutic intervention (e.g., Video Interaction Guidance, Systemic Family Practice), has allowed an increasingly well-integrated model of infant mental health provision to emerge.

More recently, NHS England has also commissioned a Specialist Community Perinatal Mental Health Service in the region, which provides assessment, birth planning and multidisciplinary intervention for women who experience moderate to severe mental health difficulties in the perinatal period (conception to age 1). This service will also be providing training to other mental health and frontline professionals, as well as supervision to the Enhanced Midwifery team who provide the maternity care for vulnerable women.

A community of practice has been established with a range of local agencies, and close partnership working is being developed between the three specialist services. The aim is to ensure that the needs of mum, baby and partner are recognised and intervention offered at whichever level of the system can provide the most effective mechanism of change. While still some way from being the single 'family mental health' service that the authors would prefer to see, this collaboration is a crucial step towards demonstrating the value of integrated and responsive perinatal and infant mental health provision across the statutory and voluntary sector.

Conclusion

This is an exciting time in the field of perinatal and infant mental health, with the emerging evidence base for interventions with both parents and infants developing apace, alongside a growing acknowledgement that investment in this area is key to promoting the life chances of vulnerable children.

However, the ability of specialist services to be proactive and responsive is influenced by the social and political climate in which they, and families themselves, are growing and developing. Those services supporting families on the frontline report a need for training, support and opportunities to reflect on their work with families, in order to develop a culture where infant and family mental health is seen as 'everyone's business' and models of care are responsive to psychological as well as physiological need.

Ultimately, in order for support to be effective, there needs to be a sense within the political discourse that parents and the parenting role are valued, and where there is an understanding of infants as sentient beings who have emotional as well as physical needs. Similarly, we need societal recognition that parenting is a complex role, that is most effectively done by a 'village' (or social network) rather than an isolated nuclear family, and that to struggle in this role is to be human – reducing the stigma and the fear of criticism that makes it so hard for parents to share their experiences.

With these tiers of support in place, we have every reason to encourage vulnerable parents to feel optimistic that they can break the cycle.

Chapter 3

Building sustainable parent interventions in early years

CAROLINE WHITE

Introduction

Early intervention

The evidence for investing in early intervention in the early years of a child's life is overwhelming. There is a large body of research evidence showing that environmental influences from conception to three years of age impact significantly on a child's academic, language, social and emotional development. Poor early life experiences can permanently impair the healthy growth of very young children's brains, while positive experiences can have the opposite effect, promoting healthy brain development. The central tenet of early intervention is that by preventing problems arising in the first place, and/or remedying problems as early as possible, families can be supported to help their children develop to their full potential. There is long-standing research evidence that parent interventions can be highly effective in the prevention and treatment of emotional and behavioural difficulties in young children (Brestan and Eyberg 1998; Gardner, Montgomery and Knerr 2015).

Alongside the scientific case to be made for early intervention and the significant potential to improve outcomes for children, economists and politicians are increasingly recognising the financial case for early intervention (Allen 2011a). There are effective, evidence-based interventions suitable for preschool children and their families which not only provide good outcomes but also have positive cost-benefit analyses. Investing funds in these interventions saves on wider public expenditure. It is therefore interesting that so few services implement these interventions robustly enough to have a major impact on improving the psychological outcomes for children (Timimi 2015;

Wolpert *et al.* 2017) and reducing the financial burden on the public purse (Scott *et al.* 2001a).

In this chapter, a model for successful delivery and sustainable implementation of effective evidence-based interventions in the early years will be discussed. This will include exploration of the role of national and local policy, of frontline and strategic managers, training and supervision of staff, and cultural beliefs and values; in addition, the barriers and obstacles commissioners, managers and workers face will be discussed.

Early childhood development

As discussed in the previous chapter, the very earliest experiences, from conception, shape a baby's brain development and have a lifelong impact on their mental and emotional health. From birth to 18 months, connections in the brain are created at a rate of one million per second. If these connections are not repeated many, many times the brain cells themselves will disappear; and it requires sensitive and responsive parenting from caregivers in order to establish critical brain mass. By 3 years of age a child's brain has reached 85 per cent of its full development.

Yet babies are also at their most vulnerable to abuse and neglect in these early months. Most deaths of children occur in the perinatal period, with babies being disproportionately vulnerable to abuse and neglect (Leadsom *et al.* 2014). In England, they are seven times more likely to be killed than an older child; and 36 per cent of serious case reviews involve a baby under one year of age. Perinatal mental health, domestic violence and substance abuse are frequently highlighted in such cases and it is estimated that approximately 26 per cent of babies in the UK are living within complex family situations. There is now good medical evidence that when a foetus or baby is exposed to such toxic stressors it can permanently raise their cortisol levels leading to a distorted stress response in later life. Research consistently shows that these early difficulties are often the precursor to preschool behaviour problems, followed by conduct disorder in later life, alcohol and drug misuse, mental health problems and, potentially, a life of social exclusion (Broidy *et al.* 2003; Fergusson, Horwood and Riddler 2005; Scott *et al.* 2001b).

In order to support optimal brain development, it is imperative that babies have the best possible start in life, and there is long-standing research evidence that a strong attachment between a baby and the caregiver provides the basis for positive outcomes in terms of academic, social and emotional development. There is good evidence that effective interventions are available for babies, preschoolers and their caregivers to reduce these risks and provide a more stable foundation for child development.

National policy

Over the past decade there has been a wealth of national policy and cross-party collaborations highlighting the importance of intervention in the early years, the basic premise being that identification of problems early in life will not only be the most effective in terms of child outcomes, but also the most cost effective in terms of public expenditure.

One of the most influential was the publication of *Early Intervention: Good Parents, Great Kids, Better Citizens* (Allen and Duncan-Smith 2008). This cross-party document concluded that, having looked at previous approaches to tackling anti-social behaviour, successive governments with multiple policies have failed to improve outcomes. It presented the case for intervening early and suggested that the major political parties put their differing views aside to tackle the intergenerational cycle of underachievement and social disorder. A follow-up report, *Early Intervention: The Next Steps* (Allen 2011b), proposed a radical new social policy of early intervention to deliver effective, evidence-based interventions, to develop an Early Intervention Foundation (EIF), and to support the development of research in innovative areas. It highlighted that child public expenditure was at its lowest when the child's development is most rapid and has the greatest capacity to change; with high levels of expenditure much later in life tackling mental health problems, anti-social behaviour and drug and alcohol addiction. A compelling case was made for preventative strategies, noting that the economic returns of intervening early were well documented.

A range of policy documents have been produced, all reinforcing the same message regarding the enormous significance of the early years. *The Marmot Review: Fair Society, Healthy Lives* (Marmot 2010, p.22) asserts that 'the foundations of virtually every aspect of human development are laid in early childhood. What happens during these early years (starting in the womb) has lifelong effects on many aspects of health and well-being.' *The Foundation Years: Preventing Poor Children Becoming Poor Adults* (Field 2010) and *The Early Years: Foundations for Life, Health and Learning* (Tickell 2011) both state the same important principles for better outcomes.

The Department for Education outlined in its service reform paper for 0–5-year-olds that 'The foundation years are vitally important both in their own right and for promoting future life chances. The moral argument is clear and the economic cost to society of failing children in the foundation years is becoming increasingly well understood' (Department for Education 2011, p.8). It emphasised the need to:

- focus on child development

- recognise that families are the most important influence on children in the foundation years

- promote effective and evidence-based early intervention

- improve the quality of the workforce.

Most recently, the EIF published two documents (Asmussen *et al.* 2016; Axford *et al.* 2015) outlining that the strongest evidenced interventions targeted the early signals of risk, which are:

- child behaviour problems

- insecure attachment

- delayed speech development

- lack of maternal sensitivity.

They also highlighted the importance of the parent or primary caregiver as being best placed to support the child's optimal development. The Department of Health's *Future in Mind* (NHS England 2015) restates the vital importance of early intervention and the need for effective evidence-based parenting interventions.

With approximately 27 per cent (and rising) of children living in poverty (Axford *et al.* 2015), and all the risks associated with child poverty, it seems clearer than ever that tackling these issues from the point of conception is essential. The real question is, why do so few services provide the kinds of high-quality care and interventions that all of these documents recommend and highlight as being of crucial importance, especially when the financial argument for early intervention is as strong as for child outcomes?

Implementation science

One of the biggest criticisms of evidence-based interventions is that they don't transport well from research trials into 'real-world' services. Implementation science is still relatively new and studies the process of implementing evidence-based programmes into real settings. Increasingly, there are models for implementation being developed and many programme developers of existing evidence-based programmes have their own research and strategies to support successful implementation. However, the evidence for successful, effective and sustainable implementations is still very limited despite these frameworks and redesign of the workforce. For example, children's services across England have, for eight years, had access to funded, accredited training and managerial support and training to transform services to deliver evidence-based interventions via Children and Young People – Improving Access to Psychological Therapies (CYP-IAPT provides a one-year, postgraduate diploma in evidence-based interventions, with a view to transforming services to improve access). Despite the success of workers trained in one-year postgraduate diplomas in relevant interventions, there are still few robust examples of sustainable implementations of this evidence-based intervention (Timimi 2015).

Another example is highlighted when taking a look at the National Institute for Health and Care Excellence (NICE) guidance for the treatment and prevention of behaviour problems (including conduct disorder and attention deficit hyperactivity disorder) and the promotion of social and emotional wellbeing in early years. Unsurprisingly, evidence-based, group parent training is highlighted as a model of best practice (National Institute for Health and Care Excellence 2012, 2013, 2018). However, very few child and adolescent mental health services (CAMHS) even take referrals for under 5-year-olds, where we know intervention is most effective, cost effective and preventative; and many CAMHS services do not provide group-based parent training as part of their care pathways for older children with these difficulties either. Equally, very few early years frontline workers such as health visitors, nursery nurses and family support workers have any remit in their job roles to deliver such evidence-based interventions. There is no doubt these professionals work extremely hard and play a vital role in safeguarding children and supporting families. However, it does leave the question about the evidence for their effectiveness in terms of measurable child outcomes and whether this is the best way to invest public funds.

Despite its relative infancy, implementation science tells us some important principles regarding the effective mechanisms involved in developing services to deliver successful evidence-based interventions. Unfortunately, the least effective strategies are the most common (Fixsen *et al.* 2005) and these include information dissemination alone and staff training in isolation. Fixsen *et al.* (2005) states the key components for successful and sustainable implementation are:

- having a longer-term and multi-level approach

- careful practitioner selection for training

- skills-based training

- practice-based coaching

- using fidelity measures

- practitioner evaluation

- programme evaluation

- facilitative administration

- being programme driven, not practitioner driven

- policy makers understanding the implementation themselves.

Interestingly, most implementation models also highlight these themes, and the CYP-IAPT programme shares the same principles and methods too, yet there are still very few examples of sustained, evidence-based implementations. It appears there is a parallel process taking place, whereby the evidence we have for successful implementation is as difficult to implement as the intervention itself!

Children And Parents Service, Manchester: a successful model of sustainable evidence-based implementation in the early years

Maybe there is something to be learned by taking a look in some detail at models of best practice, where effective, evidence-based interventions have been embedded successfully and have achieved and maintained positive outcomes for children and families over time. The Children And Parents Service (CAPS) in Manchester has consistently demonstrated impressive results using standardised, reliable and valid outcome measures, with significant improvements in child behaviour problems, and parental depression and stress. These results have been maintained over time, and data has shown that children are more ready for school and parents are more likely to get a job or go back to college as a direct result of the parenting intervention. These impacts are substantial and lifelong, so why are there not more services achieving this standard? It is possible that, while guiding principles are helpful, the actual details of applying them are worthy of more scrutiny.

CAPS is a citywide, jointly commissioned, multi-agency early intervention service that delivers effective, evidence-based interventions to preschool children and their families. It was established in 1998 following a successful bid to identify behaviour problems in young children and deliver evidence-based parent groups in community settings across Manchester. The service has delivered the same evidence-based intervention for almost 20 years and has been highlighted as a model of best practice by NICE for 'early years social and emotional wellbeing' (National Institute for Health and Care Excellence 2012).

CAPS initiated as a partnership between three organisations: health (CAMHS), the local authority (Manchester City Council) and a third sector agency (Family Action; formerly Family Service Unit and Family Welfare Association). The CAMHS-led team consisted of a clinical psychologist and two family support workers to deliver the interventions, with the provision of funding for child care available as part of the bid. In addition, an assistant psychologist was appointed to support the evaluation of the project. The service was fairly innovative at the time and followed many of the principles that were later implemented by the government initiative Sure Start.

The initial funding was for three years and was commissioned by the CAMHS commissioner as part of the NHS Modernisation Fund.

The service's main aims were to identify early child behaviour problems, to deliver effective evidence-based parent programmes and to provide a seamless referral process to other services where necessary. There is an enormous range of parent interventions available and understanding the research thoroughly in order to choose the most effective and cost effective is not an easy task. This chapter will not present the wealth of research regarding the many parenting interventions as this is already well documented in other texts (Brestan and Eyberg 1998; Furlong *et al.* 2012).

The evidence-based parent intervention commissioned was the Incredible Years® Parent Programme, due to its highly robust evidence base (Brestan and Eyberg 1998; Webster-Stratton 1990, 1997, 1998, 2000; Webster-Stratton and Reid 2012), including multiple randomised controlled trials by independent researchers, who were not the programme developer, across different settings and populations (Gardner *et al.* 2015; Bywater *et al.* 2009; McGilloway *et al.* 2014; Møerch *et al.* 2004; Scott *et al.* 2001b).

The detail behind this initial phase reveals important factors about the implementation. While most implementation models talk about the importance of a 'champion' within the service, this alone is not enough. It is also critical that the 'champion' has relevant knowledge and expertise in the evidence-based programme chosen, has a thorough understanding of what it entails to model fidelity (i.e. ensure that it is delivered in exactly the same way it was in the original research) and, crucially, has some authority for shaping the service delivery model.

It was also essential that this information and intelligence were shared and disseminated to commissioners and strategic leads so there was mutual understanding of the details. This process was established over a long period of time, via several face-to-face meetings, with a collaborative approach. This included an understanding of the programme, its effectiveness, its cost-effectiveness and the enormous commitment required to deliver it to model fidelity, in order to achieve the same positive outcomes. There are far too many examples of services with experienced, well-meaning practitioners delivering evidence-based programmes poorly, which simply doesn't work and wastes public money.

The Incredible Years® Parent Programme

The Incredible Years® Parent Programme is a series of evidence-based interventions that focus on strengthening parenting competencies to improve the parent–child relationship, promote children's academic, emotional and social skills and reduce conduct problems. The research evidence for the programme's effectiveness and cost-effectiveness is extensive and the findings have been replicated in many countries, across diverse populations over many years (Gardner *et al.* 2015). There has also been much research on which components of parent programmes make them effective (Webster-Stratton 2004, 2016). These include:

- group based
- based on social learning theory
- manualised programme
- videotaped modelling
- role play and rehearsal
- removing barriers to access
- highly skilled workforce with ongoing accredited video supervision.

A glance down this list will highlight immediately that the majority of parent and family support currently provided would not meet many of these criteria, and with just a little further examination the many obstacles to implementation become clearer.

Time

In relation to setting up CAPS, this knowledge and expertise of the Incredible Years® Parent Programme allowed the bid to be realistic in terms of timeframes, outputs and outcomes. It ensured that staff were allocated the appropriate amount of time to deliver parent courses; for Incredible Years®, a minimum of one-and-a-half days per week is recommended for both group leaders for every group delivered. As a new project, with newly appointed staff, it was realistic to expect that it would take even longer to acquire new skills, set up new referral pathways, establish good working relationships with children's centres and design a thorough system for data analysis.

Manchester is a culturally diverse city with a high-need, complex population of vulnerable families who may be seen as 'hard to reach'. The approach of CAPS was to acknowledge that it is often services that are 'hard to reach' and an assertive outreach model was adopted for parental engagement, which is inevitably time consuming and requires high degrees of skill acquisition. As a result, two-and-a-half days per week were actually allocated in the bid for group leaders to ensure enough time to do all of these elements effectively. Many implementations fail due to the absence of protected staff time in the job plan to deliver evidence-based programmes to model fidelity and they often underestimate the challenges of a totally new set-up.

Access

The stigma attached to attending a parenting course is a huge barrier, and the term 'parent training' is often perceived as 'parent blaming'. The art of engaging 10–12 potentially resistant parents, often with their own clinically significant mental health problems, in a minimum 14-week intervention for two hours per week is a truly challenging task. An enormous amount of time, effort and service redesign needs to be invested for services to break down barriers to engagement; these include providing high-quality child care and interpreters.

CAPS parent courses were delivered in children's centres but not all centres were Ofsted registered for a crèche and links were developed with other child care providers locally to resolve this. Some parents had never separated from their children so additional support was needed, prior to the course, to settle children, and this required highly skilled crèche staff. CAPS psychologists provided one-day training to frontline, multi-agency staff across early years in attachment and parenting strategies covered by the course. This ensured the wider workforce were consistent in supporting parents and also improved communication and referral pathways. In the original bid, funding was set aside for crèche provision, interpreters and refreshments for parents. Without this budget, most services are unable to provide the necessary infrastructure to enable parental access to courses.

Even when funds are available, some organisations find it difficult to change their cultural norm. For example, senior managers demanded why parents should get refreshments on the parent courses when other interventions didn't provide that, and biscuits were banned from buildings as it didn't promote healthy eating. These factors may seem petty but parents won't come to a 14-week course, for two hours per week if you don't meet their basic needs, nurture them and provide high-quality child care. These tiny obstacles can soon become insurmountable and, without the organisational support from strategic and operational managers, the intervention fails.

Materials and equipment

One of the early steps to implementing an evidence-based programme is to purchase the materials required to deliver it. For Incredible Years® this comprises a manual, DVDs and tip sheets costing approximately £1500 ($2000), and each parent requires a book (or downloaded version) and photocopies of the tip sheets. This should be one of the simplest steps but unfortunately can cause chaos within organisations. The materials must be purchased in US dollars and this can lead to an investigation about why materials are being purchased from another country, followed by a pointless tendering process to find the cheapest possible solution, despite materials only being available from the programme developer in the US. This can take months to resolve.

It is also common for managers to question the perceived 'enormous' cost of this intervention. Research consistently tells us that it costs approximately £1500 per family and has a positive cost-benefit analysis (i.e. investing money in it, saves more money). There seems an excessive desire to only use or develop 'home-grown' (UK) interventions. This seems inexplicable when the evidence base is so strong across countries and cultures and has over 30 years of research (Gardner *et al.* 2015). There are several national implementations across Europe; why is England any different? There appears to be a cultural bias towards external models despite contradictory evidence that the programme works cross-culturally. Would we have the same approach if another country had developed the cure for cancer?

Other equipment is also required for delivery: a large television or projector and good quality speakers. In community settings, it is important to establish that equipment is available for all 14 weeks, that it works, that remote controls are available, that batteries are charged and that someone knows how to use the equipment. It is the minutiae that can make all the difference; but reports of schools needing to use televisions for assembly one week, lost remote controls between sessions and no one knowing how to get sound out of the projector are all too common. The solution CAPS adopted was to purchase its own equipment, with bespoke carriers for safe transportation and protection.

All practitioners are dependent on good organisational support for letter and report writing, photocopying, access to equipment and so on. Each of these time-consuming tasks is aided massively by a single place for equipment storage and administrative support to complete all paperwork in advance.

Model fidelity

Model fidelity is the term used to describe the process of facilitators delivering an evidence-based programme as closely as possible to the developer's intentions to ensure the same outcomes as were obtained in the original research. This is key to the success of the programme.

It is useful here to compare the implementation approach to medical treatments with those for psychological interventions. In parent programmes, all too frequently, the number of sessions is reduced from 14 weeks to as few as six to eight sessions. Courses are sometimes run with one group leader instead of two, and many without ever having any supervision of their practice. In some instances, they do receive supervision, but from someone without any training or experience of the programme themselves. Now imagine this same 'dilution' of intervention if it were for radiotherapy treatment for cancer. If the research states 14 sessions are required for efficacy then this is given; and the practitioner giving the radiotherapy most certainly would have been supervised many times and had their practice supervised by someone with the qualifications to do so.

Furthermore, with the cancer analogy, if this were a pharmaceutical intervention model, fidelity refers to the 'active ingredients' that make the intervention effective. Incredible Years® has many checklists, protocols and evaluation tools to help practitioners follow the programme to model fidelity by using these 'active ingredients'. Two of the main ingredients include video modelling to promote discussion in the groups, and role play and rehearsal to allow parents experiential learning and to practise the strategies.

The video clips are of parent–child interaction in American families, and some are quite dated and even unintentionally humorous. New group leaders often feel uncomfortable using the videos, being embarrassed by the age of the material and also assuming the American accents aren't relevant to a UK audience. Parents complete weekly evaluations and new group leaders frequently report that parents rate the videos negatively. Sometimes group leaders then abandon the video clips, hence leaving out a crucial active ingredient.

The role play and rehearsal element is another barrier, with the majority of practitioners having a strong dislike and/or fear of participating in role play, and the same is almost universally true for parents too. It is therefore easy to understand why some new group leaders avoid doing role plays, for fear of parental drop out. This again often leads to the removal of a key ingredient for success.

However, accredited, experienced group leaders don't find the same resistance to the videos or to integrating several role plays at every session. This tells us something about the high level of skills required to deliver the programme collaboratively. Protocols and checklists are important tools but the only way to ensure model fidelity is by accessing accredited, video supervision from a certified Incredible Years® mentor and to have all practitioners work towards their own accreditation.

Most organisations don't consider the role of ongoing supervision for practitioners following the three-day initial training. There exists a belief that psychological interventions can be tampered with and endlessly adapted, and with parent training in particular there is a professional snobbery that it is not an especially skilled intervention. Within many CAMHS organisations, parenting interventions have disappeared from provision altogether, being outsourced to local authorities and the third sector, despite the fact that NICE guidance recommends evidence-based group parent training as the first line of treatment for conduct disorder and attention deficit hyperactivity disorder – the majority of CAMHS referrals. The challenge of attaining long-term, sustainable change in 10–12 often anxious and depressed parents, resistant to advice due to previous failures, requires complex collaborative and group processes – skills taking years to master. Would you want your cancer specialist to have only had a three-day training before administering your intervention?

CAPS benefited hugely from an individual desire by the lead psychologist to access accredited supervision and attain accreditation to ensure model fidelity. At the time, this was only possible via direct contact with the programme developer in Seattle. It was, however, also understood that this was not a sustainable model for supervision going forward. As a result, discussions took place with the programme developer to develop an infrastructure for providing more accredited training and supervision in the UK. This structure now exists internationally, making it much more accessible.

Supervision and accreditation

The Incredible Years® has a well-established training/accreditation process with four levels:

- group leader
- peer coach
- mentor
- trainer.

Each level has specific requirements involving months of training, shadowing, video submissions and delivery, with strict criteria to be achieved. To put this into context, there are currently only eight trainers in the world, 50–60 mentors and nearly 100 peer coaches. Mentors are required to attend an international meeting each year in either the US, Canada or Europe, supported by their agency.

Ideally, to build a sustainable intervention, a plan to develop accredited group leaders, peer coaches and a mentor should be considered from the start. The sooner this process begins, the sooner the organisation reduces costs and becomes more self-sustainable in providing supervision. Realistically, it takes about two years for a group leader to become accredited, another two years to become a peer coach and perhaps another two years to become a mentor. As the majority of public funding is increasingly short term, this makes forward planning challenging. A further barrier occurs when, as during austerity, organisations indiscriminately ban professional development to reduce expenditure. This is shortsighted as developing sustainable supervision within an organisation saves money.

The initial funding for CAPS was for three years and the staff were employed on fixed-term contracts. For the service to survive, it had to demonstrate positive outcomes for children and devise a proactive strategy to develop the lead psychologist to become a mentor. This enabled the service to develop the workforce and maintain the high standards of model fidelity required for success.

All parent group leaders required video supervision to shape the collaboration skills needed to be effective and achieve accreditation.

This meant that all parent group sessions had to be recorded, so video equipment was needed for every session and staff had to have training to use this equipment alongside editing software. Clinical governance policies also required this sensitive and confidential data to be handled safely and appropriately – something made even more complex when working in multi-agency settings. The technical skill and policy guidance required cannot be underestimated and requires organisational and managerial support at every level.

Part of this process involved written parental, informed consent. Many practitioners feel threatened by the prospect of video supervision and parents can be suspicious of video cameras in the room. However, well-informed parents rarely refuse consent and once an ethos of reflective practice is established these initial fears from practitioners can be overcome. It does, however, need strong leadership, organisational support and an expectation of best practice for effective implementation.

Data and evaluation

Outputs and outcomes are increasingly important for services to demonstrate, with a culture of key performance indicators and payment by results. In England, the IAPT programme has had some impact on transforming services to develop systems to analyse data, and a shift in the workforce to collect routine outcome measures. This is a good example of the influence a national driver, such as IAPT, can have in shaping organisational change long-term and challenging long-standing practices. It takes a whole organisational restructure to ensure it happens effectively. The workforce need to collect, input and analyse data while the database develops in line with service requirements. Managers need to operationally manage the timelines of each action and ensure data is accurate and complete.

For future funding, it seemed imperative that CAPS was able to demonstrate positive outcomes for preschool children and families in Manchester. Standardised, valid and reliable outcome measures were used – such as the Beck Depression Inventory (Beck *et al.* 1961), the Child Behaviour Inventory (Eyberg and Ross 1978) and the Parenting Stress Index (Abidin 1995) – to evaluate the impact of interventions, and an annual report was published demonstrating the intervention's effectiveness, with multiple demographics, highlighting risk factors and complexity of cases.

The routine collection, analysis and reporting of the outcome data for CAPS, such as the graphs shown here, has been pivotal in the continued success of the service. With demonstrable improvements in child behaviour problems and parental mental health reported annually, and sometimes more frequently, commissioners were able to make informed decisions about funding and service developments. Furthermore, this data provided a platform for dialogue with strategic leads regarding needs analysis and targets, including reach rates and uptake and retention of service users. The importance of high-quality data using the most robust outcome measures available cannot be overstated. In addition, the clear reporting and interpretation of this data is essential to make the information as accessible and transparent as possible. Explanation of the measures and clinical cut-offs to readers has proven to be more helpful than reporting statistical significance, as would be used in the research literature.

At a time when routine outcome measures were not used and computers were not on every clinician's desk, the creation and management of a database was seen as a high priority. The original bid included the appointment of an assistant psychologist to set up the database and input data. In many implementations, these 'gold' standard measures are not used simply because they cost money. While free measures are available they're not always appropriate for measuring the desired outcomes, and it can look as if the interventions had only minor impact. This is disastrous in terms of bidding for future funding, and investment in the most appropriate measures is very important.

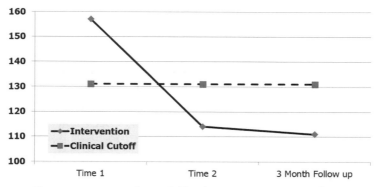

Figure 3.1: CAPS Eyberg Child Behaviour Inventory Total Score

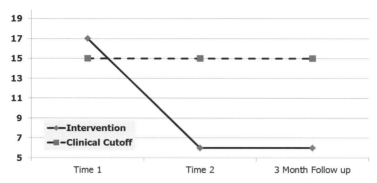

Figure 3.2: CAPS Eyberg Child Behaviour Inventory Problem Score

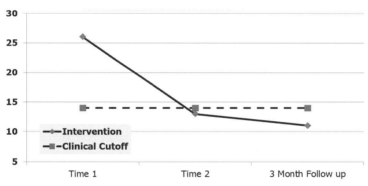

Figure 3.3: CAPS Beck Depression Inventory II

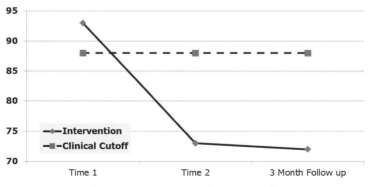

Figure 3.4: CAPS Parenting Stress Index

Local strategy and funding

CAPS was accountable to a multi-agency steering group consisting of both strategic and operational managers from each partner agency, plus the commissioner. Initially, this group met monthly, but later quarterly to ensure progress was made, targets were met and data was reported directly from the service lead. This created a collaborative forum where issues were discussed and problems resolved, and it was crucial that all partners agreed jointly with transparency. Annual reports were published, jointly owned and distributed widely to highlight the excellent outcomes achieved. This data formed the basis of all future bids and was imperative in strengthening the case for further funding and expansion.

Over the following two decades a series of national drivers and policies highlighted the importance of early years and early intervention as the foundation for life, and CAPS funding was increased with its strong track record of positive outcomes. The service lead was invited to participate in Manchester's Parent Board, Health and Wellbeing Board and Parenting Strategy. Many times there was uncertainty about funding, constant organisational change and shifts in policy. This was enormously challenging to manage and incredibly unsettling for the workforce, and yet staff turnover remained low and positive outcomes were not only maintained but improved on.

In 2011, with huge austerity measures, Manchester announced its largest cuts to public funding in history, with 2000 job losses (17% of the workforce) and a 26 per cent reduction of the budget for children's services. Over the following few years the early years budget was cut from £29 million to just £7 million and the number of children's centres reduced from approximately 50 to 12. This impacted enormously on the entire workforce across children's services. Despite this, CAPS received a significant increase in funding from the local authority, taking its total budget to £2 million, on the premise that with so little funding left, it had to be targeted and demonstrably effective. CAPS currently consists of 20 whole-time equivalent (wte) clinical psychologists, 21 wte parent group leaders and six administrative staff (including one information officer), with new partners Big Life (third sector) and Barnardo's (voluntary sector).

During the same period, Greater Manchester (GM), made up of Manchester local authority and nine others, was granted a devolved budget and an elected mayor. With this in mind, the ten boroughs were invited to participate in writing an early years pathway for all 0–5-year-olds across GM. Early years representatives from GM completed a needs assessment and a review of all interventions delivered. A staggering number of different, largely non-evidence-based interventions were identified. It took over two years, looking at models of best practice, but eventually the GM Start Well: Early Years Strategy (Greater Manchester Combined Authority 2016) was agreed. The main aims were for health visitors to complete developmental checks and implement the Healthy Child Programme, and for outreach workers to engage families unknown to services and to deliver evidence-based interventions to those in need – the priorities being group parent training and specialist speech and language therapy. Many services were decommissioned and the remaining workforce was trained in evidence-based assessments and interventions. Calculating the long-term cost benefits was integral and it was demonstrated that after approximately seven years, authorities would see a return on their investment. This was, and still is, a hugely ambitious goal and each authority is at different stages of its development.

Manchester currently has a preschool population of approximately 33,000 and estimated that approximately 20 per cent (6600) of those families needed a targeted intervention. CAPS already had a proven track record of delivering effective evidence-based parent programmes and the additional funding was to facilitate this scale-up. The service had also learned much about implementation, and shared knowledge has benefited developments in other boroughs. It is noteworthy that other local authorities have adopted different models of delivery but success has come from the application of the principles and details outlined in this chapter.

Scaling up with sustainability

CAPS has experienced two episodes of large scale-up, a challenge for most successful implementations. Usually an area trials a small-scale model and once positive results are achieved, they aim to roll it out broadly and quickly; however, training a new workforce, managing operational and administrative systems while handling the natural response to the uncertainty of change is difficult. The infrastructure of the organisation has to be sound, with good lines of accountability, excellent communication and organisational resilience consisting of effective systems and processes to ensure the maintenance of model fidelity.

As part of the development of CAPS, over several years, the psychologist workforce has also been trained in Video Interaction Guidance (VIG), another effective programme with a strong, emerging evidence base for improval of maternal sensitivity, and this is recommended in early years guidance (National Institute for Health and Care Excellence 2012). This is not part of any current commission but is an important implementation phase for effective delivery. The same principles have been applied as for Incredible Years® by developing a skilled workforce of accredited practitioners, supervisors and trainers, identifying the most accurate outcome measures and educating strategic leads and commissioners.

Change is inevitable in any organisation, let alone a large, citywide multi-agency service. What happens when your only mentor leaves for another job and it takes six years of training to replace them? How do you manage maternity leave and long-term sick leave when the locum workforce doesn't have the skills in the evidence-based programmes you deliver? How do you ensure that staff collect crucial follow-up data consistently and accurately when it's a boring part of the job and parents are difficult to contact? How do you keep staff motivated when funding is uncertain and policy is forever changing? The list of potential threats to the implementation is endless. Over the years, CAPS has developed a number of systems and processes to adapt to the ever-changing environment and to minimise inevitable challenges.

The first principle, adopted early on in CAPS, was to plan for the long term, regardless of unknown future budgets, as this was essential for forward planning. To protect staff time, CAPS developed clear job plans for each role, ensuring everyone had appropriate amounts of time to do all tasks. Also, each position's job description was reviewed and when necessary modified according to the requirements of the service (e.g., data collection was added to highlight its importance). This was done by the service lead in conjunction with the manager from each agency. An audit group was set up with representatives from each staff group, and regular audits completed (e.g., parental uptake and retention rates, referral patterns, outcome standards). At the end of each parent course, group leaders received summaries of outcomes and retention rates which was motivating and made the data meaningful. Collected data was handed in at weekly team meetings and minuted so there was transparency about missing data and an action plan could be made to rectify it. Group leaders collected data, and assistant psychologists inputted data. Scaling up created much more data management, and commissioners became much more demanding regarding demonstrating impact. As a result, a full-time information officer post was established, with responsibility for creating, developing and modifying a database specific to the needs of the service. This was absolutely crucial for long-term success as funding was dependent on demonstrable outcomes. Finally, proactive management of staff and application of performance management policies when necessary instilled an ethos of high quality.

Often when scaling up some associated costs get easily forgotten, and failure to include those costs into the budget can be fatal. CAPS consistently built in relevant additional funds for crèche staff, interpreters, staff equipment (including replacement of dated/broken equipment), administrative support, outcome questionnaires and refreshments and books for parents, accreditation fees and supervision.

A systematic approach was adopted to develop the service's capacity to provide supervision. All group leaders were expected to become accredited and this formed part of their annual appraisal to ensure progress; once accredited, all were trained and supported to become peer coaches. Two further mentors were also developed to remove reliance on one individual for future training and supervision. Most psychologists had a career path for pay progression; however, this was not true for family support workers, as with increased funding, opportunities were taken to restructure the service allowing those workers to achieve an increased pay grading once they became accredited peer coaches. This has contributed to low staff turnover and a feeling of being valued in the workforce.

To achieve model fidelity, supervision and accreditation were imperative and it was hugely beneficial that the service lead became a mentor (and eventually a trainer) in the evidence-based programme being delivered. It was advantageous for the person responsible for the implementation to know in great detail every element of the programme and what was needed for delivery. In addition, it meant that accredited supervision was consistently available for all staff 'in house' and annual requirements for attendance were set at every level. It is no coincidence that CAPS delivers the highest amount of accredited supervision of any implementation of Incredible Years® in the world and also has possibly the highest retention rates of parents (approximately 82% complete), while also working with the most vulnerable, complex and high-risk families.

CAPS maintains a commitment to model fidelity despite huge cultural pressure, especially during austerity, to deliver interventions quicker, faster, shorter and cheaper. Despite the service's established track record of success there is a constant need to exhaustively educate and disseminate to strategic leads and commissioners regarding model fidelity, why it is important and what it takes to achieve it, and this continues.

Chapter 4

Enhancing effective psychological care for families in primary care and community child health

Opportunities for integration

JAIME CRAIG

Introduction

In this chapter, the breadth of intervention in primary care and community child health will be explored, including descriptions from the research literature of different models of practice and their effectiveness. We will then pull out the key messages for practice and in particular how these might challenge service structure and the profession of clinical psychology to make most effective use of their cross-lifespan skills.

Given the complexity of interacting threats to wellbeing, and the ways in which these are displayed, no one therapeutic modality or approach will be effective in early intervention and nor can we assume that it can be undertaken effectively by those with the lowest or narrowest skillset. We will consider what models have been effective in supporting this work and those delivering it.

What do we mean by primary care?

When we refer to primary care in this chapter we mean those professionals working in a health context with children and young people as part of universal services, for example:

- general practitioners

- health visitors

- midwives

- school nurses

- school doctors/community paediatricians

- mental health/psychological practitioners working through and alongside them or in their spheres of influence.

There is clearly an overlap with topics covered in other chapters in this book, including the perinatal, physical health and education contexts, and in all of these there is overlap with social care when child protection or parenting capacity concerns come to the fore. While references will be made to these areas, the focus will be on primary care and community child health.

Despite a series of policy initiatives and attempts to highlight the importance of this work, it remains clear that professionals at this level both in education (e.g., Vostanis *et al.* 2013; Whitley, Smith and Vaillancourt 2013) and in primary care (e.g., Cousins, 2013) feel ill-equipped to work with mental health. McDougal (2011), with reference to nursing in particular, notes that the success of early intervention is dependent on a well-trained and supported workforce.

Models of effective work in primary care: innovation and translation

The research literature is not always helpful, particularly when one looks outside the UK. There are different models of service delivery context in other countries and direct comparisons may not be always appropriate. It is also the case that access to other areas of support either in social care, education or the voluntary sector will be different across the UK, which might make it difficult to identify isolated interventions and innovations that bring about effective change when context differences are considered. However, it can be useful to look at the learning from such initiatives to highlight core principles of effective practice in terms of children's emotional health, development and wellbeing.

There are several ways in which children's mental health has been targeted in primary care settings and Bower *et al.* (2001) conducted a systematic review. They suggest that these can helpfully be grouped into three models:

- Treatment/management by primary care professionals, for example general practitioners (GPs) and health visitors.

- Management by specialist mental health professionals working in primary care contexts.

- A 'consultation-liaison' model where specialists support primary care staff to manage child mental health difficulties.

Bower *et al.* (2001) note a limited research literature and that, of the studies available, few had controls. There can be many reasons why approaches may be unsuccessful in one context but not another, and good 'real-world' research design is key in aiding this understanding. Focusing on controlled studies, they found it difficult to reach meaningful conclusions about outcomes from studies of management by primary health care staff. Hewitt (1991) found little benefit in health visitors using structured interviews and information leaflets in the prevention of behavioural problems, although parent satisfaction was relatively high, but there were some encouraging results from specific behavioural interventions delivered by health visitors, for example interventions for sleep problems (Galbraith and Hewitt 1993).

However, evaluation of management of psychological difficulties by specialists working in primary care settings, particularly clinical psychologists, was more positive, for example Finney, Riley and Cataldo (1991), and Benson and Turk (1988). These studies reported significant reductions in parent-reported difficulties, behaviour and medical/primary care 'utilisation' (e.g., number of appointments, considered a key outcome in managing demand and capacity).

In terms of the consultation-liaison methods, Neira-Munoz and Ward (1998) explored the referral rates to specialist child mental health workers as a result of liaison clinics with primary care staff. They found a marked reduction in referral rate, and also that more referrals were rated as appropriate. However, only a third of the GPs felt that their knowledge and skills had increased as a result of liaison clinics. More recently, Wirral Primary CAMHS (Taylor 2017) have adopted a consultation/liaison and training model with no direct referrals to support schools who have an assigned CAMHS worker and who identify their own link worker. They offer an advice line open to anyone, including GPs, parents and social workers, and report a 40 per cent reduction in self-harm attendances at Accident & Emergency (A&E) departments, which they attribute to people using the helpline. The consultation is supported by online resources, and strategies include signposting to local organisations as well as training, brief input from primary mental health workers (PMHWs) and onward referral to specialist CAMHS liaison or advice. The work of the PMHWs on the advice line and clinically is quality assured by a CAMHS clinical psychologist.

Interagency working
The challenge of service structures

There are clearly challenges in ensuring that those in frontline positions have the competencies and access to advice when faced with the complexity of mental health, developmental and educational difficulties alongside the interplay with relationship, parenting capacity and family resilience. Identifying and targeting support most effectively in this system of interacting factors is a hugely skilful multi-modal task for any worker in isolation. The structures around services may do little to make available the additional skills needed in a timely and integrated fashion.

Previously in the UK, child development centres brought key professionals together. Child/family guidance of the 1920s has evolved into child mental health services, and where provision is poorest, services are conceptualised as targeting 'mental illness'. A side effect is that access for those in community child health to clinical psychology expertise now often sits behind these artificial barriers (which owe much to outdated models of adult mental health provision, no longer tolerated in adult services) or only within diagnosis-specific pathways. There are clear philosophical differences inherent in these different service structures in which much that was good has been lost. Co-working may be more problematic in current CAMHS than in service structures of the past. Good liaison and joint thinking often therefore falls to personal relationships and chance opportunities to meet – despite service organisation rather than because of it.

Partnership across agencies

Isolation limits the effectiveness of workers in the frontline. *Future in Mind* (Department of Health and NHS England, 2015) highlights the lack of cohesion between child mental health services and recommends a 'whole systems approach' to how assessments are coordinated and support is planned and delivered. In a systematic review of interagency collaboration in children and young people's mental health, Cooper, Evans and Pybis (2016) note that interagency collaboration was perceived as helpful by both service users and professionals. However, outcomes were mixed, with some findings indicating that interagency collaboration was associated with greater service use and equity of service provision, but others suggesting negative outcomes on service use and quality. The most common perceived barriers to collaboration were inadequate resourcing and poor interagency communication along with different perspectives and poor understandings across agencies and concerns about confidentiality issues.

Working across agencies means working across at times competing philosophies and different understandings of difficulties. Different conceptualisations can lead to conflicting advice. One example of this is that parents of children with developmental disorders showing challenging behaviour may be told that difficult behaviours are part of the condition and this prevents them looking to develop or implement strategies to improve such difficulties. Similarly, CAMHS services may utilise the same logic to refuse referrals for anxiety in children with autism spectrum disorder (ASD) diagnoses (Read and Schofield 2010).

Partnership with families

The importance of parental expectancies, including treatment satisfaction, on both children's engagement with and outcomes from interventions was highlighted by Acri *et al.* (2016). They found that parental satisfaction with an intervention for behavioural 'disorders' was predictive of both parental stress and ratings of child oppositional behaviours independently. Considering and meeting the psychological needs of the parents can challenge service structures but this study highlights what most practitioners on the ground recognise – that not doing so impacts on outcomes for the whole family. Services need to consider how to come together to provide more holistic interventions, but there is a tension here as more discrete 'treatments' may be more easily delivered than holistic or integrated ones.

Integrated approaches
The example of community paediatrics
GPs are faced with this complexity daily and will often call on the expertise of 'generalists' in community child health: community paediatricians/school doctors (depending on local service structures). *Facing the Future: Together for Child Health* (Royal College of Paediatrics and Child Health, Royal College of Nursing, and Royal College of General Practitioners 2015) articulates guidelines to ensure that specialist child health expertise and support are available directly into general practice services, 'where the needs of the child and their family are known' (p.7). The standards aim to build good connectivity between hospital and community settings; primary and secondary care; and paediatrics and general practice.

The task typically is disentangling the biological, emotional, neurodevelopmental, attachment and parenting capacity factors to understand what will often present as behavioural quandaries in primary care and community child health. It is often far from clear who holds responsibility for children presenting with 'behaviour problems' across health, social care and education, and by default many GPs, social care and education professionals refer to community paediatrics when they have concerns.

While local organisation varies, community paediatricians typically provide assessment, diagnosis, management and long-term oversight of children, with a focus on prevention, continuity of care and multi-agency team working, including across organisational boundaries, especially with education and social care (Royal College of Paediatrics and Child Health 2017).

Their expertise extends to working with vulnerable groups of children and their carers, including children with neurodevelopmental disorders and disabilities, and those with physical health needs. Their work brings them into contact with parents whose parenting capacity may be impaired by overlapping factors such as parental mental health difficulties, substance misuse, learning difficulties and possible domestic abuse. The risk of poor mental health and psychological wellbeing is therefore increased in many of the families they meet.

Community paediatricians also have several statutory duties in which their holistic 'bio-psychosocial' approach to understanding development and child health and wellbeing is needed and in which there are opportunities to act preventatively. These are:

- physical and mental health wellbeing assessments and advice for children and young people who become looked after or are in the process of being adopted

- child protection

- notification and assessment of children with special educational needs.

In each of these areas, it is clear that the role of the community paediatrician is broad and necessarily integrative, drawing on the skills and expertise of a range of others, including speech and language therapists, occupational therapists and psychologists, to augment assessments. They can take a lead in coordinating the ongoing case management of interacting factors for a child and their family.

By virtue of their role and approach, community paediatricians may often identify child and family mental health and psychological wellbeing difficulties, and do so early, but their basic training may not enable them to undertake the assessments and interventions needed for complex cases. Some will have undertaken more specialist training while others will need access to specialist skills in order to work effectively with many of these families. They may, however, face challenges in advocating for the services and interventions needed. Research by the Paediatric Mental Health Association suggests that a growing proportion of community paediatric work is concerned with responding to emotional and behavioural presentations and, at the same time, under resource pressures, a trend towards reduction in the amount of liaison and joint work between paediatrics and CAMHS (Davie 2015).

The primacy of the comprehensive assessment

High-quality, comprehensive assessment is key to effective intervention and prevention regarding child and family wellbeing, including but not limited to consideration of neurodevelopmental, attachment, emotional, social, behavioural, parenting capacity, social/environmental, trauma, educational factors. This understanding is highlighted in recent NICE assessment guidelines in relation to attachment difficulties (National Institute for Health and Clinical Excellence 2015).

The example of children with neurodevelopmental difficulties

Nowhere is this more evident than for children with possible neurodevelopmental difficulties due to the high rates of co-occurrence (Lundstrom *et al.* 2015). A skilled psychological perspective is crucial to good assessment and to avoid what Gillberg (2010) terms assessment 'dead-ends'. These will include assessments of the child and family and formal psychological assessment (including cognitive assessment) alongside gathering information about the child in different settings.

Children with neurodevelopmental difficulties are far more likely than the general population to experience poor mental health (Van Steensel, Bogels and Perrin 2011) and behavioural signs of psychological distress are easily overlooked (Read and Schofield 2010). The need for multi-professional assessment is clear and ideally would not be limited to diagnostic pathways. Even within such pathways, capacity and availability impacts on intervention, particularly preventative work.

This impact is apparent in services for children with attention deficit hyperactivity disorder (ADHD) diagnoses. As service capacity is under increased pressure, the focus on delivering evidence-based, non-pharmacological interventions for children with a diagnosis of ADHD appears to wane, as does the availability of early intervention pre-diagnosis.

Several factors can impede access, including cost and the availability of trained staff, but also a lack of clear responsibility for delivery of these types of interventions and poor coordination across systems (Vallerand, Kalenchuk and McLennan 2014). The authors make the point that these behavioural and family interventions are, maybe unsurprisingly, poorly detailed in treatment guidelines compared with pharmacological management.

Parent-level interventions may be less easily 'sold' to families. If this psychological understanding is not integrated into the process from the outset, such interventions are unlikely to be prioritised by families or services alike; it is crucial therefore that the integration is experienced by families (Hunt and Craig 2015).

Where such coordination exists, it is often down to the individuals rather than built into services strategically. However, the literature is scant in this area and many areas operate virtual teams on diagnostic pathways rather than integrated co-working as the norm for community paediatricians, school doctors and other colleagues contributing to assessments, such as clinical psychologists, speech and language therapists and CAMHS staff. There is more focus in the literature on linking physical health paediatrics with CAMHS, and psychological practice in this population is better described and evaluated in this field (see Chapter 6).

Hunt and Craig (2015) review and describe what could be considered good practice in terms of psychological services for children and young people with neurodevelopmental difficulties (autism spectrum conditions, attention deficit conditions, social communication disorders, Tourette's syndrome and motor coordination difficulties). They set out key indicators of good practice and challenge the utility of services organised around specific 'disorders'. They note the importance of recognising that services for these children span child health and CAMHS services and consider ways to improve coordination and co-working to deliver inclusive services.

They stress the importance of comprehensive and multidisciplinary assessments which situate 'diagnoses' within a wider psychological formulation of the child and family's difficulties, developing shared understanding and offering evidence-based interventions flowing from these formulations. For the vast majority of children with neurodevelopmental difficulties, they, their families and those who support them will require interventions that are primarily psychological and behavioural in nature, even when medication is indicated.

However, Hunt and Craig (2015) offer a sobering note, that in reviewing examples of good practice, further exploration often revealed that those who exemplified working in an integrated and flexible, proactive way across mental health, child health and education no longer existed or had been forced to alter their service remit in response to cuts.

The impact of poorly integrated provision

There are clearly challenges when a lack of collaboration leads to assessments or interventions in one agency being misunderstood or poorly conceptualised (or repeated) by other agencies. This can leave families vulnerable to confusion and also professionals unsure how to respond. Hutchings *et al.* (2007) give an example of a planned ignoring strategy known as 'differential attention' being negatively appraised by a social care colleague. The potential for such service miscommunication to impact negatively on families is evident, particularly in how psychological distress, difficulties and interventions are conceptualised and communicated.

Such differences may feed into identification bias. This is particularly true for behavioural difficulties. Teachers are more likely to seek help in relation to behavioural difficulties than emotional difficulties (Gowers, Thomas and Deeley 2004; Meltzer *et al.* 2003), as are GPs (Jacobs and Loades 2016). This clearly raises the question of both training and support from specialists in child mental health for these frontline workers. Indeed, several authors point to the low rate of identification of child mental health difficulties in primary care (e.g., Zwaanswijk *et al.* 2003) and a lack of confidence in offering appropriate and effective interventions at the primary care level (Cockburn and Bernard 2004).

Hutchings and Williams (2014) offer recommendations about effective joined-up services and note that a lack of *understanding* of, or training in evaluating evidence for, interventions and a general lack of knowledge about effective behavioural change principles can challenge such effective provision. Crucially, families report joint working as important in helping improve their children's mental health and report a desire for more active collaboration and communication between agencies and themselves (O'Reilly *et al.* 2013).

A related area is the experience of families where an assessment of a potential developmental disorder is indicated. Crane *et al.* (2016) surveyed over 1000 parents and found delays for diagnosis averaged three-and-a-half years. Despite several initiatives in the UK to improve ASD diagnostic services including the National Autism Plan for Children (NAPC; Le Couteur 2003), Brett *et al.* (2016) note that in the ten years that followed there was no evidence that the age at which children were diagnosed had reduced. This is crucial as there is good evidence that early intervention leads to positive results (Hunt and Craig 2015).

Palmer *et al.* (2011) reviewed 243 child development teams and found that while there had been a positive improvement in terms of the availability of a multidisciplinary team with clear assessment protocols and use of standardised diagnostic measures, only 49 per cent of those met the recommended NAPC timescale before completion of the assessment. However, there is an earlier rate-limiting step – identifying those requiring assessment. Brett *et al.* (2016) note that 'suboptimal awareness' of the features of ASD by health visitors and general practitioners could be a contributing factor to this and note that the Royal College of General Practitioners has recognised this problem by adopting ASD as a clinical priority with the aim of improving training in GPs' recognition of this disorder.

The role of training, sharing and improving practice

There is limited cross-professional, evidence-based and up-to-date training. Often this can be modality-specific and fail to address the clinical and financial imperative to offer the intervention or approach most likely to lead to meaningful change without false starts. The MindEd e-learning resource is an excellent example of cross-professional free online training for professionals and evidence-based psychoeducation for families (www.minded.org.uk). However, several authors point to limitations of training and awareness-raising alone. Bower *et al.* (2001) noted that while short courses led to an increase in confidence and knowledge in terms of children's mental health issues, there was little evidence of objective professional behaviour change or in improvement in child outcomes.

Even with training, inadequate supervision and intervention skills can impair the effectiveness of evidence-based interventions (Hutchings *et al.* 2007). Certainly, it reduces intervention fidelity and risks creating assessment 'blind spots' and ineffective interventions. Early identification only aids young people if those with the skills needed are available to readily intervene to ensure that the most appropriate and effective input is offered at the earliest opportunity (getting it right first time); this requires services to be joined up.

Delivery by primary care professionals
Health visiting

Taking a developmental perspective, intervening early naturally involves a focus on intervening early in the life of children and in the genesis of difficulties. Several initiatives have attempted to enhance the skill and competence of health visitors in particular in meeting the emotional and mental health support needs of young children and their parents.

In 2011, the Department of Health published the *Health Visitor Implementation Plan 2011–15: A Call to Action*, which fleshed out the government's commitment to increasing the health visitor workforce by 4200 by 2015 and to a new service model, and in 2014 the 2015–16 *National Health Visiting Core Service Specification* was launched.

An integrated approach to meeting the needs of young children in their families was central to these documents, as was the key role in assessing maternal mental health in order to identify those who may need additional support. The focus on promoting secure attachment and positive parental and infant mental health and parenting skills using evidence-based approaches was a key objective. Identifying early signs of developmental needs for further investigation was also a key role.

The national framework for continuing professional development for health visitors (Bishop, Gilroy and Stirling 2015) includes competence in working effectively alongside other agencies including mental health and education. Standard 2 focuses on maternal/ perinatal mental health where health visitors are seen as ideally placed to play a substantial role in both identification and early intervention and support. This early recognition role is highlighted by Cousins (2013), who notes that the universal contact which health visitors have with families with young children makes them ideally placed to support this potentially vulnerable group. However, she notes that such practice requires considerable knowledge and understanding. In particular, she notes the importance of health visitors having awareness of the impact of emotional neglect on infant mental health in order to identify early such problems and provide tailored support. Several authors (e.g., Barlett 2015) point to the need for health visitors to have access to skilled supervision and support in undertaking such roles.

A particular area of interest has been the capacity of health visitors to meet the needs of mothers experiencing postnatal depression. Morrell *et al.* (2009) reported a clinical benefit in terms of self-reporting on the Edinburgh Postnatal Depression Scale at 12 months postnatally, following psychologically informed sessions based on either cognitive-behavioural or person-centred principles for eight weeks. The health visitors were trained to use clinical assessment skills to assess the mothers' mood and to deliver manualised psychological interventions.

The health visitors had access to clinical supervision from the trainers and had monthly reflective practice sessions to ensure treatment fidelity. Interestingly, both models of therapy were equally effective. The authors note the unique position health visitors have in working with this group of women.

One model that has received detailed evaluation is the Family Nurse Partnership, an intensive licensed home-visiting intervention developed in the US which has been trialled in the UK. The model consists of family nurses supervised by psychologists trained in motivational interviewing and focused on prenatal health-related behaviours as well as sensitive and competent caregiving. There has been robust evaluation in the US and in the Netherlands showing significant improvements in, for example, tobacco use, increased birthweight and fewer second pregnancies in the 24 months postpartum, along with reduced A&E attendances and admissions (a marker of maltreatment) – see the summary in the Early Intervention Foundation Guidebook (Early Intervention Foundation 2017).

These results were not so positive in the UK pilot, which focused on teenage first-time mothers (Robling *et al.* 2016). There were small benefits in maternally reported levels of concern regarding cognitive development and child language development, levels of social support, partner-relationship quality and general self-efficacy. The authors' initial view, that the relative lack of demonstrable gains at two years made it hard to justify the continuation of the programme, was the headline taken from the study and has led to some decommissioning. However, Robling has also said that the gains that were seen had the potential to lead to long-term impact and the study is continuing in 2018. It can be difficult to make the case to wait for longer-term improvements. There is clearly a challenge in selecting those outcomes with developmental impacts, particularly when lifting these out of service and cultural contexts in other countries.

It can be challenging to find ways of providing the support to these frontline professionals that is enabling and containing but at the same time does not step on professional toes or allow the increased detection rates of children with mental health needs to cause anxiety.

Craig and Power (2010) describe a health visitor CAMHS partnership innovation in which health visitors undertook 0.1 whole-time equivalent six-month placements with clinical psychologists working in a tier 2 CAMHS service.[1] The focus was on co-work with children under 5 years, which included supervision and supervised independent work with parents. Health visiting teams reported an increased understanding of the work of CAMHS and referral processes, and saw the health visitors who had been on placement as a resource in terms of direct input but also offering reflective practice opportunities for their colleagues.

Within CAMHS, an increase in the appropriateness of referrals was noted and although an increase in the number of referrals had been feared, in fact there was a 45 per cent reduction in referrals made by the health visiting service compared with a 29 per cent increase in referrals overall in the year following the implementation of the placement scheme. The success of this led to a parallel scheme for school nurses built on a similar partnership model. School nurses were supported in delivering brief evidence-based interventions, such as anxiety management under the supervision of clinical psychologists from the service.

The school nursing role brought them directly into contact with young people experiencing mental health difficulties or developmental and behavioural difficulties. This partnership led to co-delivery of parenting courses between the services and joint consultation sessions in which CAMHS staff joined the school nurses for family sessions. What was also evident was the high level of need that was not being addressed by individualistic approaches in schools or by the high threshold criteria for CAMHS.

School nursing

The Department of Health publication, *Getting it Right for Young People and Families* (2012), spells out the vision for maximising the contribution of school nurses in terms of health and education outcomes, which includes delivering evidence-based approaches to management of mental health difficulties alongside other areas of physical health promotion and interventions. The vision is for the strengthening of school nursing services while developing multidisciplinary approaches.

---

1   In the UK, CAMHS are organised around a four-tier system – tier 2 usually refers to CAMHS specialists working in community and primary care, tier 3 usually a multi-disciplinary team or service working in a community mental health clinic.

However, Montamedi (2017) rather challenges the view that being 'best placed' is about being just in the right place. Isolated, untrained and unsupported school nurses cannot effectively intervene. Barlett (2015) notes the need for further postgraduate training for school nurses and regular supervision from a mental health specialist.

It should be noted that often the most difficult to engage families and young people fall at the first hurdle for secondary services and yet continue to be known to the health visitors and school nurses, who without supervision may have nowhere to obtain support for their work.

School nurse provision is under increasing threat in many schools and is easily swallowed up by other demands, for example immunisation initiatives. Effective liaison is crucial for those delivering mental health provision within education, but clearly challenges the ideology of some models prevalent in schools, for example person-centred counselling.

Several authors have noted the challenge for school nurses in meeting the needs of children experiencing mental health difficulties in schools. Pryjmachuk et al. (2012) used qualitative methodology to explore the views of school nurses on their potential for engaging in this work. They found that school nurses felt able to draw on established interpersonal skills and support networks. However, general workload (which includes unpredictable changes in demand, for example due to human papilloma virus (HPV) vaccinations), as well as a lack of confidence, were noted as potential barriers alongside education and training needs. Interestingly, they found that most school nurses felt that training should be provided by CAMHS professionals and, specifically, opportunities to shadow CAMHS staff were noted. School nurses were also positive about opportunities to undertake training in specific therapeutic models.

They found that CAMHS staff being available for advice or supervision was important, but good relationships tended to be between specific individuals rather than service organisations, which meant that service re-configuration was a potential threat to collaborative working. Major areas of concern for the school nurses were self-harm, depression, substance misuse, eating disorders and interpersonal issues, in particular family or friendship relationship difficulties. There were quite different models in terms of the provision of clinical supervision and support and interestingly, when CAMHS staff were not involved in this, participants generally felt that they should be, echoing earlier research (e.g., Clarke, Coombs and Walton 2003; Leighton, Worraker and Nolan 2003). Key to building these relationships was joint working, and Pettitt (2003) identifies joint training, secondments between organisations, and CAMHS staff spending time in schools as possible mechanisms to build these.

> Clarke *et al.* (2003) describe a psychology and school partnership based on a training and consultation model. This project arose from an exploration with school nurses about their current ways of working, for example drop-in sessions, and the feedback from the school nurses was of a high prevalence of mental health issues and a sense of feeling overwhelmed and lacking direct clinical support in responding to what were, at times, complex mental health difficulties. Training was based on counselling and problem-solving approaches, and augmented existing training on basic counselling skills and tailored training developed by the clinical psychology department. Clinical psychologists offered the nurses monthly group supervision involving active case discussion and there was also telephone supervision available for more immediate concerns.
>
> The feedback from the school nurses about the supervision was positive and allowed for knowledge gaps to be identified and addressed in relation to care pathways. What was evident in this process was a two-way learning. The mental health specialists became more aware that school nurses had well-developed clinical skills to build on. Although no formal therapeutic change or young person's satisfaction measures were utilised, one outcome was that most young people were contained within the structure of the project rather than requiring onward referral.
>
> One key aspect of learning from this work was the importance of enabling both staff and young people in school to identify the school nurse as a source of support. This was done by working with form tutors and pastoral heads. Another related positive outcome was perceived improved links with the local CAMHS teams.

General practitioners

The Department of Children, Schools and Families (2010) *Early Intervention: Securing Good Outcomes for All Children and Young People* stresses the role of GPs and other frontline health professionals in providing early intervention for childhood emotional health difficulties. These ideas are not new. Berger (1996) suggested the majority of child mental health difficulties could be dealt with in a primary care context with specialist support, thereby overcoming many of the problems associated with secondary care referrals. The key element here may be the specialist support.

Historically, GPs have not demonstrated high rates of identification of childhood mental health difficulties, tending only to respond when there are high levels of emotional distress. Sayal and Taylor (2004) found that less than half the children with psychiatric disorders are recognised in primary care and, of those recognised, only half are referred on to specialist services. Interestingly, of those referred, Hinrichs *et al.* (2012) found that GP referrals are over three times more likely to be rejected by specialist mental health services than those from any other referral source. For adolescents, Martinez, Reynolds and Howe (2006) found that for 13–16-year-olds, GPs correctly identified individuals with clinically significant symptomatology in just over 6 per cent of cases but only made a management plan or follow-up plan for around a third of them.

The luxury of referral criteria is not available in primary care and, inevitably, GPs maintain their involvement even when secondary care services refuse to become involved. This can leave GPs and others in an unenviable, helpless position at times that mirrors that of the families. In this situation, GPs will often turn to their community paediatrician colleagues who see a range of physical health difficulties and have expertise in both developmental and emotional health and wellbeing, including an awareness of overlapping developmental and emotional factors in this age range.

Roberts and Bernard (2012) describe an initiative to explore the potential of GPs to work with young people presenting in primary care with common mental health problems.

Children and young people were seen by their GP for a bio-psychosocial assessment, usually over several appointments, followed by a formulation and management plan. The study found that:

- the service was highly valued

- there was a reduction in referrals made to secondary care

- only 18 of the first 50 children seen were referred to CAMHS, several with symptoms or signs suggesting possible neurodevelopmental difficulties, early exposure to domestic violence, attachment difficulties or parental mental health problems.

Crucially, other key elements of good liaison were evident in this model:

- Contact was made with key teaching professionals or other health and social care professionals involved with the young people in order to gather collateral information.

- There were onward referrals within education to educational psychology or school counselling, school nurse or behavioural support worker as well as referrals to local voluntary agencies, such as Young Carers.

- The GP was offered clinical supervision by a child and adolescent psychiatrist working in the local CAMHS service, along with liaison with the primary mental health outreach worker from CAMHS.

- The GPs offered a variety of interventions directly consisting of, for example, brief behavioural interventions (e.g., sleep hygiene), and a mixture of eclectic interventions including active listening, non-directive counselling, narrative therapy and elements of cognitive behavioural therapy.

- Young people typically attended for three sessions of around 20–30 minutes, with a smaller subgroup (with problems that were normally associated with enduring familial conflict) seen for longer.

The authors propose that what may be crucial for overstretched GPs is time to hear family difficulties, something which is supported by other studies (e.g., Mercer and Reynolds 2002) highlighting the impact of consultation length in primary care on clinical empathy. However, this model may not be attractive to all GP practices, as the demands on them are huge.

The authors note that while there is clearly a time demand, the parallel with adults with mental health problems being actively supported by their GP should encourage more flexible ways of working to support young people to be made more commonly available in primary care. They acknowledge that GPs generally consider themselves unskilled in terms of child and adolescent mental health and can be reluctant to make mental health diagnoses.

Primary care-based specialists – including primary mental health workers (PMHWs)

Other models in general practice have focused more on liaison from CAMHS outreach workers, called primary mental health care workers (PMHWs), or from direct delivery of child mental health interventions by specialists working out of GP practices. Gale (2003) sets out the core activities of effective PMHWs:

- consolidation and development of skills in primary care

- training

- facilitating communication between primary and specialist services

- building networks and partnerships

- assessment and intervention at tier 1.

Wiener and Rodwell (2006) describe an evaluation of a CAMHS in primary care service for general practice which had several aims, including enabling and supporting professionals working in general practice and providing direct clinical work for children and young people who the GP may not otherwise have referred on to specialist CAMHS.

The service consisted of two workers engaged as primary mental health workers, a clinical psychologist and a clinical nurse therapist, working part time in a primary care service and part time in the specialist tier 3 CAMHS team.

Both unstructured and structured consultation liaison activities were monitored:

- Structured sessions included education, training and case consultation meetings, either with groups or individual members of the primary care team.

- Unstructured activities included telephone advice and informal face-to-face discussions or attending primary care team meetings.

The primary mental health workers saw children and families individually or jointly with primary care staff. Interestingly, professional groups utilised the service differently and reported different motivations:

- Health visitors referred cases when they felt there were no more therapeutic options they could be involved with.

- School nurses tended to be keen to learn new skills and were keen to engage in joint work.

Overall, unstructured consultation liaison was used the most, with joint work used less than direct referral for clinical input.

The study found that staff generally did not feel that the provision enabled them to 'hold' cases for longer, and there was an increase in referral rates to tier 3 rather than the anticipated drop.

Why might the service have led to an increase in referrals?

- The PMHW screening process (which included discussion at weekly specialist CAMHS meetings) may have led to this increase in referrals, with children and young people who seemed too complex for the PMHWs alone being accepted as referrals to tier 3 CAMHS, meaning that families who may not previously have been considered as appropriate for referral were being identified.

- It may be unrealistic to consider that input at primary care level necessarily reduces referral to tier 3 CAMHS, or to anticipate that this provision might enable primary care staff to hold on to families for longer before making a referral.

- Assessment by specialists can indicate ways in which specialist skills are needed, not evident in a referral alone or which are harder to ignore. Increased detection might be expected if services are more compatible with ease of access standards (Department of Health 2004).

It does, however, raise important learning in terms of how different professionals in primary care access and value this support mechanism/ resource. There is clearly much to learn about how this fits with the pressures on the individual professionals, how they conceptualise their role in terms of emotional health and wellbeing, and the extent to which they can put into practice skill developments.

In their evaluation of the impact of primary mental health workers on referrals to CAMHS, Whitworth and Ball (2004) found no overall change in referrals to CAMHS, but an increase in attendance rates.

However, they acknowledged that professionals in primary care found the model constraining at times – the workers needed diplomacy and service-selling skills. School staff were positive about the improved communication, but attention to boundaries was needed when behavioural support workers and educational psychologists were involved. Bradley *et al.* (2009) also found that there were key personal characteristics that were necessary to perform this interface role, which were not explicit in job descriptions and competency frameworks.

PMHWs come from a range of professional groups, will have different levels of training in assessment and therapeutic interventions, and variable access to supervision from specialists. This will influence their offer, as will their context. PMHWs operate in a wide variety of ways depending on local arrangements, and there are large differences in the amount of direct therapeutic input they deliver and the location of such work – primary care or schools. Terry (2006) found that in Wales, most PMHWs who responded were providing emotional health provision in school or education settings – most commonly consultation. Less than half of respondents offered direct therapeutic work with clients and less than half also reported that they measured the effectiveness of their input. There are examples of therapeutic input being evaluated – for example, Creswell *et al.* (2010) described a guided cognitive behavioural therapy self-help programme for parents of children with anxiety delivered by PMHWs under the supervision of clinical psychologists. They found significant improvements in both child and parent report measures of anxiety and low mood. There was good treatment adherence by PMHWs and high levels of parental satisfaction with this approach.

A unifying theme of the 'what works for whom' literature for children and young people's mental health is that even when individual therapies are indicated, they are most effective when embedded within systems, and families in particular.

Abrahams and Udwin (2002) describe a primary care-based clinical psychology service providing psychological assessment and intervention for children and young people presenting with emotional, behavioural or family difficulties which predominantly offered brief interventions that focused on cognitive behavioural therapy within a family therapy context.

Most referrals were for behavioural difficulties, difficulties with toileting or eating, sleeping anxieties and trauma or stress reactions, in that order. There was quite a similar pattern in the comparison group of referrals to the local secondary child clinical psychology service.

The wider system was attended to through provision of consultation and training to primary health care teams in psychological skills and child mental health issues, and also facilitated access to secondary or tertiary services when necessary. Health visitors and GPs took up these consultations and there were also visits to schools and nurseries in the area.

The families seen in the practice-based service were seen more quickly than those in the secondary service and this was felt to be due to the significantly lower number of sessions required to complete intervention in the practice-based service. In terms of clinical outcomes there were no differences between the two models, nor were there any differences in terms of DNA rates or disengagement. The feedback from GP practices involved was very positive and included an increased confidence in the quality of the service provided, with the practice-based psychologist being perceived as an accessible source of information, advice and support on child mental health issues.

Delivery with families in mind – are we 'thinking family' yet?

What emerges from the literature is that effective interventions are typically those embedded within systems and families; these challenge typical individualistic conceptualisation of children's, or for that matter adults', difficulties. One of the challenges, but also a potential strength of supporting families at the primary care level, is that more often families' difficulties as a whole are better known and may be less compartmentalised by specialist service structures. The same general practitioner may be supporting a parent with their mental health difficulties alongside hearing about their concerns about their child's behaviour or development. Increasingly, simplistic within-child models of understanding children's emotional wellbeing are being challenged.

The Social Care Institute for Excellence (2015) estimates that around a third of children known to child and adolescent mental health services have parents with a 'psychiatric disorder' (Kearney, Levin and Rosen 2003). Robson and Gingell (2012) highlight the interaction on either side of the parent–child relationship when either or both experiences poor mental health, impacting on the progress of the other and exacerbating symptoms or impeding recovery.

These factors are compounded and while the authors press for closer professional liaison between adult and child mental health teams, they also recognise that poor parental mental health is linked with both prolonging the involvement of child mental health services and early 'default' from treatment. Importantly, they found that for children whose parents had pre-existing mental illness diagnoses, the majority of referral letters that did not contain this information were in fact from their GPs. Although only 31 per cent of them were under the care of adult psychiatric services, all of the parents were being supported by their GP in relation to their mental health. The authors called for integration at a strategic level and establishment of family-focused mental health care alongside improved interprofessional liaison. The move towards increased service specificity has not facilitated this; good quality psychological formulation-driven models of meeting need will necessarily challenge these artificial boundaries.

Delivery by integrative practitioners?

Somewhat perversely then, clinical psychologists trained across the lifespan and in multiple models have become constrained in sharing these integrated skills by the structure of secondary services. It may be time to see a more radical integrative approach which may see a recognition of a greater conceptual overlap with colleagues in primary care.

There are pilot projects attempting to deliver just this. An example in the West Midlands provides 'generalist' clinical psychologists based in GP practices seeing 'all-comers' in what is described as a striated, stepped care model, with expert assessments up stream, as opposed to stratified models which require onwards referral to be seen by clinicians with more than one model of psychological theory and intervention to draw from – often leading to false starts. In this pilot, clinical psychologists offer assessment, formulation and interventions across the lifespan, from children to older adults, those with learning difficulties and psychological issues related to health problems and relationship difficulties. Alongside this is consultation and support to practice staff and, when appropriate, more accurate onward referral.

Conclusion

What emerges from the literature is the clear message that well-trained and supported professionals working in or into primary care can deliver effective interventions to improve child and family emotional wellbeing, but that such working requires effective communication, integration, liaison, co-location and relationship building *enabled* by service structures. It is also crucial that those in the frontline are equipped to intervene with the approach most likely to be effective first and early, so that families' experience is coherent and 'false starts' in assessment or intervention do not erode resilience. This requires all sectors working to the same common evidence base and challenging dominant modalities when their effectiveness cannot be demonstrated. Regardless of context, interventions grounded in evidence and embedded in systems and families are most effective and lead to sustained change.

To meet the preventative agenda there is an appropriate challenge to secondary service structure and philosophy, particularly those configured as child 'mental illness' services which seem less well formed to meet a preventative approach than others in primary care and community child care, and there is a strong case for bringing multi-skilled integrative professionals like clinical psychologists upstream and early in the setting 'where the needs of the child and their family are known' (Royal College of Paediatrics and Child Health, Royal College of Nursing, and Royal College of General Practitioners 2015, p.7).

Chapter 5

Promoting psychological health and early intervention in schools

JOE HICKEY, ANNA PICCIOTTO, WAVENEY PATEL AND KATIE HUNT

Introduction

Schools play a unique and significant role in the lives of children and young people; they are formative contexts where children learn not only academically but also socially and emotionally: a bi-directional influence between mental health difficulties and educational attainment that is well-documented (Johnston *et al.* 2014; Public Health England 2014).

Vulnerable children and those experiencing adversity in their lives, such as violence (Fry *et al.* 2018), bereavement and loss (Parsons 2011) and maternal mental health problems (e.g., Augustine and Crosnoe 2010), tend to have poorer educational outcomes, poorer school attendance, less psychological connectedness to school and fewer peer relationships. A good school environment can, however, exert a protective influence against psychological problems, and can mitigate difficulties elsewhere in children's lives.

The concept of resilience – defined as a child being able to resist adversity, cope with uncertainty and recover more successfully from traumatic events or episodes (Newman 2002) – is a useful framework for understanding these benefits (Masten 2001), since resilience is influenced by the child's environment as well as their individual characteristics and traits. Risk factors can also be reduced via protective mechanisms that change a trajectory in a child's life or lessen their exposure to risk (Rutter 1987). Schools create academic resilience but they can also support emotional resilience, for example through a good attachment relationship with a teacher (Verschueren and Koomen 2012).

It is also the case that schools can present unique risk factors for children's mental health, with difficulties such as anxiety and depression being triggered or exacerbated by school-based problems such as bullying and victimisation, exam stress and learning difficulties. Together with school exclusion, these have been shown to impact negatively on mental health in adulthood (e.g., Ford *et al.* 2017; Lereya *et al.* 2015), with the impact for children with disabilities, illness or other adversity likely to be greater due to the cumulative effects of risk factors.

With 10 per cent of children and young people aged 5–16 years thought to have significant mental health difficulties but only 25 per cent of those needing help receiving it (Public Health England 2015, 2016), schools are increasingly being encouraged to see mental health as part of their core business. Some of the barriers to getting help, such as limited resources, stigma, physical access to services and opening times, may be mitigated by locating mental health services in schools. For some children, however, including those at risk of exclusion, school will not be the right place for interventions to take place, and starting therapeutic work they cannot finish (due to being excluded) will be counterproductive.

There are challenges with locating mental health support within a school, including working with families and the long school holidays, but schools can provide support for the emotional and mental health needs of students and their families in a variety of ways. These include employing school counsellors, linking with local mental health services, linking with local authority services, and making specific contracts with specialist providers or independent practitioners. Matching the experience and qualifications of potential providers to the role is important and it can be hard for individual schools to make those judgements; adult counsellors are, for example, not necessarily trained in working with children or adolescents, and organisations may promote their services to schools in ways that look attractive but in reality lack an evidence base or do not match the needs of the school.

Being a psychologically healthy school requires work at multiple levels:

- creating an environment where children learn and develop socially and emotionally, as well as academically

- developing and promoting resilience for students

- providing early identification and intervention for psychological difficulties with established links with more specialist teams and agencies for more complex difficulties.

(Adapted from Department for Education 2017)

In many schools, different members of the staff team have a role in providing this support through pastoral care and safeguarding pathways, and through local links to external agencies in health, local authority, private and voluntary services. This work needs to include senior staff involved in supporting children and young people with special educational needs or disability (SEND), since they are more likely to require support around their psychological wellbeing. Thinking about mental health and special needs and disability as separate streams within a school will not benefit the children.

In this chapter, we will discuss the different levels at which schools can play a role in prevention and early intervention in children and young people's mental health difficulties:

- *Universal* – whole-school approaches to creating 'psychologically healthy' school environments.

- *Selective* – approaches aimed at children and young people at greater risk of developing mental health difficulties.

- *Indicated* – approaches aimed at children and young people with emerging mental health difficulties.

We will look at the evidence base for intervention at these different levels and examine models of implementation and challenges for schools and outside agencies in delivering these interventions, along with illustrations using case studies. In the final sections, we will make recommendations based on both evidence and clinical experience about how specialist services and agencies can work together with schools to create psychologically healthy environments and support education staff to fulfil this role.

Interventions and evidence

The best outcomes for young people are found when schools employ a comprehensive range of teaching, pastoral, organisational and interagency practices to promote psychological wellbeing (Weare and

Nind 2011), and different parts of the school system work coherently towards this aim (Weare 2015). This 'whole-school approach' to wellbeing is public policy in many countries, including the UK (Department for Education 2016). Guidance from Public Health England (2015) defines eight dimensions of whole-school approaches:

- ethos and environment
- curriculum, teaching and learning
- student voice
- staff development
- identifying need and monitoring impact
- working with parents and carers
- targeted support and referrals
- leadership and management.

Translating these principles into a workable package of specific interventions is not easy for school leaders but is a task supported by a significant body of research into school-based interventions.

Provision in a school community

Staff and pupils together often comprise hundreds or thousands of individuals, at different developmental stages, connected in turn to wider networks of parents or carers, family and professionals. Schools are complex organisations that can provide a wide range of activities alongside their provision for teaching, learning and assessment, which may include different types of intervention.

Before we describe research in this area, it is important to acknowledge that schools are often working at different levels simultaneously, and so not all interventions can be neatly categorised. Some common interventions, such as staff training, may be classified as universal, indicated or selective, depending on when and how they are offered. In addition, preventative interventions are often tailored to local requirements and often only evaluated within the organisation.

Supporting the school community

Over a period of three months, a high school had referred a high number of Year 10 (14–15-year-old) students to specialist CAMHS with presenting difficulties around depression and self-harming behaviours that included cutting and overdoses. School staff were particularly anxious as a Year 11 (15–16-year-old) student had died by suicide the previous year. At a consultation meeting between the local CAMHS clinician working with the school and the designated lead and support staff, it was agreed that over the following term the CAMHS clinician would provide:

- confidential consultation times for staff who may need extra support

- training to staff on depression, self-harm and managing difficult conversations with young people

- information for teaching staff about NHS-endorsed digital resources, availability of local services to support students, raising awareness of local services and the reporting and support processes available in school

- stress management training for students and parents running up to exam time

- workshops on sleep hygiene for students and parents

- clinical support for those identified as being most in need of support and referral on to specialist CAMHS if required

- discussion with senior leadership team about positive mental health and resilience approaches that can be used in personal, social and health education and across the school as part of policy and governance structures.

Theories of how organisations work psychologically can provide helpful insights into how school communities promote or hinder students' psychological wellbeing. Teams or institutions typically develop customs or patterns ('defences') that have the effect of reducing or dissipating anxiety, doubt or distress for staff (Menzies Lyth 1960). Other approaches emphasise the child's interaction with multiple systems that exist within a single school (e.g., peer group, class, subject groups), which all influence the outcome of interventions planned elsewhere in the ecosystem (e.g., senior leadership team) (Bronfenbrenner and Ceci 1994).

Complex systems theory suggests that schools will not operate simply as the sum of their parts, but will evolve or adapt in connection with neighbouring systems, may show unpredictable patterns of cause and effect, and will self-organise in the absence of central direction or policy (Snyder 2013). This means that preventative interventions may work in unplanned ways, such as when a pupil with undisclosed anxiety gains a treatment effect from a preventative whole-class intervention. Wellbeing interventions never start from a 'clean slate' and each new initiative must take account of school culture and practices to be successful.

Mental health provision is just one of the ways that schools seek actively to influence students' health, with other streams of work, including focusing on sexual health, substance misuse, violence and reducing obesity. The World Health Organization's Health Promoting Schools (HPS) model proposes that schools can effect change through (Langford *et al.* 2014):

- the formal health curriculum

- school ethos and environment

- engaging with families and communities.

Within this framework, evidence is relatively lacking for mental health prevention, for interventions engaging parents and adolescents (Langford *et al.* 2017), and over the course of this chapter, we hope to suggest some ways in which these gaps may be closed.

The value of training and consultation

A crucial part of mental health support to schools is through training to school staff on key mental health issues, including the roles that schools can play and the ways they can link with local services (Weare 2015).

Formal training is, however, just one way in which expertise can be shared and school staff can develop skills in supporting students' mental health. Ongoing consultation from mental health specialists to key school staff may be offered by local services or commissioned by schools to inform staff understanding of children and young people's behaviour, helping them to make links between behaviour they find concerning or challenging and the young person's psychological, emotional and family contexts.

Intervention through consultation

A school used 'pupil premium' funding to buy in specialist clinical psychology provision to support the psychological health of students, with input consisting primarily of fortnightly meetings with key school pastoral care staff, the special educational needs coordinator and the school counsellor. Parental permission was sought to discuss young people of concern; the aim of the consultation meetings was to reach a shared understanding of young people's behaviour and increase staff understanding of what may lie beneath the behaviour. Consideration was also given to whether onward referral to child health or child mental health services was indicated. For some young people, individual sessions were offered (including their parents) to gather more information to inform the shared understanding. All points of view were considered equal in reaching the shared understanding.

The school worked hard to release staff for the fortnightly meetings, and evaluation of the service after the first year showed that staff felt much more likely to consider explanations at the level of mental health and emotional wellbeing for young people showing behaviour of concern.

Universal provision

The evidence base for whole-school interventions covers a wide range of approaches to psychological wellbeing, including:

- cognitive behaviour therapy (CBT) – a prominent framework

- positive psychology (The Positive Education Programme; Elfrink *et al.* 2017)

- interpersonal therapy (Interpersonal Psychotherapy – Adolescent Skills Training (IPT-AST); Young, Mufson and Gallop 2010)

- child development (The Solihull Approach; Douglas and McGinty 2001; Hassett 2015)

- developmental trauma, and many others.

Universal interventions have been developed for common internalising problems (such as anxiety and depression) and externalising problems (such as rule-breaking behaviour and aggression) (Paulus, Ohmann and Popow 2016), which include teacher training and parent-focused components, with studies showing positive outcomes for staff and pupil behaviour change (e.g., Adi *et al.* 2007a; Durlak *et al.* 2011). Classroom-based interventions that raise awareness of suicide and provide skills training (problem solving and stress management) also seem to be effective in reducing suicide attempts in adolescents, and are recommended by the World Health Organization (World Health Organization 2017).

Social and emotional learning

Social and emotional learning (SEL) programmes aim to promote wellbeing and emotional development, with the most effective using interactive teaching (role play, games and group tasks), and whole-school activities, involving parents and starting at younger ages (Weare and Nind 2011). The evidence shows that they can have small to moderate effects on outcomes such as social and emotional skills, positive social behaviours, academic performance and conduct problems, with benefits maintained over more than a year (Taylor *et al.* 2017).

Anxiety and depression

Most anxiety-focused interventions derive from CBT and have been evaluated when delivered by school and mental health professionals (Neil and Christensen 2009; Stallard *et al.* 2014).

The FRIENDS programme (Barrett and Turner 2001) is a well-established and effective example where pupils work in groups over ten sessions to learn cognitive, behavioural and physiological strategies to identify anxiety, challenge anxious thoughts and problem solve. FRIENDS has been evaluated as a universal intervention in several UK studies, one of which showed significant improvements compared with control groups in self-reported anxiety and self-esteem when FRIENDS was delivered to 9- and 10-year-olds by school nurses (Stallard *et al.* 2005), and showed continued improvement in self-report at 12 months (Stallard *et al.* 2014). Interestingly, Stallard *et al.* (2014) found that the programme impacted only on anxiety rather than on general emotional wellbeing and also that the programme was effective when delivered by health staff but not by school staff.

Reasons for this are complex, but Stallard *et al.* (2014) suggest that adherence to CBT models (including an understanding of the role of 'homework' in CBT approaches to consolidate newly learned skills) and use of supervision may be important factors.

The picture for universally delivered interventions for depression appears more mixed. A meta-analysis of universal interventions for depression (Hetrick *et al.* 2016) found that studies tended to be of relatively low quality, and notes that for depression, 'prevention programmes delivered to universal populations show a sobering lack of effect when compared with an attention placebo control' (Hetrick *et al.* 2016, p.2).

There is some suggestion that different groups of children may respond differently to universal interventions; for example, an evaluation of the UK Resilience Programme (a targeted intervention for building resilience) showed it had a larger measured effect for children receiving free school meals and those with special educational needs. Those children with higher initial scores on an anxiety and depression measure showed a larger measured impact (Challen, Machin and Gillham 2014).

More work is clearly needed to develop universal depression prevention programmes with meaningful results in real-world conditions (Stallard 2013). Given the importance of family risk factors for childhood depression, Gondek and Lereya (2017) have recently argued for school-based depression prevention to take a more family-focused approach.

Trauma-informed schools

The trauma-informed schools movement in the US advocates for school environments that are sensitive to the neurobiological, psychological and relational impacts of adverse childhood events and developmental trauma on pupils (Chafouleas *et al.* 2016). Programmes are multi-tiered (Phifer and Hull 2016) and organised by the aims of a trauma-informed approach:

- *Realisation* of the pervasive effects of trauma.

- *Recognising* the signs of trauma in pupils.

- *Responses* by staff that are grounded in evidence-based practice that *resist* retraumatising young people (Substance Abuse and Mental Health Services Administration 2014).

Examples such as San Francisco's Healthy Environments and Response to Trauma in Schools (HEARTS) programme have shown changes in staff knowledge, and reductions in the behaviour problems and symptom levels of trauma-affected pupils (Dorado *et al.* 2016).

Bullying

The example of bullying demonstrates the links between universal, selective and indicated support.

Research over the past decade has shown that bullying by peers places young people at increased risk of becoming depressed in young adulthood, relative to those who have never been victimised (Bowes *et al.* 2015), with some studies suggesting that peer bullying may place young people at greater risk of later mental health problems than physical, emotional or sexual abuse (Lereya *et al.* 2015).

In this context, the importance of preventing bullying is clear. Universal bullying prevention programmes and whole-school anti-bullying strategies have been trialled extensively, many based on the Olweus Bullying Prevention Programme's principles (Olweus 1993) that adults at school should:

- show warmth and interest to pupils

- set firm limits for acceptable behaviour

- give consistent, non-hostile but negative consequences for rule breaking

- model desired behaviour as authority figures.

The Linking Interests of Families and Teachers (LIFT) programme adapted these core elements for younger children, producing positive results three years later on outcomes relating to conduct problems (involvement with delinquent peers, alcohol use and arrests) (Reid *et al.* 2000).

Other approaches include CBT (targeting thoughts and beliefs linked to aggressive behaviour), and restorative justice (resolving conflicts through a process of acknowledging and repairing harm) (Morrison 2002).

Overall, interventions specific to bullying or violence show positive effects on reducing or mitigating harm, and on school attendance and exclusions (Adi *et al.* 2007b; Department for Education 2014).

For children affected by bullying, however, other interventions will be needed: at a selective level, bullied pupils can receive extra support, and those who continue to show signs of psychological distress (such as low mood, reduced self-esteem, intrusive memories or raised anxiety) should be considered for indicated work and, in some cases, specialist assessment.

Targeted interventions

Targeted interventions are those which assign students based on known risk factors (selective) or emerging psychological difficulties (indicated). They concentrate resources more closely on pupils with greater needs, with the corollary that help may only be provided once the child has experienced significant adversity.

There is overlap between the content of selective and indicated programmes, with the main distinction being the point of enrolment. Some universal programmes can be delivered on a selective basis, including FRIENDS (Barrett and Turner 2001) for anxiety and depression. Other established interventions include various adaptations of the Coping Cat CBT programme (Flannery-Schroeder and Kendall 1996), and school groups based on interpersonal therapy (IPT-AST).

Analysis of targeted programmes is mixed and shows that for depression the effect sizes are bigger than those for universal interventions, but not for anxiety prevention (Werner-Seidler *et al.* 2017), with the age of the children receiving the intervention affecting the overall impact.

The need for psychological assessment in school

Psychological assessment is a crucial part of the process of providing interventions at any level, but its importance is often under-recognised or neglected. Assessment of children's mental health is a specialist task that should be carried out by appropriately trained and registered clinicians. The following case studies help to illustrate why assessment is of paramount importance.

The overlap with SEN

A 13-year-old boy (Ryan) was referred to an in-school mental health service staffed by a clinical psychologist due to increasing concerns about his behaviour, which was seen as deliberately disruptive. He was walking out of lessons, refusing to work and disrupting others, and was struggling to make expected academic progress.

Ryan was discussed with the clinical psychologist and his parents were then invited to meet with the psychologist and pastoral leader as part of the process of developing a different understanding of his difficulties. It became clear that there was a strong family history of literacy difficulties and, as a result, an assessment of Ryan's reading and language skills was suggested.

This assessment revealed significant difficulties with reading and language skills and, from further clinical assessment with Ryan, it became clear that he was struggling to access the written elements of lessons. His need to hide this had resulted in a pattern of behaviour that diverted staff attention away from his poor reading onto his behaviour.

A specific reading intervention was recommended to the school, which was implemented on a daily basis with a direct improvement in Ryan's behaviour in class, and a significant improvement in his relationship with pastoral and teaching staff.

The overlap with family factors

An 11-year-old girl (Elise) was seen by an in-school mental health service following referral from the school's behaviour lead. Elise had presented with a refusal to work and disruptive behaviour and was at significant risk of being excluded or moved to another school.

She had been dealt with initially by the school's behaviour lead using the standard behaviour management policy but this led to a deterioration in her behaviour.

The mental health worker met separately with Elise and with her mother, and it became clear that there were significant difficulties within the family, with very different parenting styles. Telephone calls from the behaviour manager (as per the school's policy) resulted in Elise being 'grounded' by her mother and there was a deterioration in the already strained relationship between her parents. This had a directly negative impact on Elise's ability to cope emotionally at school, leading to the further deterioration in her behaviour in the classroom.

A specific request was made (with the parents' permission) for the school's standard policy to be varied for Elise to enable difficulties at school to be dealt with at school and not communicated home. This resulted in a reduction of pressure on her, enabling her to develop a supportive relationship with the school counsellor, who she had previously refused to see due to concerns about communication of her difficulties with her mother.

Adolescent skills training based on interpersonal psychotherapy (IPT-AST)

In contrast to the CBT-based interventions, IPT-AST has shown promise as a group prevention programme for adolescents. It is based on an interpersonal model of depression that recognises the importance of interpersonal risk factors in some young people's relationships and vulnerability through their patterns of communication with others.

IPT-AST is delivered at an indicated level, with adolescents identified by high scores on a depression screening tool. It takes place over 12 weeks using activities including psychoeducation, exploring links between interactions and feelings, role play and rehearsal of new communication skills, and strategies to reduce conflict and build support in relationship networks. It links emerging symptoms of depression to interpersonal problems such as conflict in important relationships, disruptive transitions, unresolved grief or long-term isolation.

Evaluations of IPT-AST has shown it outperforms an active control group (school counselling) post-intervention, though not at the 12-month follow-up (Young *et al.* 2010). Adolescents receiving IPT-AST reported more improvement in symptoms of depression, and showed greater clinician-rated improvements in general functioning, six months post-intervention (Young *et al.* 2016). Future research will investigate longer-term follow-up and seek to refine the model.

Aggression and bullying

For aggression and bullying, effective targeted programmes tend to combine behaviour modification strategies, training for pupils in social skills and problem solving, consistent playground supervision and parental involvement. Studies suggest that interventions have led to reductions of around 20 per cent in the frequency of bullying and victimisation (Ttofi and Farrington 2011) but that outcome is also affected by participant age, with stronger results generally observed for pupils over 10 years. Evidence shows that better results for bullying and aggression interventions are seen in selective and indicated interventions (Weare and Nind 2011). Interestingly, group interventions for children carrying out bullying seem actually to increase the problem (Weare and Nind 2011).

Limitations of the evidence base

There are a number of limitations in the evidence base for universal, indicated and selective programmes, despite some positive findings (for reviews see, e.g., Clarke *et al.* 2015; Martin *et al.* 2018). A common criticism is that effect sizes tend to be small (Weare and Nind 2011), meaning that change may not be meaningful in clinical terms. There have also been very few replications of large-scale trials demonstrating the biggest effects. Even so, small effects may be comparable with educational interventions generally (Taylor *et al.* 2017) and still meaningful in prevention terms (Werner-Seidler *et al.* 2017).

Where approaches have been successful, it is not always easy to generalise the findings to other schools or replicate interventions to produce the same effects, in part due to concerns about the external validity of some multi-component protocols (Wolpert *et al.* 2013). Research needs to be focused on future innovations that can increase the reach and impact of existing universal interventions, and demonstrate effectiveness as well as efficacy. Research practices are also evolving new ways of testing complex interventions, with an increasing focus on process issues, such as how interventions are implemented, identifying mechanisms of change, and local context (Moore *et al.* 2015), which should be particularly beneficial to preventative work in schools.

Surprisingly, the impact of mental health prevention on academic outcomes is not measured in many studies, and where it is measured, there are methodological issues (Werner-Seidler *et al.* 2017), with any impact on attitudes to learning and on attainment found to be small when measured (Weare and Nind 2011). As an example, meta-analysis suggests that universal SEL programmes may not deliver the meaningful benefits to attainment they were once thought to (Corcoran *et al.* 2017), indicating a need to integrate psychosocial and academic outcomes in future work. It is perhaps not surprising that many studies of school-based prevention are not rated as high in quality because of their designs since they are investigating new interventions.

The importance of implementation

It is clear, then, that gains from prevention work may be small, and that there are significant variations in the efficacy of apparently similar universal programmes. Any benefits for schools seeking to replicate these effects may, therefore, depend greatly on process variables, including how a programme is implemented.

In the UK, for example, the most widely adopted SEL programme has been the Social and Emotional Aspects of Learning (SEAL) strategy (Department for Education and Skills 2005, 2007). Despite its wide reach, quantitative evaluations of the programme are disappointing (Humphrey, Lendrum and Wigelsworth 2013). Follow-up analysis, however, suggests that changes in school ethos are the key link between the whole-school adoption of SEAL and beneficial attainment, attendance and social outcomes (Banerjee, Weare and Farr 2014).

Durlak *et al.*'s (2011) analysis suggested that effective SEL interventions demonstrate four implementation principles (SAFE):

- *Skills* development follows a logical sequence.

- *Active* learning approaches are used.

- Time to *focus* on the programme is available.

- Components *explicitly* address social and emotional skills development.

Despite developing understanding of how schools can best deploy effective programmes, a significant gap between research and practice remains (Barry, Clarke and Dowling 2017), due to factors including limited staff time, unfavourable staff attitudes towards SEL (Humphrey, Lendrum and Wigelsworth 2010), limited transferability of programmes from other countries, and schools seeing increasing rates of more severe psychological problems in their students.

Given the scarcity of resources across NHS and local authorities, together with the principle role of teaching staff being learning and assessment, it is important to ask: who should deliver these school-based interventions?

The available evidence suggests that a wide range of clinical and educational staff are already involved:

- In the US, teachers were sole providers of 18 per cent and involved in 41 per cent of the interventions reviewed by Franklin *et al.* (2012).

- In a UK study, Sharpe *et al.* (2016) found that specialist provision for psychological wellbeing or mental health was provided most often by educational psychologists (81%), followed by counsellors (62%) and clinical psychologists (20%).

For at least some interventions, outcomes may vary according to who delivers them. Werner-Seidler *et al.* (2017) meta-analysis found that depression programmes delivered by providers external to the school showed larger effects but for anxiety there was no such difference. Stallard *et al.* (2014), however, found that for the FRIENDS anxiety programme 'training teachers to deliver mental health programmes was not as effective as delivery by health professionals' (p.185).

Making it work

It is clear that when considering effective interventions in schools, we need to attend to what is delivered, the process of delivery, and the key elements that support effective implementation. We explore this further below, looking at how challenges in each area may be met.

Interagency working towards mental health promotion

Successful collaboration between schools and other organisations (interagency working) is essential to the success of almost all work to promote good psychological wellbeing in schools, both in terms of the delivery of interventions by external professionals, and child safeguarding. Serious case reviews consistently show that failures in sharing information and concerns between services put children at greater risk of harm (National Society for the Prevention of Cruelty to Children 2018). Unsurprisingly, children, young people and parents also tend to prefer service delivery models with greater integration and interagency communication.

Cooper, Evans and Pybis (2016) found that collaboration across services was facilitated most by good communication, joint training, shared understanding, mutual valuing of respect and trust.

Specific frameworks for interagency working between schools and mental health services include the CASCADE model (Anna Freud Centre n.d.) and the Theory of Action (Oberle *et al.* 2016), which emphasise a number of priorities, including:

- auditing existing resources and skills in schools

- outcome, impact and evidence-focused interventions that inform ongoing work

- shared vision and clarity of roles between partners

- integration of learning and skills into a whole-school approach.

Schools are hierarchical organisations with high levels of accountability, and senior leaders have key roles to play in creating a positive school culture to enable change and innovation (Day and Sammons 2014). With leaders modelling and endorsing mental health initiatives, teachers can be more easily engaged to take part and to hold them in mind as a priority for their students (Department for Education 2017).

Integrated working takes an investment of time and energy to embed, and school and mental health contexts need to understand each other (Dowling and Osborne 2003). In planning and implementing services in schools, it is vital to engage with and inform all levels of the school organisation. Clarifying work practices, governance and roles between organisations when the work is being established can avoid confusion, misunderstanding and frustration (Mattison and Fredman 2017).

Contacts between schools and specialist services

Working relationships between individuals are an important aspect of interagency collaboration. This is especially true for school-based mental health work, where contacts between services (e.g., referral discussions) often take place at moments of stress following incidents, concerns or exclusions at school. The importance of a designated 'school link' member of staff, responsible for liaising with specialist mental health services, who builds expertise in areas of mental health, links with local services and effectively signposts (Neave and Patel 2014; Picciotto 2014) has been shown to increase mutual understanding and frequency of contact between schools and CAMHS and improve staff knowledge (Day *et al.* 2017). There may be particular value when this is a senior member of school staff (Department for Education 2017).

'Team Around the School' (TAS) meetings also facilitate contact and cooperation between schools and partner organisations. These are multi-agency meetings and joint planning forums, attended by professionals designated to a particular school, including educational psychologists, school counsellors, SEND services, school nurses and statutory, voluntary and community services. The TAS meeting can provide swift access to expertise, consultation and referrals, enabling earlier detection and intervention for children and young people.

Crucially, over time, through these repeated points of contact, a shared language for psychological wellbeing can develop between professionals. This enables joint reflection on the needs of the students and the school and contributes to the development of creative interventions.

Screening and consultation

The mental health clinician's skills in formulation can help contribute to a fuller understanding of a student's needs on an individual, family and school level, including how these interact with each other. This is a complex task that requires a high level of skill by the clinician and robust clinical supervision and management structures to support the work and provide a useful, safe and effective service.

Integrating consultation, screening and intervention

A CAMHS clinician was allocated to be the designated worker for a primary school.

The clinician's agreed role was to provide a fortnightly consultation space to the school's designated mental health lead and three other support staff. A school counsellor, directly employed by the school, also attended. The link role also involved half-termly training sessions for staff on mental health issues on a rolling programme across the school year.

At the start of the clinician's work, he completed a mental health screening across Years 4 and 6 (8–10-year-olds) for anxiety and depression using a standardised pupil-report questionnaire. Results showed high levels of mild to moderate anxiety presenting in the Year 6 group.

This information was discussed at the consultation meeting. It was agreed he would discuss approaches to managing class anxieties regarding performance in statutory assessment tests (SATs) with the senior leadership team. He also held a separate consultation with the Year 6 teachers to talk through their own anxieties and experience of secondary school and parent expectations about the SATs results. After receiving the informed consent of parents and carers, and the informed assent of identified pupils, the clinician also ran a group for the eight children presenting with the highest scores and completed a piece of direct therapeutic work with one child who was later referred into specialist CAMHS for a more intensive intervention.

Supporting teachers to promote mental health

Teachers' core task is to help their pupils to learn, but they and other school staff are a key resource for their pupils' mental health. They typically:

- have relevant knowledge of child development

- can closely observe individuals and groups of students on a repeated daily basis

- have daily access to large groups of children of the same age as a normative comparison group

- are adept at noticing changes in behaviour and tracking change over time.

Staff can only support pupils effectively if they have sufficient psychological and practical resources of their own on which to draw. Limited staff capacity is a key barrier to greater engagement in mental health work in schools (Patalay *et al.* 2016). Teachers report being inadequately trained to manage mental health needs that arise in school (Straw, Tattershall and Sims 2015), feeling overwhelmed or de-skilled by students' needs and distress and experiencing a high level of workload and pressure, with increasing numbers of teachers planning to leave the profession as a result (*The Guardian* 2016). This is significant since lower perceived teaching efficacy is linked to higher teacher stress (Collie, Shapka and Perry 2012).

Increasing teacher knowledge and understanding of mental health may also enable teacher participation. Without awareness of the links between academic achievement and social and emotional wellbeing, teachers may find it difficult to prioritise mental health initiatives

(Weare 2015). Mental health awareness training for all staff can increase their ability to notice problems earlier and respond in ways beneficial to students, and enable rapid access to support (Durlak *et al.* 2011).

Opportunities for staff to develop skills in mental health can be further supported by individual or group consultations and reflective practice. This can help staff who manage complex and demanding roles to explore the impact of their work on themselves, and improve the mental health and wellbeing of staff as well as increasing the 'reach' of the mental health specialist. Such consultation can provide staff with the opportunity to discuss behaviour and emotional health and wellbeing together in a supportive context that enables them to identify problems at an early stage and encourage thinking about creating psychologically healthy environments for their students. The remit and governance of this work should be contracted clearly before it starts, to differentiate it from supervision or therapy, and make agreements about confidentiality.

Supporting evidence-based practice in schools

Mental health services have a strong focus on evidence-based practice, but it has less of a focus in education, leading to uncertainty for teachers about how to make best use of an evidence base and to select approaches from it (Cooper 2011; Toda 2011).

Teaching staff are well practised at the ongoing assessment and monitoring of pupils. This sets the stage for closer working between CAMHS and schools to develop practice-based evidence for effective approaches to identifying and helping students with mental health needs. Using evidence alongside sound audit and baseline information for the whole school, groups or individuals means that change can be tracked and progress monitored. Practice-based evidence then adds to the growing body of data about what will work best for schools. An emphasis on evidence and evaluating impact can also guide schools' decisions about spending precious resources and commissioning services to best meet the needs of their students.

Both CAMHS and schools are keen to involve students in contributing to school policy and interventions. Schools already have student forums (e.g., school councils) which feed back their views and ideas and can enable the co-creation of relevant and accessible services for students of all ages and enhance other service-user involvement strategies.

Conclusion

Children and young people need more accessible mental health support at an earlier stage, so they can receive the right interventions at the right time, and in the right place. Schools have a vital role in children and young people's mental health, and it must be the shared responsibility of education and mental health professionals to help schools create psychologically healthy environments in which children and young people can flourish and learn.

Working more closely together will require a transformation of approach by both CAMHS and education services if barriers to joint working are to be overcome and shared goals and language developed. The evaluation of approaches and interventions is developing and improving, for example external validity and outcome measures that are directly relevant to schools. If schools are to fully accept their role in children and young people's mental health, then government may also need to expand the targets against which they are assessed to include emotional wellbeing.

Chapter 6

Promoting the psychological health of children and young people in hospital and with long-term physical health conditions

Evidence, theory and practice of effective integrated care

SARA O'CURRY AND SALLY BENSON

Introduction

In this chapter, we consider how services, from primary care to tertiary centres, can identify and minimise the risks, promote resilience and address specific difficulties in order to improve the mental health and wellbeing of children and young people in hospital and with long-term physical health conditions. The whole range of physical health care is considered, from infants in neonatal intensive care units (NICU) and children who have been in accidents or are critically ill in paediatric intensive care units (PICU) to children and young people with long-term health conditions such as diabetes, cancer, cystic fibrosis, craniofacial conditions and children presenting with medically unexplained symptoms. It is beyond the scope of this chapter to discuss barriers to joint working or suggest changes in commissioning and public health (see The Kings Fund 2016 for a comprehensive analysis) or the range of highly specialist treatments provided by psychological services, which can be found elsewhere (Faulconbridge *et al.* 2016).

Chapter 1 identified people with long-term health conditions as being at greater risk of experiencing psychological difficulties than their healthy peers. In addition, repeated hospitalisation and invasive procedures put children and young people at increased risk of developing procedural anxiety and post-traumatic symptoms (Center for Pediatric Traumatic Stress 2005). It is therefore necessary to put psychological wellbeing at the centre of child health services to ensure that harm is reduced and to improve children and young people's experiences of health care, which, in turn, influences their engagement with health services in the future (Doyle, Lennox and Bell 2013). A positive experience of treatment and care is rightly viewed as an important health outcome in itself (NHS England 2014).

According to The King's Fund (2016), 'Integrated care initiatives in England and elsewhere have paid insufficient attention to the relationships between physical and mental health' (p.4). It cites four related challenges that evidence the need for better integration of physical and mental health services for adults, three of which are pertinent here:

- High rates of mental health conditions among people with long-term physical health problems.

- Poor management of 'medically unexplained symptoms'.

- Limited support for the wider psychological aspects of physical health and illness.

Given that many long-term physical health conditions and chronic medically unexplained symptoms begin in childhood (Hotopf *et al.* 1999), there is a unique opportunity to get things right in services accessed by children and young people in order to influence their long-term physical and mental health trajectory and also reduce the costs of care in the NHS in adulthood.

This chapter will explore the evidence, theory and practice of effective integrated care for children and young people with physical health conditions using the Pediatric Psychosocial Preventative Health Model (PPPHM), see Figure 6.1 below (Kazak 2006). This model is based on a public health framework and is a useful way to conceptualise families with varying levels of psychosocial risk, in order to identify appropriate levels of intervention. We provide examples of ways in which existing services have developed their workforce and integrated care at each level and suggest areas that might be usefully developed.

A note on language: the terms 'psychological medicine service' and 'psychological practitioner' will be used to refer to, and interchangeably with, specialist mental health services and staff. These can include paediatric clinical psychologists (who are usually embedded in a particular paediatric medical speciality), child psychiatrists, specialist mental health nurses, hospital social workers and counsellors, all of whom, in the current models of care, usually only become involved when certain mental health criteria are met.

We propose that all of this expertise could be better harnessed to provide training, joint working, consultation and supervision to physical health staff so that mental health and wellbeing can be promoted through policy and practice development. This will skill up and support frontline staff and provide specialist assessments and treatments where necessary.

Background

Between 10 and 30 per cent of children and young people in the UK have a chronic illness or physical health need (Kush and Campo 1998) and ten per cent of young people under 19 years of age are admitted to hospital every year (Department of Health 2010). It has been stated that 'families facing serious paediatric illnesses are essentially normal families confronting an abnormal stressor' (Kazak 1997, p.147); however, children and young people with health conditions and their families experience four times more psychological distress than their healthy peers (Bøe et al. 2012). This increases the risk of developing psychological and behavioural difficulties that impact on their emotional, social and educational development and future occupational opportunities (Glazebrook et al. 2003; Meltzer et al. 2000).

The long-term process of adjusting to and coping with a medical condition, managing symptoms and treatments, coping with setbacks and disease progression, as well as having to navigate complex medical systems, are all significant challenges, particularly in the context of the developmental changes of childhood and adolescence. Each child, young person and family has a unique set of vulnerability and resilience factors that determine their ability to cope. These include demographic variables, the nature of the diagnosis and prognosis, family structure, financial resources, pre-existing family difficulties, social support, the child or young person's ability to access education, their personality, peer relationships and coping styles. In addition, the demands of treatment, including medications, procedures and any special dietary needs, frequent hospital appointments or overnight admissions, missing school, parents having to take days off work and organise child care for siblings, all compound the stressors for the child and family. Parents' adjustment and coping, whether acute distress or mental health difficulties, need to be identified and addressed because they can have a significant impact on children's ability to cope (Ramchandani *et al.* 2006).

In focusing on prevention and early intervention we cannot ignore the impact and role that poverty, social deprivation, race, religion and gender have in relation to children and families accessing the right services at the right time. The tendency for services to label specific communities and populations 'hard to reach' invites us to pay attention to the fact that it is exactly these so-called hard-to-reach populations that so often report experiencing professionals as 'hard to reach' and inaccessible. If we are to take prevention, early intervention and the integration of physical and mental health services seriously, we must invest in a realistic appraisal of the barriers to accessing the best health care in the NHS. A proactive and preventative framework can offer some of the best opportunities to engage children and families and, at the same time, make a critical contribution to mobilising *service users and carers* in providing peer support, help with self-management and support for family and carers.

If, as the evidence suggests, we consider that children and young people with long-term physical conditions are significantly more at risk of developing mental health problems than their peers (Bøe *et al.* 2012), this means that many children and young people need to access both physical and mental health services rather than be bounced between the two. There is now a large body of evidence for the effectiveness (Palermo 2014) and cost-effectiveness (Janicke and Hommel 2016) of targeted psychological interventions in paediatric (physical health) populations.

However, what is needed from frontline staff, in order to provide preventative care and early intervention, is the delivery of person-centred care and therefore an understanding of the child and young person in their family, community, school, social and economic context. The centrality of the bio-psychosocial model here cannot be overestimated. Attending to any distress, and identifying and addressing bio-psychosocial risk factors rather than simply focusing on the medical condition is an essential component of integrated care. In order for staff at all levels to have the confidence to do this, they need access to expert training and consultation and to be able to refer on children for timely intervention.

The existing psychological provision for children and young people in acute hospitals is grossly inequitable. All children's hospitals and most teaching hospitals in the UK have some paediatric clinical psychology provision and some have liaison psychiatry, counselling or family therapy. Very few district general hospitals or community health services have any psychological support and there are almost no child and family psychological practitioners in primary care. Paediatricians simply have nowhere to refer children and young people, unless they meet mental health service thresholds. Moreover, there is inequality between medical conditions. Some service specifications mandate psychosocial or clinical psychology provision, for example the National Institute for Health and Care Excellence (2014) Guidelines for paediatric oncology or NHS England (2013) service specifications for diabetes, paediatric intensive care (Paediatric Intensive Care Society 2015) and cystic fibrosis (Cystic Fibrosis Trust 2011). In contrast, most other conditions have none whatsoever. This renders service delivery acutely vulnerable to specific factors such as local leadership, commissioning, service priorities and budgeting.

When psychological provision is embedded in the medical team, children, young people and their families have access to excellent, holistic care, with the psychological practitioners playing a key role in keeping psychological wellbeing at the centre of multidisciplinary discussions, during consultations and in helping the medical team to manage difficulties with, for example, adherence to medical regimens. They also deliver teaching, supervision and consultation to frontline staff such as clinical nurse specialists who are often best placed to deliver initial psychological treatment because they have pre-existing relationships with the family, while the psychological practitioners take on only the more complex cases for specialist intervention.

Psychological practitioners treat a range of problems that result from living with a long-term physical health condition, including anxiety, depression, family conflict and school or peer difficulties. This allows for the complex interplay between medical and psychological symptoms to be addressed, for example pain management in young people with rheumatology or gastroenterology conditions, or anxiety and depression symptoms that mimic or exacerbate respiratory or cardiac conditions. However, these services are not equipped to deal with complex psychiatric problems that require specialist assessment, medical treatment or multidisciplinary mental health management, and few services have robust pathways of care from the acute hospital to mental health and community services. This means that children and families experience delays in having their mental health needs met, which can impact on their physical health and psychosocial functioning. It means they can fall through the net, undergo unnecessary re-assessments and duplication and there are inequalities, depending on their presentation, where the child and family live in their ability to access services. What children and young people need are defined pathways and joint clinical management of medically unexplained symptoms and risk between acute, community, child health and mental health services.

The King's Fund (2016) defined the *professional attributes* required to provide effective integrated care, such as being able to take a 'whole-person' perspective and including communication and consultation skills. It also defined the *system attributes* such as coordination of care and proactive care, and emphasised the *role of service users and carers* in terms of peer support and self-management as well as support for families and carers. A continuum of integrated physical and mental health provision has been described elsewhere (Faulconbridge *et al.* 2016). If all frontline staff were to take a holistic view of wellbeing and saw both physical and mental health as their responsibility regardless of their roles, we would get much closer to genuine integration between physical and mental health.

How could this be achieved? It requires workforce development so that this integration is part of the training of the whole workforce, as well as supervision and consultation structures to support frontline staff delivering psychological interventions. It would also require joint continuing professional development across professions, sectors and services to enable people to learn from each other and develop working relationships, in order to facilitate communication, joint working and integration. Finally, it would require structures such as regular cross-sector meetings for complex case management and the development of policies and pathways.

At the other end of the continuum, what is needed is for practitioners expert in the psychological wellbeing of children with long-term conditions to deliver universal, preventative skills training on the psychological aspects of long-term conditions to school nurses, teachers, social care staff, health visitors and primary care physicians who are working with children, young people and their families every day. This would enable problems to be identified and dealt with quickly and would prevent more complex difficulties from developing and creating an additional burden for young people, their families and services.

Pediatric Psychosocial Preventive Health Model

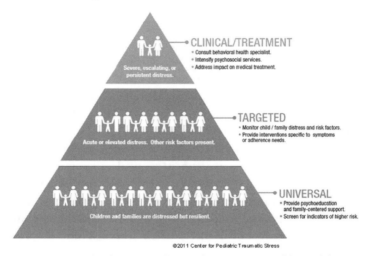

©2011 Center for Pediatric Traumatic Stress

Figure 6.1: Pediatric Psychosocial Preventive Health Model
Reproduced with permission from the Center for Pediatric Traumatic Stress (CPTS) at Nemours Children's Health System © 2017–2018. All rights reserved. The PPPHM image may not be reproduced in any form for any purpose without the express written permission of CPTS. To obtain permission to use or reproduce the most recent version of the PPPHM, please contact CPTS at psychosocialassessmenttool@nemours.org.

At the base of the pyramid in Figure 6.1 are *universal* families, who are understandably concerned or distressed about their child's health problem but who are generally resilient and able to cope with and adapt to their child's illness and treatment. The middle tier consists of *targeted* families, with pre-existing concerns or difficulties that may contribute to continuing or escalating vulnerability during treatment.

At the tip of the pyramid are *clinical* families, with one or more pre-existing, chronic and complex problems, resulting in greatest need for prompt and often intensive intervention.

In the remainder of the chapter we will seek to illustrate service examples of universal, targeted and clinical interventions.

Level one: universal (prevention and early intervention)

Many hospital services for children and young people with long-term physical health conditions provide care that will address the needs of *universal* families. Professionals involved in delivering this care can include clinical nurse specialists, physiotherapists, dieticians, hospital social workers, hospital play specialists and chaplains. These professionals can provide psychoeducation and family-centred support and care from diagnosis through to transition to adult services and can help families adjust to life with a long-term condition. They can also prepare children, young people and families for transitions such as starting school, managing new medical regimens and helping young people to gradually take on more responsibility for their health care. These professionals can screen for indicators of higher risk and can provide some specific interventions where a greater, targeted level of intervention is needed to address risk factors, specific concerns or difficulties with adherence to treatment. Such an approach enables problems to be identified and dealt with quickly, preventing more complex difficulties from developing and creating an additional burden on the health care system.

Training can also help staff address psychological factors that can play a significant part in complex decision making, for example in relation to high-risk or highly aversive but potentially life-saving surgery or treatments, or decisions to cease treatment and move to symptom management or end-of-life care. Involving a child, young person and their family in complex decision making requires health care staff to conduct a bio-psychosocial assessment of the issues, taking into account the child's developmental stage and level of understanding, the parents' perspective, the level of distress and family resources, and identifying any mental health or psychological factors in the child or family that might be interfering with their ability to make informed decisions (e.g., hospital phobia, pre-existing anxiety or depression), and involving psychological medicine practitioners where necessary.

Workforce development

According to The King's Fund report (2016), 'all health professionals play a key part in delivering closer integration' (p.5). At the universal level, workforce development strategies can ensure that all staff have sufficient skills to provide evidence-based psychoeducation and family-centred support to promote wellbeing and prevent the development of mental health difficulties. The King's Fund also asserts that 'a meaningful definition of integrated care must include provision of integrated psychological support to help people adapt and manage their health effectively' (p.9). Of its recommendations for how to do this in adult services, those that are pertinent to the scope of this chapter are:

- new approaches to staff training and development so that physical health staff are equipped to identify and address mental health issues, either directly or through signposting to appropriate services. These might include peer support services run by service users and carers, information, resources and support groups provided by voluntary sector organisations or specialist psychological medicine services

- the development of integrated service models that facilitate skill transfer between physical and mental health professionals.

One of the main findings in The King's Fund's (2016) research was that people most frequently commented on being seen only through the lens of their condition, with consultations tending to focus on a particular part of their body or particular symptom. They tended only to be asked closed, condition-specific questions such as 'How are your HbA1c levels?' rather than open questions such as 'How are you coping?' (p.14), which broaden out the scope of a clinical encounter and invite people to talk about psychosocial stressors or difficulties.

Managing medical consultations differently requires skills not only in how to broaden out the consultation but confidence in managing the response to these questions. This means that mental health training should form part of the core training of all professionals working with children, young people and their families. Interestingly, however, England (The King's Fund 2016, p.69) found that while many GPs already have the right skills to support physical and mental health in an integrated way, they often lack the confidence, support or time to use these skills to their full potential. To this end, there are an increasing number of local training initiatives for GPs to help support and enable them with the integration of psychological principles and models in their everyday working, thus supporting the development of skills in bio-psychosocial assessment and therefore early intervention and appropriate signposting if required.

The Royal College of Paediatrics and Child Health (RCPCH) has given clear guidance to its members for there to be 'parity of esteem' (E. Blake and J. Valente, RCPCH, personal communication, 29 September, 2017) – the principle by which mental health must be given equal priority to physical health. However, this has not been reflected in paediatric training until very recently when the RCPCH rewrote the curriculum to integrate mental health throughout. Mental health will now be part of the core competencies of all paediatricians and is also included in greater depth in the training for GPs. Furthermore, there are a very small number of sub-specialisation posts available for paediatricians in child mental health, although the future of these is uncertain.

The RCPCH supports the trainee paediatrician in developing the skills and knowledge required to work safely and confidently as a child mental health paediatrician – a doctor who has expertise in promoting mental wellbeing, 'parity of esteem' and working with children and families with mental health difficulties. Currently, training places are in single figures but as the programme expands, there will be more child mental health paediatricians who have a thorough knowledge of theoretical aspects of mental health, including psychological, social and neurobiological aspects, and will be able to apply it in a clinical and advisory capacity. They will be involved in developing formulations, managing complex cases and liaising with other mental health specialists, paediatric sub-specialists and local teams in order to enhance holistic care. They will have the ability to provide specialist regional advice in complex cases. A child mental health paediatrician is an excellent example of how professional training programmes can directly influence services and the integration of physical and mental health.

The Royal College of Nursing (RCN) has also been grappling with its training within the context of working with the 'whole child' and prioritising a bio-psychosocial approach. In a similar vein to the RCPCH, the RCN has long called for a 'child health nurse' recognising the 'holistic nature of nursing, with people's response to and experience of health, illness or disability in any setting' and who is 'capable of working across organisational boundaries and with multi-agency services' (F. Smith, RCN, personal communication, 13 October 2017). Again, while many universities have been ensuring that children and young people's mental health is given parity with physical health within their curriculum, nurses report feeling ill-equipped to deal with mental health difficulties alongside physical health problems where their training has been in general nursing.

The University Hospitals of the North Midlands (UHNM) provide a good example of what one group of hospitals has chosen to do to address the significant unmet mental health needs of their patients. In response to staff increasingly reporting that they felt ill-equipped to adequately meet the needs of the ever-expanding numbers of children presenting on wards and in the emergency department with mental health needs, they created a new post: the clinical lead nurse in mental health. This senior divisional specialist role was devised to encompass a range of leadership and clinical responsibilities, not least to raise the profile of mental health in the acute hospital. The role is responsible for developing policy and practice in order to support the most vulnerable patients and for creating an environment where mental health is fundamental to nursing and medical practice. UHNM report that by appointing a mental health lead they have enabled an innovative redesign of the workforce to meet the needs of some of the most vulnerable children and young people, improved patient and staff experience and promoted parity of esteem across the health economy (S. Scott, King's Fund Top Managers Programme, Module 2: Working across boundaries: connecting self and system, personal communication, 3 July 2017).

The paediatric psychology workstream within NHS Education for Scotland (NES) has been developing and delivering training in psychological skills to multidisciplinary paediatric health care staff for the past seven years with great success. To date, over 2000 staff have attended the Training in Psychological Skills Paediatric–Healthcare (TIPS-PH) skills-based workshops. These are on a range of modules designed to help staff integrate psychological care into their daily practice, thereby improving children, young people and families' ability to cope with the psychological demands of having a long-term health condition, and supporting families with managing adherence, concordance and self-care (Adkins *et al.* 2006).

In addition, NES has commissioned University College London (UCL) to develop a Paediatric Competence Framework that defines the psychological skills needed for all staff, across all professions, working with children in hospital or with long-term conditions.

Co-location

Co-location of psychological medicine practitioners or other integrated service structures such as regular multidisciplinary meetings could facilitate the promotion of mental health and wellbeing and allow better use of resources through, for example, joint working, consultation, supervision and teaching on specific clinical areas (such as management of medically unexplained symptoms or pain management) or specific techniques (motivational interviewing, behavioural management of medically unexplained symptoms, relaxation).

Children and young people presenting with 'medically unexplained symptoms', ranging from symptoms for which no organic cause can be found, such as unexplained recurrent abdominal pain or unexplained seizures, to an exacerbation or mimicking of symptoms of an existing medical condition that cannot be explained and is likely to be related to stress, anxiety, low mood or other psychosocial difficulties, are without doubt in need of an integrated approach. At an early stage in their presentation, bio-psychosocial assessment of the difficulties can help the child and family to develop an alternative explanation for their symptoms, introducing the idea that psychological and coping factors might be playing a role in exacerbating or maintaining their symptoms. This in turn can help to develop appropriate coping strategies, supporting a gradual return to normal levels of functioning and thus reducing the need for further medical investigations or treatment.

At a primary care level, such an assessment would not have to be conducted by a specialist psychological medicine practitioner, but could be done by a GP or health visitor, as long as they had sufficient training, sufficient knowledge of services and resources and access to consultation from a psychological medicine practitioner. Similarly, children who have existing medical conditions and are presenting with unexplained symptoms could be assessed by their clinical nurse specialist, dietician or physiotherapist.

A good example of partnership working that promotes integrated child need based care is the Virtual under 5s team in Western Health and Social Care Trust. This is a bi-monthly multi-agency meeting including representatives from looked-after children services, autism spectrum disorder services, CAMHS, children's disability, paediatric clinical psychology, a consultant paediatrician and lead nurses from Public Health. This team meets to progress complex cases through joint thinking and will become directly involved if necessary. The team has found that, while resource-intensive at the point of the meeting, it is an effective and productive way of partnership and system working that allows teams to bring difficult cases and to gain insight into how different professionals and parts of the organisation interface.

Case study – Gemma

Gemma is a 3-year-old with significant sleep and feeding issues. She was referred by the paediatrician to paediatric clinical psychology due to concerns about feeding. She was also known to the autism spectrum disorder (ASD) service. She was brought to the Virtual under 5s service for discussion by both the paediatrician and the clinical psychologist. They were concerned that neither service was meeting the family's needs and that Gemma's difficulties were having a significant impact on the family. While there were clearly feeding difficulties, in part as a result of hypersensitivity, that for another child would be a key issue, for Gemma and her mother it was down the list of priorities. Keeping Gemma safe was the mother's number one priority and, for the paediatrician, there was concern about the impact on her siblings as they had presented as fatigued when they attended a clinic with their sister.

Discussing Gemma at the Virtual under 5s meeting meant a referral to the CAMHS intellectual disability (ID) service could be made directly. Usually the service requires referral, triage and assessment, including cognitive assessment, to determine if a child meets the requisite criteria. However, in this case, the consultant psychiatrist was able to listen to a description by two consultants who had seen her and agree that she met criteria based on what they said. The health visitor was present and able to give valuable insight into the home situation and the remarkable resilience of a mother who wanted the very best for her child who had multiple needs. Multi-professional discussion, alongside the information given by Gemma's mother, allowed a reformulation of the case with all agreeing that practical support for the family was a priority. A representative from social care also attended this meeting and was able to advise on the best route to this, and the health visitor was able to then take the information back to Gemma's mother. The ASD service was able to add to the information and discuss the resources already received as well as provide ongoing social support until the ID service was in a position to see the family and set up an appropriate package of care.

The joint discussion relieved the pressure within the family system by providing practical and emotional support and it permitted a joint understanding of the child, her needs and who was best to meet them, without putting the child and her family through the arduous process of referral from one service to another. There are undeniable economic and resource benefits for the services and reduced frustration and improved quality of life for the family system. Gemma was spared from having to attend multiple appointments, which she found difficult to tolerate, and the situation was not allowed to deteriorate as it inevitably would had she been passed from one waiting list to another to try and find a service that best met her needs, when realistically, all she needed was bits of different services to work together.

Improving self-management

Providing universal tools that teach children, young people, families and staff psychological self-management strategies to reduce hospital and procedure-related anxiety, improve communication, promote choice and involve them more effectively in decision making is an essential part of universal care. NES has successfully developed the Hospital Passport Coping Kit (Donnan *et al.* 2016) to deliver these universal tools. Here, online apps are proving transformative in increasing access to universal mental health tools. The Paediatric Psychology Department at the Royal Hospital for Children in Glasgow and the Glasgow Children's Hospital Charity (2016) have developed a free app for children regularly visiting hospital called 'HospiChill'. The app was developed from the Hospital Passport Coping Kit.

There are also good examples of integration within education, such as the e-learning platforms MindEd and RCPCH e-learning for health care (e-lfh Hub). This material was developed by an interprofessional working group including specialists in paediatrics, paediatric psychology, psychiatry, nursing and public health. MindEd is designed for universal access and e-lfh is available to all NHS employees, so the material is aimed at an interdisciplinary group of learners. There is also a suite of programmes making up CYP-IAPT (Children and Young

People – Improving Access to Psychological Therapies) that is available on MindEd. There is a lot of potential for these resources to be used in integrated interprofessional learning contexts, particularly across training programmes for health professionals, including medicine and psychology.

Furthermore, providing staff with the opportunity to reflect on their own beliefs, attitudes, behaviours and emotional wellbeing and how these can impact on their work helps them to deliver more compassionate, patient-centred care (Archibald, Maidment and Casey 2017). A good current example of this is a drop-in mindfulness initiative developed for staff at Noah's Ark Children's Hospital for Wales. An introduction to mindfulness practice was delivered to 80 staff members via fortnightly drop-in sessions and additional teaching sessions. Feedback confirmed that the intervention had a positive impact on staff members' wellbeing, focus at work and work-related stress (N. Parish and S. Majumdar, personal communication, 15 October 2017). This model enables the support of a large number of staff where there is also a high volume of staff turnover.

Systematic screening

Finally, systematic screening for risk factors is an important aspect of universal care that ensures inclusion of all groups, not just those who find accessing services easier. Screening helps identify treatment needs and a need for further in-depth assessment, monitoring and treatment. The Psychosocial Assessment Tool (PAT; Kazak *et al.* 2015) is a brief (5–10 minute) parent-report measure of psychosocial risk in the context of children in hospital or with long-term conditions. It is based on the Paediatric Psychosocial Preventative Health Model and is composed of items that assess potential stressors and risks associated with the child, family and broader systems. The number of items varies according to the age of the child and siblings, and some versions have been adapted to add disease-specific questions.

The domains covered in the generic PAT include demographic characteristics, diagnosis, family structure, family resources, social support, child knowledge of their condition, school, child problems (internalising, externalising, peer or cognitive), sibling problems, family problems, family beliefs and stress responses. It was originally developed in the US for use with families of children with cancer but has been adapted for use in other paediatric settings, including chronic pain, obesity, congenital heart disease, diabetes and irritable bowel disease, and it has been translated into a number of languages and adapted for the UK, Canada, Australia and New Zealand.

Level two: targeted

Where children, young people and their families are presenting with acute or elevated levels of distress or difficulty with adherence to medical regimes, early intervention is necessary to address the difficulties and prevent them from escalating.

Tree of Life groups are an excellent example of a group intervention that can be used in the early stages, following diagnosis, to support children and young people. Tree of Life groups are a group therapeutic approach drawing on narrative therapy ideas (Ncube 2006). The groups were initially developed by professionals working with vulnerable children in South Africa, who wanted to find ways of allowing the young people to tell their story in a safe and contained way, and to assist these young people to shape their own futures and sustain change beyond the groups (Archibald *et al.* 2017). The approach uses the tree as a metaphor for the young person to think about their identity, life experiences and hopes for the future, with different parts of the tree representing different parts of the young person's life story.

These groups have been adapted and are now widely used with young people who are living with chronic health conditions. The aim is to build resilience and self-esteem, develop a positive sense of self and identity separate from their medical condition, and to receive peer support through sharing their experiences with others who may have had similar experiences. Feedback from young people who attend these groups is very positive, and suggests that these groups help young people by reducing the sense of isolation that young people living with medical conditions may feel, giving them an opportunity to meet others and space to feel listened to and understood, having their strengths and positive attributes witnessed and reflected by other group members, and sharing and hearing stories of coping (Archibald *et al.* 2017).

Home-based behavioural health interventions are rapidly developing and can offer useful targeted and early intervention opportunities. Examples include managing adherence in type 1 diabetes

(Adkins *et al.* 2006) and a computerised cognitive behavioural therapy programme for chronic pain (Velleman, Stallard and Richardson 2010). These can be used as early interventions for difficulties, guided by or done in collaboration with health care staff already involved in the child or young person's care (such as their hospital or community nurse or physiotherapist). These health care professionals can then monitor the effectiveness of the intervention and refer on to a psychological medicine practitioner when necessary.

In many tertiary hospitals, psychosocial meetings are routinely held where children, young people and families with elevated levels of distress or for whom risks have been identified, are discussed by a multidisciplinary team who formulate the presenting difficulties, coordinate and evaluate interventions and manage risk. There is evidence that psychosocial forums provide an efficient means of delivering specialist psychological medicine consultation (Douglas and Benson 2014) and there are many examples of effective psychosocial meetings across the UK. Psychosocial meetings serve to facilitate working across professions and agencies and coordinate care, and can thus be seen as forming part of both targeted and clinical/treatment levels of care.

At Addenbrooke's Hospital in Cambridge, the Neonatal Intensive Care Unit holds weekly psychosocial meetings. These are attended by a diverse group of professionals from both the acute and community setting in order to coordinate acute care, continuing care and discharge planning. The range of professionals who attend includes: the maternity safeguarding nurse, doctors and nurses from the ward, the ward dietician, the speech and language therapist and play specialist, a hospital chaplain, the WellChild nurse, who is responsible for the coordination of the care of children with complex needs, a community neonatal nurse, a representative from the local hospice, a family and baby worker (from a local children's centre), a specialist clinical psychologist and counsellor, a specialist breast-feeding nurse and an expert in newborn behavioural observation/assessment. There is compelling evidence that early intervention to promote bonding not only improves infant–caregiver interactions but also has an impact on cognitive and behavioural outcomes in later childhood (McCusker *et al.* 2007), therefore a major focus of the coordinated support given to families early on is devoted to alleviating barriers to bonding and providing a range of interventions that promote it.

Level three: clinical/treatment

As mentioned earlier, service specifications and NICE guidelines only exist for a small number of conditions. Some guidelines specify a minimum mental health resource that is required for a service and where these minimum standards exist they are often integrated within tariffs, enabling a service to secure funding for an interdisciplinary service. This ensures the integration of mental and physical health care delivery, but for long-term conditions, where standards do not exist, there is an unequal distribution of resources at the targeted and highly specialist levels both in terms of the medical condition and geography. It is high time that these inequities were addressed. It is our hope that by highlighting some examples of good practice and the innovative ways in which services have been integrated to make the best use of resources, the value of these will be appreciated, facilitating the improvement and development of services for children with long-term health needs.

Neuropsychological rehabilitation

The Cambridge Centre for Paediatric Neuropsychological Rehabilitation (CCPNR) is a good example of a complex tertiary service that has integrated interdisciplinary interventions that support the improvement of physical and mental health.

The CCPNR was developed because after a brain injury a child's needs cannot be well met when mental and physical recovery are treated in different services. CAMHS are not equipped to meet their complex sensory, motor, communication, cognitive, emotional and behavioural needs. The service recognises that after a brain injury, the recovery and development of a young person's skills (be it walking, talking, bike riding or accessing the curriculum) require specialist input from professionals from different disciplines. The assessment and treatment of all the young people is managed by a multidisciplinary team of professionals including neurology, neuropsychology, psychology, psychiatry, occupational therapy, speech and language therapy and specialist teaching. Professionals from third-sector organisations (such as The Child Brain Injury Trust) and local collaborations (e.g., Cambridge Kung Fu) are welcomed into the team to support specific interventions as appropriate. The professionals in the team, who are embedded in acute and community services, come together to work with other professionals supporting the child and family to deliver context sensitive rehabilitation that maximises the child's participation in their own community (home and school).

The literature tells us that family functioning is one of the greatest predictors of outcome for children with acquired brain injury (Butler *et al.* 2008) and family supported rehabilitation is more effective than direct clinician delivered intervention (Braga, Da Paz and Ylvisaker 2010). Parents are often traumatised and grieving after their child has been in a road traffic collision and do not have the resources to support the mental health of their child. They need psychological support to be able to cope with their own distress or mental health so that they can support their child with daily living skills and the implementation of therapeutic interventions.

The Children's Acquired Brain Injury Consultation Service (Children's ABCS) based at Belfast Children's Hospital offers an innovative regional service to support professionals working in this specific area. It describes itself as a 'service-facing service' providing an advisory and consultative focus for professionals and services that are supporting children, young people and their families following an acquired brain injury. The multi-professional team consists of clinical psychology, speech and language therapy and occupational therapy. This is an interesting model for delivering staff support alongside service development, best practice and ultimately the integration of mental and physical health care pathways and service delivery.

Child development centre

Peterborough Child Development Centre is a good example of a multidisciplinary integrated neuro-developmental assessment team. The main part of the multidisciplinary team (MDT) work is within the neurodevelopmental pathway. Following a general developmental assessment with a paediatrician, the team completes a joint MDT assessment with occupational therapy, physiotherapy, clinical psychology, dieticians and speech and language therapy. Working in an integrated way reduces the time needed to complete assessments overall and minimises duplication of information from the parents and child. The final assessment report is jointly written. Feedback is routinely given by the paediatrician and another team member. Interventions are often joint and multidisciplinary. Joint working allows the team to deliver a coordinated care plan and prevents the duplication of work and overloading of families with strategies.

Palliative care

Life Force is a multidisciplinary community-based paediatric palliative care service covering three London boroughs and is a good example of the integration of care in relation to children and families living with life-limiting conditions. The service accommodates families moving between acute and community health care provision, working with a 'whole-family approach' and offering coordinated multidisciplinary support and interventions. In terms of psychological working, Life Force works from a systemic perspective with the families and provides the following range of interventions:

- Joint work with other professionals from the Life Force team and community teams (e.g., community physiotherapists to support rehabilitation post hospital stay and/or impact of treatments; community dieticians to advise on managing eating while receiving chemotherapy or while fed by a nasogastric tube).

- Regular consultation to and supervision of Life Force multidisciplinary team, children's community nurses and carers (who work shifts to support the child).

- Pre-briefs and debriefs offered to the system involved in the child's care (Life Force MDT, community MDT, children's community nurses, schools, hospices).

- Additional consultation or one-off supervision sessions offered to children's schools, for example around managing deterioration and 'Do Not Attempt Cardio-pulmonary Resuscitation' orders in a school setting.

- A link with local and national charities around children's palliative care.

Liaison psychiatry

Where children, young people and their families are presenting with severe, escalating or persistent distress, specialist psychological medicine practitioners are needed to provide high intensity input and address the impact on medical treatment. The Department of Health (2015) found that only 16 per cent of acute hospital trusts in England had access to a comprehensive liaison service and recommended that all acute trusts have lifespan mental health liaison services in emergency departments by 2020/21.

RISE (Rapid Intervention Support and Empowerment) provides an excellent example of a rapid response acute service meeting the needs of children presenting in mental health crisis in acute settings (Derbyshire Healthcare NHS Foundation Trust 2018). The service is based on a children's ward at the Children's Hospital, Royal Derby. It is probably best described as an outwardly facing psychological liaison team. RISE works predominantly in children and adults' emergency departments. Approximately 70 per cent of its referrals of under 18s presenting with suicidal ideation and self-harm come via the emergency department. One of the difficulties with a rapid response service for emergency departments is that it can inadvertently encourage inappropriate attendance, in order to expedite access to services. To this end, RISE encouraged referrals from GPs and other professionals, and self-referrals. The team then endeavoured to speak to the family within one working day, and see the patient within five working days.

RISE recognises that each time a young person is moved between teams or workers there is a significant drop-out from service, rendering the child and family more vulnerable and increasingly more likely to access crisis services. In order to address this risk and promote continuity of care along a clear pathway, it endeavoured to work with the young person for a nominal 'up to eight sessions'. This also significantly increased multidisciplinary and agency working around the young person and their family (Evans 2017).

This service has had a significant impact on improving access to services when children are in crisis (a 230% increase in children and young people being seen on the same day as their arrival in the emergency department). There has also been a significant reduction in CAMHS-related admissions to the children's wards (over a three-month period there was a 47 per cent average reduction in the number of children admitted from the emergency department onto a children's ward). Unsurprisingly, cost savings have also been considerable – an estimated £326,275 of savings in acute hospital care in 11 months (Early Intervention Foundation 2015).

RISE has successfully demonstrated the benefits of integrating physical and mental health care crisis services for young people and their families.

Conclusion

What is clear from the examples shared in this chapter is that, in keeping with The King's Fund findings (2016), some innovations have allowed staff to redefine their 'core business', enabled skills transfer, bridged the gaps between services, redesigned the workforce and reduced the stigma associated with using mental health services. However, access to psychological expertise continues to be inequitable between conditions, between secondary and tertiary care and between geographical locations. The King's Fund points out there are a number of factors that are critical to overcoming the barriers to integrated care, including: investment in leadership and leaders committed to change; workforce development; changes to finance and commissioning; agreement on outcomes and how to demonstrate value; and harnessing digital technologies. It is notable that most of the prevention and early intervention with this population occurs in acute hospitals and that staff in primary care and community settings have little or no access to specialist psychological professionals for joint work, psychosocial meetings, supervision, consultation or training.

We argue that commissioning should expand the scope of psychological medicine and mental health services to ensure robust patient pathways from acute inpatient care to community care follow-up, support and care coordination and, where indicated, rehabilitation. Empowering young people and families to help others is also an effective, non-stigmatising and cost-effective way of delivering care at the universal level. If commissioning models could change from an emphasis on face-to-face contacts to other metrics, including staff competence and confidence in the assessment and management of psychological issues, pathways and the timeliness of interventions, training and support for young people and parents to provide peer support, then integration would be easier to achieve and psychological expertise easier to reach.

Acknowledgements

The authors would like to thank the following individuals for their contributions to this chapter: Emma Blake, Harriet Conniff, Nicola Doherty, Janie Donnan, Jess Douglas, Chris Kirk, Megan Maidment, Sarah Majumdar, Eunan McCrudden, Nicola Parish, Fiona Smith, Jacqui Stedmon, Krystina Turner, Jane Valente, Suzanna Watson.

Chapter 7

Creating change that works for vulnerable families

Effective psychological services for children, young people and families involved with youth justice and social care

JENNY TAYLOR AND LISA SHOSTAK

Introduction

The concept of early intervention when working with children and families involved with social care and youth justice is somewhat different from that in other areas. By virtue of being involved with social care or youth justice, children and families have *already* been identified as struggling with managing themselves or their interactions with others in a psychologically healthy fashion. However, even within this context there are interventions which, if offered earlier rather than later in a young person's life, are likely to reap exponentially higher benefits, both for that young person and for any younger siblings. Integrated work is key in this field, where the primary agency seen as responsible for managing these young people is often the local authority, rather than the local health care trust.

Considering the World Health Organization (WHO) definitions of good mental health in children (see Chapter 1), families are frequently involved with social care due to concerns about the soundness of family relationships, and with youth justice due to evidence that young people are not engaging in productive social relationships (in that they are acting in a way that infringes on the rights of others in a significant way). It is therefore interesting that there continues to be a lack of universal acceptance of the need for psychological assessment and thinking regarding these children and families.

In terms of diagnostic categories, it has been repeatedly demonstrated that the populations of young people involved with youth justice services (e.g., Ford *et al.* 2007) and/or in the care of local authorities (e.g., Chitsabesan *et al.* 2006) have significantly higher rates of mental health difficulties than the general population. Furthermore, closer analysis and clinical experience suggest that many of the young people within this group who do not meet diagnostic thresholds still have very apparent psychological needs, and while their behaviours may defy easy categorisation – for instance, presenting with both self-harm (internalising) and aggressive (externalising) behaviour – they are nonetheless behaviours that indicate significant distress and poor mental health (Ryan and Mitchell 2011).

Commonly, children involved in children's social care or youth justice are divided up into those who *are* considered to have mental health problems (restricted to those with a diagnosis from the *Diagnostic and Statistical Manual of Mental Disorders* or the *International Statistical Classification of Diseases*, although still often excluding those children who meet the criteria for a diagnosis of oppositional defiant disorder or conduct disorder), and those that *aren't*, despite them all meeting the WHO definitions of having problems with their mental health as noted above. This means that current mental health systems frequently fail to adequately engage with creating change for these children and their families, despite the significant cost of failing to do so, to them, their families and wider society, and despite the existence of evidence-based psychosocial approaches to creating change. Applied psychological approaches have a vital and under-utilised role in these fields in the co-development of formulation driven, multi-modal approaches to creating change for some of our most concerning and vulnerable children and families.

In this chapter, we'll be reviewing a range of approaches to creating change as early on as possible in the trajectory of a child's involvement with social care or youth justice, looking at integrated models of practice and the evidence collected so far as to effectiveness. The next section will attempt to stimulate thinking about the range of opportunities to intervene systemically to improve children's psychological wellbeing, which largely do not involve traditional individual therapy, and which are often viewed as beyond the scope of traditionally organised child mental health services. What we will not have space to do in this chapter is to go into the detail of practice delivery in relation to each of these stages – for this the reader is advised to consult texts such as *Clinical Practice at the Edge of Care* (Smith 2016) and *Young People in Forensic Mental Health Settings: Psychological Thinking and Practice* (Harvey, Rogers and Law 2015), which have more detailed expositions on a range of innovative intervention practices.

We'll also be introducing the concept of 'STAIRS approaches' to creating change with complex family problems as a way of identifying and developing approaches that are innately collaborative, formulation driven, and focused on community sustainability.

Children's social care

A key difference in focus for psychological practitioners working with children in children's social care, as opposed to a more traditional child and adolescent mental health service (CAMHS) setting, is that the child's home environment has clearly been identified as struggling to meet that child's needs. While that may of course also be the case for children referred to tier 3 CAMHS, it is a necessary component for children being referred to children's social care, meaning that it is always necessary to take a systemic rather than individualistic approach to understanding and creating change for these children.

Intervening pre-birth

Can we intervene to reduce the number of children born into circumstances where there is very good reason to think that these children will be removed from their parents' care under child protection legislation? This question is politically controversial, as 'intervening' in these circumstances can be seen as attempting to have control over the basic reproductive rights of others. But can it also be seen as a reasonable 'early intervention opportunity' – an opportunity to support potential parents to wait and instead have children in circumstances that are more likely to be conducive to them managing to raise those children and have positive relationships with them? We know that people do try to conceive, or allow themselves to conceive, even when they know that they are unlikely to be able to keep those children safe from harm, or keep them at all. This should lead to genuine open-minded questions as to why this is so, and there are interventions that might be used appropriately to help people better understand these decisions. For example:

- Where women are choosing pregnancy as a way to gain a sense of self-worth or status from others, interventions around improving self-esteem or developing alternative social roles might be focused on.

- Where experiences of removal or loss of children have been so traumatic that the person is unable to consider or process that experience but instead avoids thinking about it, work on processing such experiences may help provide space to make a more measured decision about when to have more children. Innovative projects such as Pause (www.pause.org.uk) involve psychologically trained staff trying to help understand what motivates decisions to conceive or at least not take measures to prevent conception, and provides multi-modal interventions as appropriate to that particular woman. Initial evaluations of Pause in Hackney and Southwark have been positive, and by the end of 2018, 17 teams will be in operation across England (McCracken *et al.* 2017). Such an approach might be considered with men as well as women.

Intervening to support parents who are likely to struggle

Another area where preventative approaches have been developed is working with parents who are deemed likely to struggle with safely parenting their children, due to being affected by a number of the sorts of life events or circumstances that are known to impact on individual wellbeing and the ability to develop and manage interpersonal relationships. Approaches such as the Family Nurse Partnership (see Chapter 4), and various parenting programmes (see Chapter 3) aim to support those at risk of struggling with parenting to be able to develop safe secure attachments to their children and manage the considerable day-to-day challenges that parenting brings 'well enough'. To be effective, such programmes need to understand the specific issues an individual may have that make it harder for them to bond well or manage safely, and provide the appropriate multi-modal interventions. For example:

- Careleavers who have experienced multiple disrupted attachments may need particular support managing the emotional aspects of being the attachment object for another person.

- A person with intellectual disabilities may need support in developing strategies to manage the multiple demands of caring for an infant.

- Someone who is parenting on their own and is socially isolated may need help accessing or creating the sorts of networks that are necessary to manage the daily 24-hour needs of an infant.

Parenting programmes with an evidence base in improving child wellbeing, increasing prosocial behaviour of young people and reducing the risk of the young person becoming involved in crime, violence and anti-social behaviour often focus on developing skills that enhance parenting practice, mental wellbeing in parents and a supportive network. For example, Family Foundations focuses on developing the skills needed to improve the quality of interparental relationships such as communication and conflict resolution and creating a supportive network (Feinberg 2008; Feinberg *et al.* 2014; Kan and Feinberg 2014, 2015). For more detail regarding parenting programmes, especially the Incredible Years® and the current evidence base, please refer to Chapter 3. It is also worth noting that the Early Intervention Foundation provides a useful and regularly updated summary of programmes available and the evidence for these (and the quality of the evidence) in its guidebook (2017).

Intensive interventions for families with younger children on the child protection register

When children have been deemed by children's social care departments to be experiencing significant levels of neglect or abuse, a decision is made as to whether the children can remain in the household or need to be removed immediately. If they are remaining in the household, this should be because there is a belief that change can occur, *and* because considerable resources are going to be used to support that change occurring. Unfortunately, in many children's social care departments, limited resources and lack of in-house methodologies for creating change mean that families are actually monitored rather than intervened with, while they continue to struggle. This can mean that the children continue to experience significant harm for prolonged periods, and then are ultimately removed anyway, thus disrupting their initial attachment relationships and frequently creating internal narratives of unlovability and lack of safety in interpersonal relationships.

Where there are external services available, for example from the voluntary sector or the NHS, families may be referred to these services, perhaps for input around domestic violence, or parenting skills, or individual therapy for an issue that is affecting their parenting such as drug use or depression. But this approach of making referrals and then monitoring whether they are 'complied with' fails to acknowledge that it is unlikely that anyone would fail with the parenting task (to the extent of their children becoming subject to child protection proceedings) without there being a whole host of factors that are getting in the way of them being able to understand the impact of their current parenting, or being able to engage with change interventions.

As we say when training staff to work in this field, 'If it was simple, they'd have done it already.' This is a complex area where simply making referrals to different agencies for the obviously identifiable 'problem behaviours' without a good multi-level formulation is unlikely to create change. Access to good psychological formulation around the reasons for neglect or abuse should greatly increase the likelihood of being able to develop multi-modal intervention plans with a reasonable chance of success. Multi-Systemic Therapy – Child Abuse and Neglect (MST-CAN, Swenson et al. 2010), a variation of Multi-Systemic Therapy (Henggeler et al. 2009) that focuses on child abuse and neglect, Signs of Safety (an approach for whole social care systems) (Bunn 2013), and FAMILY (a training package designed for small case-holding teams of social workers with embedded clinicians) (Bostock et al. 2017) are all examples of approaches that attempt to co-develop a complex multi-level formulation of the reasons why a family is struggling in order to develop a multi-level intervention package. Evidence for these approaches is promising, although there is not yet enough longitudinal data to allow us to comment confidently on the impact on long-term outcomes for children.

An initial randomised effectiveness trial of MST-CAN demonstrated that it was significantly more effective than what the authors termed 'enhanced outpatient treatment' in reducing young people's mental health symptoms, parental psychiatric distress, parenting behaviours associated with maltreatment, and out-of-home placements for the young people targeted by the interventions. Interestingly an additional finding from these studies was that MST-CAN was also significantly more effective at improving natural social support for parents (Swenson *et al.* 2010).

Regarding Signs of Safety, a review of the literature by the NSPCC concluded that the approach helped practitioners assess and intervene with the danger and harm factors in a case and clarify concerns, especially with more difficult cases and during periods of crisis. It also helped practitioners to be more specific about child protection issues, ensuring that they described behaviours and frequencies rather than just said the child had experienced 'neglect'. This also helped practitioners think of families as individual families, each different, rather than just having a certain 'type' of problem. Signs of Safety methods also increased the participation, cooperation and engagement of parents/families and there was some evidence that this meant that action and change were more likely to happen. However, there is limited evidence so far on whether Signs of Safety improves outcomes for children, and further research is needed to evaluate the effectiveness of this model (Bunn 2013).

Initial evaluations of FAMILY indicated that working from this framework provided a better quality of children's services than normal practice, with highly positive feedback from the families involved. Data from the initial 119 children who were part of this evaluation (and had been referred to the service from multi-agency resource panels due to being at high risk of being taken into care) indicated that 79 per cent remained at home, with only 25 children (21%) subsequently receiving some form of care (Bostock *et al.* 2017).

Intensive interventions for families where teenagers are at risk of entering care

Teenagers at risk of entering care is another key area where using more resources in a more psychologically strategic way earlier may lead to considerable benefits. Teenagers appear to benefit least from the intervention of being placed in statutory care, frequently either choosing to abscond from their care placements, or having care placements that end prematurely as the carer feels unable to manage the teenagers. Many foster carers struggle when trying to integrate an adolescent into a new family when, developmentally, they are going through the process of differentiating themselves from family life. This means that teenagers who enter care are disproportionately placed in residential care. Residential care accepts a less intense bond between young person and principal carer than is aimed for in foster care, due to the residential setting where there are multiple carers. This can allow residential carers to 'cope' with more emotionally and physically challenging young people than foster carers, but at the cost of the young person no longer having a home with a principal adult caregiver. As well as providing a less containing adult bond, residential care provides a peer environment of other young people not safely bonded to a principal adult carer and who are likely also to be struggling to fit into societal expectations, thus in some cases increasing rather than decreasing the young person's move away from socially acceptable behaviour. There is therefore a significant interest from local authorities in programmes aiming to reduce the accommodation of teenagers where they might instead be able to safely remain at home.

Intervention approaches currently being used to try and reduce the accommodation of teenagers, such as Functional Family Therapy (FFT) (Sexton and Alexander 2003; Sexton and Turner 2010) and MST (Henggeler *et al.* 2009), take a systemic, collaborative and analytical approach to creating intervention plans with families. Christofides (2016) provides a helpful round-up of the thinking behind and the evidence for these sorts of approaches in her chapter in *Clinical Practice at the Edge of Care* (Smith 2016).

Interventions to prevent alternative care placements from breaking down

Where children are placed away from home, there are clear correlations between the outcomes for them and the stability of the out-of-home placement. Research has clearly demonstrated that children and young people crave stability and that disruption may significantly undermine their wellbeing and feelings of self-worth (e.g., Jackson and Martin 1998). While there is uncertainty within the literature about whether difficult behaviour is the cause of placement breakdowns, or the driving factor, there is clear evidence that instability is related to poor outcomes (e.g., Minnis and Devine 2001). One study found that children who did not demonstrate any behavioural problems before being in care were badly affected by placement moves (Newton, Litrownik and Landsverk 2000). It is clear that where possible it is in the best interest of children and young people to have placement stability.

Interventions aimed at supporting and maintaining alternative care placements such as KEEP (Knibbs, Mollidor and Bierman 2016; Roberts, Glynn and Waterman 2016) and AdOPT (Harold *et al.* 2017) are frequently based on the same core approaches as group parenting programmes, but with additional components to reflect the differences in parenting a child with a history of disrupted attachments and neglect and abuse. Approaches such as MST and FAMILY have also been used to support foster and adoptive caregivers, and although there is not a separate evidence base regarding their effectiveness with this group, there is good reason to assume that these approaches could be effective in maintaining alternative care placements.

Interventions with careleavers to reduce their likelihood of needing adult mental health services/social services support in parenting their own children

'Careleavers' is the term used for young people who have reached their 18th birthday when in local authority care – some of these young people may have spent the majority of their life in local authority care, for example having experienced an early failed adoption, numerous foster placements, and then finally residential care. Others may have entered care as young adults and been placed in semi-independent accommodation. What they all have in common is the experience of loss of at least one adult attachment relationship before adulthood. Many careleavers unsurprisingly struggle to manage independent living at the relatively young age of 18, in the context of disadvantageous early experiences followed by entering adulthood unsupported by the usual friends and family network. Being in care during childhood has been shown to be associated with adverse adult socio-economic, educational, legal and health outcomes in excess of those associated with co-existing childhood or adult disadvantage (Viner and Taylor 2005).

Yet services for this client group are probably the least advanced – young careleavers no longer have access to the sorts of multi-modal and flexible psychosocial interventions detailed above. Unless they have already had children and had difficulty with parenting those children (and thus gone full circle and become eligible for the sorts of services this section started with), they are usually trapped between two types of mental health services, neither of which may meet their needs. At the more accessible community level we now have a range of IAPT services across the country, but many careleavers do not fit neatly into the categories of disorder these services exist to treat (mild to moderate anxiety or depression), and even if they do, they may struggle to engage in a new therapeutic relationship without considerable outreach work of the sort most IAPT services are unable to provide.

At the other end of the spectrum are the community and inpatient mental health teams that work with people with more severe and enduring mental health problems. These services are again diagnostically led, and therefore are not always able to accept referrals of careleavers with significant psychological and interpersonal difficulties if they do not have existing diagnostic categories. This is, therefore, a group ripe for the development of early interventions to enable these young people who have already experienced so much trauma to have the best chance of being able to develop sound family relationships and engage in productive social relationships. An example of an innovative attempt to address these issues is the Department for Education Innovations funded project being undertaken by Southwark Council and Catch 22, which is looking at how to extend the multi-modal approaches to care detailed above to careleavers up to the age of 25. This is likely to be achieved through the Personal Advisors (the social care staff employed to support young people leaving care with the transition to full independent living) having access to clinically trained staff embedded within their team, to support their ability to understand and meet those young people's needs, but also the development of clinical intervention services based on the impact of emotional difficulties on day-to-day functioning, rather than on diagnostic criteria.

Youth justice

There is significant overlap between the group of young people considered to be at the edge of care and/or in the care of the local authority and those involved with the youth justice system. Research has consistently demonstrated that young people looked after by the local authority have a significantly higher official recorded rate of offending than young people in the general population (e.g., Schofield *et al.* 2012).

Therefore, the interventions listed above can be considered to also be early interventions for the group of young people involved with youth justice. Many of the young people involved with the criminal justice system have had complicated and chaotic lives. Many have experienced trauma, abuse, bereavement, been excluded from school, experienced drug- or alcohol-related dependencies and have mental health problems or personality disorders.

There are a number of intervention packages with an evidence base in specifically supporting young people who have been identified as on the edge of involvement or are already involved with the youth justice system. These aim to either avoid formal involvement or have such involvement last for as short a time as possible and prevent repeated involvement. Throughout discussion of these programmes and the rationale for them it may be noted that there is significant overlap in the methodologies found to be effective in creating change across both this group of young people and the group of children and young people involved with social care. The elements that are common to effective interventions will be explored further in the discussion of the STAIRS framework at the end of this chapter.

Intervening with young people at risk of criminal involvement

It is perhaps useful to consider two distinct but overlapping groups when thinking about intervening with young people at risk of entry into the youth justice system. The first is the group who are currently exposed to a number of the known risk factors which significantly increase the likelihood of entry, such as low socio-economic status, low school achievement, child abuse or parental conflict, poor parental mental health or substance misuse problems and parental contact with the criminal justice system. The second is the group who are already known to be either directly engaging in illegal activity or spending time with others who are directly engaging in illegal activity but who have not yet entered the system (i.e. been caught). It is often the case that networks around young people are well aware that they are on the cusp of contact with the youth justice system for some time before their formal entry into it.

In the National Institute for Clinical Excellence (NICE) guidelines on conduct disorder and anti-social behaviour, interventions offered to the first group described – those whose risk of developing a conduct disorder is significantly higher than average, as evidenced by individual, family and social risk factors – are termed as selective prevention. Recommendations include classroom-based emotional learning and problem-solving programmes for children aged typically between 3 and 7 years in schools which are intended to increase children's awareness of their own and others' emotions, teach self-control, promote positive self-concept and peer relations and develop children's problem-solving skills. It is suggested that the programmes should typically consist of up to 30 classroom-based sessions over the course of a school year. It is interesting to note the individual, as opposed to multi-modal, nature of this sort of intervention. Such approaches would presumably be most likely to succeed if the main reason that the child was at risk of offending was because of their individual difficulties in emotional recognition, self-control, and problem solving, rather than if there were significant family and social factors creating the risk.

The NICE guidelines indicate that the research from these sorts of approaches (e.g., Webster-Stratton, Reid and Stoolmiller 2008) has demonstrated that teachers trained in this type of intervention used more positive classroom management strategies and that their students showed more social competence and emotional self-regulation and fewer conduct problems than control teachers and students. Interestingly, these teachers also reported more involvement with parents. Overall, NICE concluded that findings show some promising evidence for the efficacy of a preventive curriculum, such as described above, for enhancing school protective factors and reducing child and classroom risk factors faced by socio-economically disadvantaged children.

As regards the second group – those known to be offending or close to offending but not yet formally within the youth justice systems – various government-led initiatives have aimed to try and target this group, including Youth Inclusion Support Panels (YISPs) and Youth Justice Liaison and Diversion (YJLD) schemes, by offering multi-agency support to identified young people and their families to attempt to make changes that prevent entry. Practice in this area is often characterised by the involvement of a number of professionals and community services working to create change using different approaches. While there was some evidence suggesting potential efficacy of these types of programmes in preventing re-offending for some young people (Haines *et al.* 2012), reductions in funding and overall pressures on limited youth justice and local authority budgets have meant a reduction in number, scope and efficacy of programmes over the last few years.

Intervening with young people known to be involved in offending behaviour

The outcomes for young people who enter the youth secure estate are poor. Effective community-based interventions rather than custody can therefore be seen as a form of 'early intervention' in the trajectory of a young person who might otherwise spend multiple periods in custody.

There is growing evidence that multi-modal interventions may offer more effective (in terms of reducing likelihood of re-offending) and more humane alternatives to custody (e.g., Henggeler *et al.* 2009; Butler *et al.* 2011). Multi-modal interventions take an ecological approach to assessing and understanding offending behaviour (Bronfenbrenner 1977). They focus on the creation of collaborative formulations to drive a range of interventions aimed at influencing change in whichever aspects of the systems surrounding the young person, or the young person themselves, are indicated by the formulation.

The NICE guidelines for conduct disorder and anti-social behaviour in children and young people recommend that multi-modal interventions should involve the child or young person and their parents and carers and should:

- have an explicit and supportive family focus

- be based on a social learning model with interventions provided at individual, family, school, criminal justice and community levels

- be provided by specially trained case managers

- typically consist of three to four meetings per week over a three- to five-month period

- adhere to a developer's manual and employ all of the necessary materials to ensure consistent implementation of the programme.

Other less intensive approaches with promising evidence to support them include Functional Family Therapy, which also focuses on collaborative systemic interventions.

Intervening with young people in custodial settings

There are three options for the placement of young people who receive a custodial sentence: secure children's homes (SCHs), secure training centres (STCs) and youth offenders' institutes (YOIs). These increase in size and decrease in staff-to-young person ratios from the SCHs to the YOIs. As mentioned above, two-thirds of young people placed into custodial settings re-offend within 12 months. Re-offending rates are also substantially higher among young adults in the criminal justice system than older adult offenders, indicating that we really are still struggling to come up with effective ways of creating change for these young people while they are in custodial care. In fact, there are concerns that for some young people, time spent in a custodial setting increases rather than decreases the likelihood of future offending.

There are a number of reasons why it is particularly hard to create change for this group of young people in these settings. By virtue of being placed in a custodial setting, these young people are separated from their families and networks, and the staff working with them are usually doing so in isolation from working with their family or network. Even where institutions have the scope and resources to take a broader approach, the closure of some institutions and restructuring of the secure estate has meant many young offenders are in custody so far from their home that such work is not practically viable. The only peer relationships available to young people in secure settings are with other young people with offending histories. Gang involvement is problematic in secure settings. The regime and the support available are not consistent between youth and adult systems, which means that those who move between establishments to complete their sentences experience the same sorts of issues with transitions as young people moving between CAMHS and adult mental health (AMH) services in the community.

Despite all the issues raised above, a young person being 'secured' in an environment where there is a range of staff with training in health and social care in theory provides a real opportunity for changing their trajectory. NHS England's CAMHS Health and Justice workstream embarked on an ambitious CAMHS transformation programme in 2016 to look at how mental health input to the children and young people's secure estate could be organised differently to create better outcomes for young people.

One of the core principles behind the new programme was that the environment and the relationships within it (rather than specialist in-reach services) were likely to be the primary agents of change for young people within secure settings. This led to the idea that the residential and custodial staff at the establishments should be at the centre of creating change, supported by mental health staff, rather than 'mental health interventions' occurring separately and in a vacuum for a small number of young people who fit specific diagnostic criteria. This focus on the creation and maintenance of a therapeutic environment with well-supported staff with an understanding of the impact of trauma and other social and developmental challenges on young people was seen as a critical and essential task in its own right in terms of improving psychological wellbeing. The transformation programme coined the acronym 'SECURE' to outline the key components of such a milieu: specialist skills, emotionally resilient staff, cared for staff, understanding of key psychological theories by frontline staff, reflective practice opportunities for frontline staff, and every interaction matters as a cultural norm for frontline staff (see Taylor *et al.* 2018 for further details).

Much of the impetus for this shift in focus within the secure estate from interventions aimed at the young person to interventions aimed at the whole system emerged from the DART approach developed through working with young people presenting with high-risk behaviour and particularly complex needs in the Willow Unit in Hindley YOI (Rogers and Budd 2015). However, this work itself draws on a myriad of other innovations that would be consistent with this type of approach such as Trauma Systems Therapy (Saxe, Ellis and Kaplow 2007), The Sanctuary Model (Bloom 2005), the Enabling Environments initiative (Johnson and Haigh 2011), psychologically informed environments (Haigh *et al.* 2012) and the Psychologically Informed Planned Environments (PIPEs) approach (Bolger and Turner 2013), to name but a few.

The second aspect of the programme was to look at the possibility of supporting establishments to develop a STAIRS approach to creating change for young people. In STAIRS approaches, clear 'destination targets' are collaboratively identified, formulations are collaboratively developed with young people, their families and the key professionals around them, and whole-system interventions are then planned based on those formulations.

The SECURE STAIRS programme is looking, with establishments, at creating smaller groupings of young people to be staffed by a relatively consistent group of frontline staff. In the smaller establishments, for example in most of the SCHs, this is already standard practice, but in the larger establishments this is rarely the case. These staff (residential and attached educational, social care and health staff) would have weekly multidisciplinary meetings regarding their residential grouping, which would provide the internal engine for the interventions for young people. The result of this joint thinking would be establishment-wide intervention plans for each young person, based on a shared understanding of the causes of their difficulties.

A major challenge for the secure estate, as indicated earlier, is the separation of the young person from their 'natural' environment, meaning that there is a far greater challenge in trying to support changes that would sustain across environments. This is an explicit component of any STAIRS approach, and the secure estate is looking at innovative ways (e.g., using video suites) of working more closely with young people's family and 'home' networks during their custodial stays.

Introducing the idea of STAIRS

How might we recognise approaches likely to be effective in children's social care and youth justice and help develop new ones? As a result of their work across children's social care and youth justice, the authors of this chapter were interested in how to identify and support the development of effective practice in these settings. In order to successfully create change in children's trajectories, psychological staff need to focus on how to support integrated effective working practices. The concept of a STAIRS approach to creating change developed out of consideration of the challenges to effective integrated work in these settings and of the key elements of interventions that do have a good evidence base within these settings.

In children's social care and youth justice, professionals with a range of different training are working to create change in complex patterns of behaviour between people – between parents and children, young people and their peers, young people and their communities. One of the key challenges for social work, youth justice and residential staff and their service managers is in being able to critically assess and choose between the myriad of specific intervention packages on offer.

The increase in information around evidence-based approaches (development of NICE, Social Care Institute for Excellence, Research in Practice) has been helpful in supporting social care and youth justice staff to access massed data on the likelihood of any particular intervention helping with any particular problem. What is not always understood is that it is just the likelihood of being able to create change that means that an approach is the recommended approach, rather than any certainty. Some well-evidenced and well-respected approaches which are nationally implemented are only expected to be effective for less than half the population. Thus while standardised evidence-based approaches are certainly the appropriate starting point for any particular presenting problem, their impact needs to be assessed rather than taken for granted, as the young person may be, for example, one of the 40 per cent for whom the approach is not effective, rather than one of the 60 per cent for whom it is. In addition, in order to even be able to start thinking about whether there is an evidence-based approach that might be appropriate, a young person's difficulties need to be properly identified.

This means that the process of assessing a problem, choosing an intervention appropriately, and then assessing its impact and revisiting and revising as necessary is crucial. However, that analytic process is not usually embedded in professional trainings in social work or youth justice, yet those staff are often expected to be the ones making decisions as to which 'treatment package' to offer a young person.

Another core issue in relation to work in this field in particular, is the balance of power between 'professionals' and 'clients' (using the term 'professional' to mean anyone paid to try to create change, and 'client' meaning the person the 'professional' is trying to change). Unlike work in other specialities of mental health and social care (such as treating an adult for depression, or providing support to a family with a child with a disability), most of this work is carried out because someone other than the clients themselves considers there to be a problem. This means that the clients may be ambivalent about or actively antagonistic to the professionals' conceptualisation of the problem. Unless the interventions are seen as addressing issues that the clients themselves see as problems, they are unlikely to be interested in the evidence-based nature of those interventions or collaborate in their delivery. This means that many young people or families are written off as 'impossible to engage', or appear to engage when in fact they are just following the path of least resistance. Collaborative practice is therefore at the heart of all the effective intervention approaches in this field.

Lastly, many intervention approaches in this field do not have a significant focus on ensuring that the people who are expected to change understand the processes of creating and sustaining change, and have the skills and capacity to notice future problems and address them without ongoing professional input. So while professionals are often able to create change while involved with clients, they frequently then see them 'relapse' once that additional support is removed, or when a new challenge arises. Effective approaches place a considerable emphasis on considering issues of sustainability throughout the intervention. These issues together provided the impetus for articulating a collaborative and analytic approach to creating change that could be easily communicated and kept in mind by professionals who might come from a variety of different backgrounds, and be relevant whatever the presenting problems and range of interventions – the idea of a STAIRS approach to creating change for children and young people in complex social care settings. The STAIRS acronym was developed as a way to both identify intervention approaches that are collaborative, systemic and analytic in their components, and also to provide a scaffold for the development of new approaches. Both the FAMILY approach mentioned above and the NHS England SECURE STAIRS project were specifically designed by applied psychologists using the STAIRS framework.

What components are needed to make an approach a STAIRS approach?

Scoping

Scoping refers to collating sufficient information to be able to understand as precisely as possible what the problems actually are, and their history and mediating factors. This is important in this field for a number of reasons. Vague or inaccurate information about problem patterns of behaviour increases the extent to which the professional will 'fill in the gaps' in their information according to their own internal models of such behaviour patterns and their causes. This can be particularly tricky when the problem issues are of a social interactive nature, such as violent or abusive behaviour, or concerns about parenting, as unlike changes in blood pressure, these sorts of interpersonal behavioural problems are ones that all human beings tend to have emotive responses to, coloured by their own experiences. Thus, a description of a person 'repeatedly acting in an aggressive fashion' will be interpreted in a myriad of different ways by different people, affected by their own relationship to the concept of 'aggression'.

Lack of clarity regarding the actual specific nature of the problems impacts on the professionals' ability to accurately assess risk, to see patterns, and to notice whether or not change is taking place. Diagnostic categories on their own will also not suffice in terms of providing the information required to assess risk, notice patterns, and notice change, as diagnostic categories in mental health allow two people with the same diagnoses to present with very different versions of similar problems. In any STAIRS approach, professionals are expected to have the skills to work with the clients to gather FIDO-type information (information on the frequency, intensity, duration and onset of the phenomenon in question) and to be able to explain to clients *why* they need to be clear about this information, in terms of elucidating the reasons given above.

A second core feature of the sort of scoping required in any collaborative analytic approach is clear information about the resources and the desires of the client and the non-professional system around them. If from the start of any work we are aiming to support clients to be able to sustain any positive change without professional input, we need to know what the potential resources are that can be harnessed to achieve that aim – who are their family, friends, neighbours, school, workplace; who cares about this problem and who has influence over it? Who are the 'stakeholders'?

Lastly, but most importantly of all in terms of laying the groundwork for a collaborative approach to change, we need to understand what the client and other key stakeholders actually want to be different – in a STAIRS approach, as in solution-focused therapy approaches, this is a conversation had early on in the process. What is being asked is not how they think we should help them, but what they would want to be different if our involvement had been helpful. Clarifying what those who are involved in or have influence over the issue wish to change both encourages the client and others involved to think about an alternative future and allows an open discussion of what is actually realistic and in the scope of the professionals' task. It also provides the information necessary for the next stage of negotiating a clear destination which would indicate that the intervention task was complete.

Target identification

The next stage in a STAIRS approach is core to the majority of effective approaches to social and mental health work – identifying the endpoint. The T in STAIRS stands for the importance of identifying, with the client, what the final targets are for the work with the professional. These final targets may not be the endpoint of what the client would want to achieve in that area, but would be the signal that they are functioning at a level that wouldn't normally require professional involvement. Truly collaborative target-agreeing is a complex therapeutic endeavour, where the professional looks at how they can weave together the hopes of the client and the other various stakeholders with the purpose of their service, and what is realistic in the timeframe. This is particularly important in contexts where there are significant power differentials and the client is, to a large extent, an involuntary client. Here, as an absolute minimum, clients can usually be engaged in agreeing that they would like a life where professionals didn't think they needed to be involved with them. But for most clients there are other aspects of their lives that they would like to be better, or things they would like to achieve differently if only they believed that was possible – a good understanding of the problems but also the client and their networks, hopes and dreams is therefore very important.

In addition, there is then the task of working out with the client exactly how improvement in relation to the agreed targets will be measured, by whom, and how often. This is important for two main reasons. First, it is in order to ensure clarity between the professionals and the client about how change is being measured, making sure that this is discussed in an open and non-combative way at the beginning. Second, both client and professional, as human beings, will tend to interpret information according to a number of factors such as their mood or their world view. This can get in the way of either the client or professional having a balanced view regarding whether progress is being made or not, or patterns in the change process.

Activators

Activators in STAIRS terminology are the factors that lead to, or allow, the problems to occur. An understanding of these is required in order to create an informed intervention plan, and this understanding of the activators is what is normally described as a 'formulation' in applied psychology practice. Key features of a collaborative approach are that these activators are identified with the client, and the client is taught how to try to identify them and why that matters. What the professional brings to these discussions is their theoretical and professional knowledge as to the sorts of things that tend to cause these problems – but the client should always be invited to check whether they think those are the relevant activators in their case, and to offer their suggestions as to likely activators.

In the STAIRS framework, the reason the process of trying to understand the activators only takes place after identification of the targets is in order to have some boundaries on what activators, of what, are considered. This is in recognition of the complexity of the human condition, rather than an attempt to be reductionist. The human condition, and particularly interactions between humans, is so complex that a general attempt at understanding all the activators of all aspects of a client's functioning risks leading both client and professional on a never-ending journey. Although much understanding may be gained on such a journey, there is a danger that no specific interventions are actually identified and no actual change therefore takes place.

Interventions

While understanding by the client of the causes of their difficulties is a desirable condition for change, understanding alone is unlikely to be sufficient to lead to sustained change in entrenched patterns of interaction, which leads us on to the process of co-developing new ways of doing things with the client, based on their understanding of the activators of their difficulties. The term 'interventions' in this context refers to anything anyone is doing in a deliberate attempt to create movement towards the collaboratively agreed targets. Thus 'interventions' may be enacted by the professional or the client or other stakeholders, they may be practical or interactional or therapeutic or may be an individual change in thought processes – the essential point is that they are chosen because it appears likely that they will impact on a collaboratively agreed activator of the problems. The exact nature of formulation-driven interventions should vary between clients with the same 'presenting problems'. The concept of a STAIRS approach is not theory specific – if a particular understanding makes sense to a client and professional and suggests a particular intervention, then that would be the appropriate intervention to try first.

This is where the knowledge base of the professional becomes important, as what they are ideally bringing to the discussions with the client is their knowledge of what sorts of interventions are likely to work for what, given the evidence base. In a collaborative approach, the decision as to which intervention to try when would, wherever possible, be led by the client, as this will obviously increase their engagement with the intervention, and interventions should always be entered into in a spirit of experimentation – 'we are trying this, as we think it would impact on that, which would reduce the problem, but if it doesn't we'll have to rethink' – see below...

Review and revise

The process of collaboratively reviewing progress towards the collaboratively agreed targets, and revising the interventions if no progress is being made is an essential part of the therapeutic endeavour. Reviewing collaboratively allows the client to give their view on the impact of the intervention, and provides the client with an opportunity to learn through direct experience about this sort of problem-solving approach. Any intervention that doesn't appear to have an impact is an opportunity for a conversation between client and professional as to whether a) they think it didn't have an impact as maybe that activator wasn't as important as one or other or both of them thought, in which case it clears the way for an intervention aimed at an alternative activator, or b) whether while the activator was important, this intervention couldn't easily change it, in which case an alternative intervention for the same activator might be considered, or switching to a different activator that is easier to change might be considered. Making sure this process of thinking and discussion is followed tends to greatly increase collaboration and reduce conflict about causes and blame.

Sustainability

Lastly, but arguably most importantly, for something to be considered a STAIRS approach there needs to be a belief by the professional that their ultimate aim is for the client to be able to manage without their input in the longer term. This means that from the outset, interventions that can occur without professional input are favoured over those that rely on professionals – the professional's skill is in helping the client to work out what the interventions need to be, not necessarily in being the one to deliver them. It also means that where signs of progress towards targets are evident, the client and professional have an open discussion about what has led to that progress, rather than pre-supposing that any progress has necessarily been caused by the professional intervention. Core to effective approaches is that any interventions or indeed accidental circumstances that have led to positive change are considered with the client in terms of how those interventions or circumstances can be maintained without the use of professionals in the longer term. This aspect of the work should be seen as the bulk of the work in a truly sustainable approach, with all of the preceding work serving the function of understanding what needs to be different.

STAIRS: a case study

Bradley is a 15-year-old young man. The documents that follow Bradley from service to service describe him as a very angry violent young man who is putting his younger siblings at risk by being violent home, being heavily involved in a gang and engaging in lots of anti-social and illegal behaviour. They say that his mother is unable to control him and that his dad is not involved. There is some mention of a new partner but no detail. They report that Bradley sometimes lives with his grandmother who is also unable to control him. At the point of referral, Bradley's younger siblings have recently been placed on the child protection register due to 'a violent outburst' from Bradley during which the police were called.

S – Scoping

Clarity regarding presenting problems, who the key players are in the child or young person's life and what change is wanted by whom.

Scoping involves really finding out who is important in the family and extended network, including completing a genogram (a pictorial representation of family relationships, see Jolly *et al.* 1980), what these key individuals really want to be different, what the strengths are of the young person and the systems around them and specific details about the behaviours that everyone agrees they want to see less of.

What everyone wants

Bradley:

- Mum and Harry to get off my back.

- Everyone to just leave me alone.

- Less shouting at home.

Mum:

- Social services to get off my back.

- School to not call all the time about Bradley.

- Bradley to show some respect at home.

- To have my life back.

Uncle:

- Bradley to go to school.

- Bradley to treat adults with respect.

- Junior and Damon to go to bed in the evenings.

Junior (brother):

- Mum to not be cross all the time.

- Bradley to not be naughty.

- Bradley to play with me.

Social worker:

- Bradley to be in school.

- No physical or verbal aggression from Bradley towards his mother or younger siblings.

- No use of physical chastisement at home.

- Younger children to be in a routine.

- Mum to not drink so much.

Strengths within the system

- Individual: friendly, affable, enjoys praise from adults.

- Family: committed to Bradley, warm relationship between Uncle and Bradley.

- School: good relationships between Bradley and some teachers.

- Peers: good at making friends.

- Community: local prosocial activities club.

Table 7.1: Specific details presented in a FIDO table

Problem	Frequency	Intensity	Duration	Onset
Verbal aggression	6/7 (nearly every day of the week)	Not shouting but threats to hurt/kill	Since September 2014	Starting secondary school
Physical aggression to property	1/14 (couple of times/month)	Actually breaks furniture – doors/tables	Since Christmas 2016	Don't know
Physical aggression to people	2/365	Pushes me hard	Since February 2017	Since Dad stopped any contact

T – Targets

Going through a process of checking what is wanted by whom in order to agree what we're aiming for with as many people as possible, and an agreed way of tracking our progress.

What everyone involved (including Bradley) wants for Bradley, and how frequently and intensely the problems occur, is all thought about together to try to come up with realistic targets for change that are specific and measurable and worded so that as many people as possible (ideally including Bradley) will feel they can sign up to them.

For Bradley to be attending school and enjoying it as measured by:

- teachers reporting he is there every day

- no exclusions.

For everyone to be treated with respect at home as measured by:

- no slapping or hitting reported by Mum/Bradley/little ones

- no use of f*** or c*** words, as reported by Mum

- no destruction of property, as reported by Mum

- no pushing Mum, as reported by Mum.

Mum to feel like she has her life back as measured by:

- younger kids in bed by 8pm, as reported by Mum

- Mum to be drinking less than four units a day, as reported by Uncle

- Mum to start Zumba classes and attend weekly.

A – Activators
Collaboratively identifying the multi-level activators of the problems with reaching our targets.

Within the STAIRS framework, before we start any interventions, we consider all the activators that make that behaviour more likely to occur. To do this we look, with the young person, family and carers at a specific circumstance where a target has not been met and what the things were that contributed to that. In this case, within the first week of the goals being set Bradley reports an incident where his mother slapped him. To understand this, we think about all of the activators that lead to this, and find a way to share them pictorially with the family, for example using a 'fit circle' as used in MST (Hengeller *et al.* 2009):

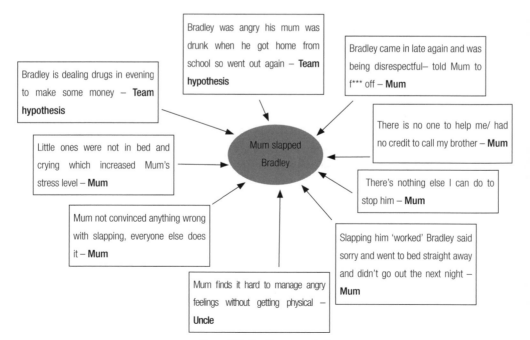

Figure 7.1: Bradley case study

I – Interventions

Interventions in a STAIRS context means anything anyone does, from the practical to the therapeutic, with the aim of impacting on the activators.

Interventions are aimed to address specific activators. The process of deciding which activator to intervene on is collaborative. The team has a hypothesis that the most powerful activator is Bradley's mother's drinking but Mum does not agree and therefore the team agrees to initially trial whether Mum is able to manage to abstain from hitting Bradley by working on her gaining a better understanding of the sequence that leads to the violence and identifying with her other options for exiting the sequence earlier. Mum is not convinced it is wrong but is clear that she wants social care 'off my back' and that she needs to stop hitting Bradley in order for this to happen.

- Chosen activators: 'There is nothing else I can do to stop him.' Mum finds it hard to manage angry feelings without physical violence.

- Intervention: Work with Mum on drawing out the sequence that leads to the slapping and identifying alternative exits and/or strategies. Role playing these with Mum. Support Mum, by phone if necessary, at times where the sequence is likely to be activated.

R – Review and revise

Real-life monitoring of movement towards targets and modelling going back and revising formulations and plans – experimenting together.

This initial intervention is unsuccessful and Mum hits Bradley again within 48 hours of making the alternative plan. Mum is able to acknowledge when reviewing why the plan has not worked and that once she has 'had a few drinks' she no longer 'has the strength' to do the plan. Mum therefore acknowledges that drinking on nights she is alone with the kids is a key activator of her then 'losing it'. The intervention is then revised to do direct work with Mum on her drinking.

S – Sustain

Sustainability thought about from the outset in terms of types of interventions offered and plans for maintaining progress after closure – the bulk of the work!

Once Mum has managed to not hit Bradley for a period of three weeks a positive map of the activators leading to the positive behaviour of 'no violence towards

Bradley' is completed with Bradley and his mother. They are able to identify a number of changes that have impacted on this change:

- Mum using different strategies to manage Bradley's abusive language via clear consequences.

- Mum ensuring her brother or neighbours are around when she is having a few drinks.

- Bradley and Mum recognising the sequence and being able to 'exit' earlier.

- The winter coming so Bradley is coming in earlier anyway.

Work is then completed to think about:

- how Mum/Bradley can keep all of these positive changes going, for example Mum to continue to use the family calendar to record when poor language occurs, and to continue to link phone credit to language

- identifying what might go wrong in the future and how they can get things back on track when things do go wrong, for example what if Mum feels that the consequences for Bradley are no longer working and his language has become unacceptable again? Mum will a) look at the list of all the possible consequences we developed during our work together, b) take this list and discuss with her brother (Bradley's uncle) how they might change the plan, c) once agreed, Mum and her brother will both sit down with Bradley and give him the new rule which will be monitored in the same way as before but with the change in consequence.

Conclusions

Children's social care and youth justice are fields where applied psychology has much to offer in terms of both early intervention and integrated ways of working. This field benefits from flexible, systemic, formulation-driven approaches, rather than more traditional diagnostic individual therapy approaches. STAIRS is an example of a framework developed by psychologists that can be shared with other staff to support formulation-driven and collaborative care. There are already many evidence-based approaches in this area that make use of the idea of collaboratively developed and shared psychological formulations to drive multi-modal interventions, but there is still considerable scope for the development of psychosocial work in this field. Psychologically trained staff are ideally suited to work alongside social care and youth justice staff to increase the delivery of effective, integrated care.

Chapter 8

People in their whole context

Promoting social justice and community psychology as a means to prevent psychological distress and improve wellbeing for children, young people and their families

LAURA CASALE, NATALIE SEYMOUR, MARK
CHENTITE AND SALLY ZLOTOWITZ

The authors would like to dedicate this chapter to the young people in the communities we have joined who have lost their lives in the context of serious youth violence. Their commitment to making personal and social change through their active participation in MAC-UK and our partners' projects will not be forgotten.

Introduction

This book serves to demonstrate how resources can be used more effectively to decrease psychological distress and increase wellbeing. In this chapter, we will share ways of using these resources by working in and with communities, outlining the rationale and evidence base for community working and providing examples of this increasingly popular approach. We will demonstrate that community working provides a hopeful response to the challenges posed in the introduction to this book.

Why community working?

There is clear, well-supported evidence that key determinants of mental health include social, cultural, economic, political and environmental factors (Purdie, Dudgeon and Walker 2010; World Health Organization and Calouste Gulbenkian Foundation 2014; United Nations Human Rights Council 2017). Poor mental health and low wellbeing are consistently strongly associated with social context factors, such as levels of unemployment, isolation, inequality and low income (Melzer, Fryers and Jenkins 2004; World Health Organization Calouste Gulbenkian Foundation 2014). For example, many social and environmental conditions are associated with suicide rates, although their relationship may be dynamic and contextual to a country and culture. These include unemployment and precarious employment, income and the economy, government health spending, religion and female workforce participation (Milner, McClure and De Leo 2012; Milner *et al.* 2013). Poverty has frequently been researched as a predictor of anti-social and related behaviour (e.g., Costello *et al.* 1996; Eamon 2001; Patterson, Kupersmidt and Vaden 1990; Velez, Johnson and Cohen 1989).

If these societal factors have a significant impact on mental health and wellbeing, it follows that mental health interventions need to impact on these factors (Kagan 2008) *and that interventions might have significantly more success if they did.* Conversely, if these are some of the key factors affecting mental health, an intervention focus which *does not include any of them* is likely to show limited effect and impact on preventing the future distress of others. Yet currently, individualised and reactive responses to psychological distress are widely used in UK statutory services. Prescriptions of psychiatric medication continue to increase, as does demand for individual therapy (Harper 2017) while preventative practical social interventions like youth clubs, safe community spaces and women's refuges continue to decrease due to austerity measures. There are long-standing and well-evidenced criticisms of this approach to distress (e.g., Kinderman 2014). We suggest that we will improve outcomes if we shift from 1) *reacting* to distress to attempting to *prevent* it and 2) from focusing the cause of distress and the path to recovery in individuals to *wider contexts or structures.*

Working in communities

If we know that the current individual focus is limited, what are our other options? Certainly, we can turn to community psychology, which attempts to widen the focus and engage at community and societal levels of change (Kagan *et al.* 2011). Community psychology is a way of shaping services to improve the societal determinants of health. Within this approach, wellbeing is defined at a level beyond the individual. Wiseman and Brasher (2008) suggest that wellbeing is 'the combination of social, economic, environmental, cultural, and political conditions identified by individuals and their communities as essential for them to flourish and fulfil their potential' (p.358). Nelson and Prilleltensky (2005) suggest that community wellbeing includes 'clean environment, freedom from discrimination, safe neighbourhoods, good schools and employment opportunities. Communal goods that benefit everyone' (p.10). Finally, Kee and Nam (2016) argue that a sense of community is also a factor in wellbeing.

It is important to remember that community psychology is not the same individualised approach just practised in community-type settings. Holland (1992) reminds us that 'Mental health workers... cannot assume that merely to be "in the community" is in itself socially progressive' (p.75). Instead, the focus, methodology and evaluation of the work moves from individual or family-focused talking therapies towards preventative and community-led change (Casale, Zlotowitz and Moloney 2015), seeking to expand beyond traditional psychotherapy to promote wellness within wider groups. The work is action orientated and explicitly led by values of social justice and stewardship, with practitioners working in partnership with marginalised and disempowered groups (Prilleltensky, Nelson and Peirson 2001). The aim of interventions is to identify and change the conditions and systems that lead to oppressive and disempowering experiences, all of which lead to ongoing distress (Fryer, Duckett and Pratt 2004; Kagan and Burton 2001). This approach will be outlined in the remainder of the chapter.

Fundamentals of community working

While there are various approaches to applying community psychology in practice, one approach we have found useful is outlined in Kagan and colleagues' textbook *Critical Community Psychology* (2011). This lists clear stages of action, some of which we have used to structure this section. The textbook offers a range of examples to refer to; however, as practitioners at the charity MAC-UK, we will focus on our work there, referring to our projects and services with communities of excluded young people, including those affected by serious youth violence in their communities, and with young people who have experience of the care system.

Stage 1: Problem definition
What is the problem?

Problem definition is often conceived from an individualistic point of view, which can lead to a stance of 'blaming the victim' (Ryan 1971) or their carers. Whether this blame is intentional or not, the responsibility then becomes that of the individual or immediate family. Community psychology approaches seek instead to define the problem within the social context and identify the strengths of communities in overcoming adversities and the resources in the communities to address the problems they face (Rappaport 1977). By attending to wider life circumstances and conceptualising an individual's difficulties in social and environmental terms, practical support and other types of interventions (such as policy change, service reform or social action) can be developed, which can lead to positive psychological outcomes (Smail 1994). For example, in terms of services, currently many young people are required to meet the needs of CAMHS, and education and employment services rather than these services adapting to meet the needs of the young people. Young people talk of having to attend at particular times, with people they do not know, in places they do not feel safe, in order to talk about negative, often shaming aspects of their lives. If they do not attend after several invitations, they are generally recorded as not engaging and are discharged. If they attend and do not feel comfortable to engage with the allocated person, the same is likely to occur. Similarly, within the school environment, the impact of repeated school testing and reduced resources for the creative arts (a consequence of educational policy) is often not defined as part of the problem when discussing young people's 'problematic' behaviour or their increasing anxiety, despite evidence that this is the case (see Hutchings 2015).

Community psychology interventions are built around the wider social and political problems that lead to poor wellbeing for young people and their families, particularly those most marginalised in society. This is because, although everyone may experience poor mental health, we know that groups facing multiple disadvantages are significantly more likely to because of the multiple stressors they face with fewer resources to support themselves. We will focus on two groups that experience marginalisation to highlight the impact of social, political and economic inequalities on wellbeing, and therefore the importance of intervening with these issues and not only the individual or family.

What is the problem – criminal justice?

It is a shocking statistic that one in three young people who offend have an unmet mental health need (Hagell 2002). Furthermore, though two in three young people may not attract a clinical diagnosis, they have high level mental wellbeing needs due to the complexity of the challenges which prevent them from leading fulfilling lives (Youth Justice Working Group 2012). Currently, serious youth violence costs society £4 billion a year. However, the young people behind these statistics are often the poorest and most marginalised in our society; dealing with domestic violence, abuse, neglect, leaving care and homelessness (Home Office, HM Government 2011). Young offenders are far more likely to experience complex interpersonal and life stresses, like poverty, educational exclusion, homelessness, domestic violence and leaving care (Youth Justice Working Group 2012).

Research has consistently demonstrated a powerful link between social inequalities and mental health difficulties for this cohort, with poverty being the primary contributor to poor mental health and wellbeing (Murali and Oyebode 2004; Wilkinson and Pickett 2010; Marmot *et al.* 1997). The Department of Health *et al.* (2009) and Ministry of Justice (2010, 2011, 2012) reported compelling statistics on the inequalities affecting young offenders, including that less than 1 per cent of ex-offenders living in the community are referred for mental health treatment and, before being in custody, 58 per cent of prisoners are unemployed and 47 per cent are in debt.

Many such young people do not seek help, do not recognise that they need help or that help is available and for many, approaching mental health services is simply not an option. Consequently, their mental health problems are overlooked until it is too late. (Some approaches to working with this cohort are outlined in Chapter 7.) More recently, there has been a shift to creating innovative, community-based, assertive outreach and youth participation interventions. These are, however, often difficult to implement for services with staff trained to work in individual and traditional ways, and when commissioning has been set up to fund more specific, individualised interventions.

What is the problem – looked-after children and careleavers?

Young people who have been in care gain poorer educational qualifications, have high rates of homelessness, higher levels of unemployment, suicide, mental health diagnoses and offending behaviour (e.g., Christensen *et al.* 2012; Courtney *et al.* 2001; Dixon and Stein 2005; Stein 2006; Tarren-Sweeney 2008). In addition, black and minority ethnic young people in care can experience identity problems due to racism and discrimination (Barn and Harman 2005). As discussed in Chapter 7, there is an increasing understanding that careleavers' needs are not being met by existing services, with these concomitant health inequalities (Atkinson 2012). Social care can too often be defined and described from an individual or individual family point of view but this can be a largely oversimplified viewpoint which leads to discourses of 'inadequate parenting' (Gillies 2013). Isolating young people and families' distress or behaviour from their social context is misleading. Young people in care are likely to have experienced serious social inequalities, with evidence suggesting strong and statistically significant correlations between measures of deprivation and rates of looked-after children and child protection proceedings (Bilson and Martin 2016) and with regression analysis showing that over 50 per cent of the variance in looked after children rates can be explained by deprivation scores (Bywaters *et al.* 2016). We must widen our perspective and consider the impact of the multiple social disadvantages they face caused by structural inequalities.

The research evidence makes a good case for the problems of inequality, marginalisation and a poor living environment (such as overcrowding) leading to lower wellbeing. However, the mental health research and evidence base often only represents the 'medical model' of mental health in which individualising psychiatric diagnoses are the focus of the research (e.g., see Johnstone and Boyle 2018). According to one report, 45 per cent of the national mental health research budget in the UK (which is already small) is spent on brain function or dysfunction research (MQ 2015). This is disproportionate and comes at the cost of under-resourcing for prevention and new intervention research. These issues highlight the power and resources of those who get to define the problem but who may not have lived experience of the issues. Moving away from the brain (and so the individual) as the source of problems, community psychology approaches seek to rebalance power and define the problem *alongside* the population seeking support, and in so doing, develop an intervention together that best creates the changes they wish to see; this is likely to also bring individual change and benefits.

Stage 2: Community engagement

Noting this change in emphasis on how and who defines the problem, this section speaks to ways in which practitioners can begin to work in partnership with communities.

Stakeholders and stakeholder analysis

We define stakeholders as the people across any systems who have an influence on or are influenced by a social issue. They are key to community working, and it is important to identify stakeholders at the beginning of any project. Ideally, they will be drawn from a number of disciplines and include both statutory and non-statutory organisations representing different aspects of a young person's life. They can also be members of the community, like shopkeepers. Stakeholders include people in education, health and housing systems and often play a number of roles. They can enable the delivery and governance of the project, and provide support, advice and guidance about the local area and resources in the form of staff and knowledge. Stakeholder organisations can sit on a steering group to ensure it is delivering against its objectives and outcomes safely or can be more actively involved in the intervention. They can also provide local intelligence and assessment of risk, which is vital for the project's safe running.

Working in partnership with stakeholders is a key part of addressing needs in a more holistic, joined-up way and can also support evaluation. This allows stakeholders to recognise the factors affecting the development of mental health needs, and therefore what preventative work could contribute to better mental health outcomes and a more psychologically healthy community.

Getting to know the community

As each community is different, it is important for an organisation working with a particular community to get to know the area and the particular needs and strengths of the people living there in depth. This is also the time to build relationships and from the outset to co-create a service that reflects the specific community it is intended for. This stage demonstrates the asset-based approach; communities are viewed as resourceful, resilient and engaged in creating a cohesive environment (Kramer *et al.* 2011). There are various ways of doing this, including community audits, community profiling, drawing on local statistics, and going on community walks (for more information, refer to Kagan *et al.* 2011). There are many projects and organisations that focus on 'getting to know the community' as the first point of engagement.

The National Association for Mental Health (Mind) commissioned a project called Up My Street, which was delivered by three community-based projects in Birmingham. The initiative was focused on improving the resilience and mental health of African Caribbean men by understanding it from their perspective and context. The projects ran community events, developed co-produced films and ran social media campaigns to get to understand the perspectives of the group (Khan *et al.* 2017).

There are many good examples of community profiling and asset mapping that facilitate this process (e.g., Foot 2012; Lazarus *et al.* 2014). Mapping the community assets is a process by which individuals can come together and identify the strengths, capabilities and resources that can be utilised and maintained, rather than identify problems that need fixing (Kerka 2003). Amsden and VanWynsberghe (2005) suggested that community mapping was an effective tool for engaging young people in the research of health service delivery, with the main challenges being at the end of the process – how to communicate the findings and respond to them.

At some MAC-UK projects, staff have started by spending time literally 'hanging out' in an identified community location and gradually introducing themselves to young people in that area. A careful assessment of risk needs to be carried out prior to this, generally informed by the knowledge and experience of local stakeholders and 'gatekeepers' – well-known and well-embedded members of the community who may be able to support relationship building (Zlotowitz *et al.* 2016). In other projects, 'gatekeepers' have been asked to identify and introduce some young people in the area who might be willing to meet in order to ask for their help beginning a project. Once a core group of young people or their families has been identified, they are invited to work alongside staff to shape and design what a project would look like, drawing on local need and determined by the interests of the young people in that area. This can include creating a name for the project and deciding on its initial activities, for example a music, film, sports-based or social action project (more on this below). This process of co-production enables people to feel ownership of the project and empowers them to be agents of change (Zlotowitz *et al.* 2016).

In some cases, in order to ensure the project is truly community-led, the core group of community members can invite or peer refer their friends and neighbours to get involved in the activities and become a part of the project. This is a very effective way of engaging excluded young people, as seeing peers who are locally known and have influence can encourage others to engage with the project. Young people know who is in their peer group, and what they might want to access support for. Through peer referrals to the team, staff are coming with a credible bridge to a trusted relationship, and peer referrals therefore also support the project to maintain safety.

Building relationships and alliances

Building relationships is the platform on which all community work with young people is based. This phase is important because it allows the professional/practitioner to get to know the community and the people within it, including other community groups, and may involve the use of community gatekeepers (for more on building partnerships with community groups see British Psychological Society community working guidelines (Thompson, Tribe and Zlotowitz 2018)). In addition, meeting young people in an environment they are more accustomed to also enables a power shift and allows young people to feel more comfortable in the surroundings. During the initial engagement, the focus of the intervention is to build trust. This requires flexibility, openness to new ways of being with young people and a willingness to get things wrong to enable relationships to go through ruptures and repairs. By focusing on engagement and working in a young person's environment, and at their pace, a different relationship with a staff team can be developed (Durcan, Zlotowitz and Stubbs 2017).

The Up My Street projects (Khan *et al.* 2017) identified the importance of positive role models from the community. These role models were able to engage and mentor other young men, while also being able to understand their social and cultural values. All projects provided a 'safe space', that was culturally and psychologically informed, in order to develop relationships where young people were able to trust staff and access support (Khan *et al.* 2017).

Stage 3: Initiating actions to create change

Having engaged with the community, this stage explores methods of action to create further change.

Co-production

Co-production attempts to flatten the power balance between help-giver and help-seeker, effectively allowing the help-seeker to have more power over services in their community. Co-production in this context can be described as 'a relationship between service provider and service user which draws on the knowledge, ability and resources of both' (Scottish Community Development Centre 2011, p.3) in order to develop and deliver services that respond effectively to locally relevant issues. In addition to forcing a change in the balance of power from the practitioner towards citizens, it shifts the approach from 'caring for' or 'doing to' towards enabling and facilitating, 'recognising that people have assets not just problems' (Scottish Community Development Centre 2011). However, from a community psychology perspective, co-production should lead to *transformational change* in services and/or communities, that is, change to the contextual (potentially oppressive) factors which are impacting people's wellbeing or experience of services. Otherwise, there is a risk of tokenism or using the community to maintain current power and discourses.

MAC-UK's pilot project, Music and Change, acted as a platform for talented but marginalised young men from deprived communities to co-design and deliver a mental health-based project that worked for them in their context (Zlotowitz *et al.* 2016). This was achieved through trusted, meaningful relationships between the practitioners and young people being developed over a period of time and consulting with the group on all decisions relating to the project. The sense of ownership that was felt by the group subsequently led to many of them volunteering to build skills, while some were later employed by the project to develop professional skills and experience employment. They were then supported to take on more senior roles over time.

This inclusion gave the young men the opportunity to share what they had learned among their peers (see the practice example below).

Peer support is a positive way of developing mental health support focused on inclusion, recovery and social context (Repper and Carter 2011). Interventions that are developed at a community level can be a preventive measure that contributes to improved wellbeing for young people. The Centre for Mental Health evaluated MAC-UK's partnership and multi-agency projects (Durcan *et al.* 2017). Across three projects, over 360 young men, who found conventional services hard to reach, engaged with the projects. Young people consistently reported relationship building, trust, peer involvement and community proximity as key reasons for engagement. Self-report and staff-reported data showed improved awareness of mental health, increased wellbeing and reduced stigma towards mental health among young people. In addition, one project increased young people's access to employment from 43 per cent to 74 per cent.

The report describes some of the changes to wider systems that occurred in the projects' local communities, including the development of other co-produced services in other areas and local policy shifts. These wider transformational changes were harder to capture but stakeholder interviews suggested a borough-wide impact of the approach. Community projects can also have a cumulative effect. For example, adolescents who report higher involvement in community activities and being able to make positive changes report a greater amount of positive future expectancies (Stoddard and Pierce 2015).

Action planning and transformational change

Systems change involves disrupting the way things are being done and social action is used to challenge and transform harmful cultural and societal norms which perpetuate inequality and exclusion and turn these practices on their head. Creating opportunities to enter dialogue with young people about their experiences can activate new ideas and perspectives, as in liberation psychology too (Afuape and Hughes 2016). This draws on the ideas of Paulo Freire (1993) of 'conscientisation'; the goal being that a dialogue or interaction raises 'critical consciousness'. This means that people have analysed the wider context of their problem *in order to change* their situation rather than just understand it and adapt to it. Narrative practices in which others 'bear witness' to oppression and exclusion can also lead to benefits for the members of those communities (Afuape and Hughes 2016). This provides room for psychological change in young people and the people in their communities, plus the potential for a more integrated view of society and an increased sense of agency and interdependency.

Community psychology approaches look for resources at all levels of a system that could both protect against possible negative outcomes and promote wellbeing (see Foot 2012; Glasgow Centre for Population Health 2011). The emphasis is on balancing the two aspects of work (meeting current needs and nurturing strengths and resources) in order to improve quality of life, while also working to address the structural causes of health inequalities. This includes involvement in dialogue that promotes a strengths-focused narrative which can improve self-efficacy in young people and provide alternative narratives to their experience. (See other practice examples in Afuape and Hughes 2016.)

Another means of including and empowering marginalised groups is through participatory action research (Prilleltensky 2010). Participatory action research (PAR) shares power with the 'researched' so research and evaluation is 'done with' not 'done to'. One example of many is the Social Youth Action project in Melbourne, Australia (Morsillo and Prilleltensky 2007). The project engaged with a group of 12 male and 12 female adolescents (15–16 years old) from an area of low socio-economic status, poor school attendance and high unemployment. Young people, alongside community collaborators, developed youth-led approaches to tackling social issues, including a drug-free party, a community theatre group that challenged homophobia and an aboriginal garden intended to build skills and create a community space. Thematic analysis of video interviews and self-report data showed increased levels of wellbeing among those involved, particularly in relation to increased socio-political awareness, enhanced sense of responsibility, increased hopefulness and an improvement in community participation skills. The project also changed the community by increasing youth involvement in social action and raising awareness of the homophobia that young people faced.

Stage 4: Reflection

This stage highlights the importance of reflection; a core element of the process at every stage if the work is to remain grounded in lived experience and evidence and if traditional power dynamics are to be resisted.

In any community psychology work it is important to be reflexive and consider issues such as unintentional consequences of any interventions as well as the role of power and privilege in the work. Within MAC-UK, for example, although we employ many young people from our projects who do progress, we are still aware there are several white middle-class females in the senior leadership team and are working through this with external supervision from a liberation psychologist. (A psychologist who seeks to understand and enables changes, to address the socio-political oppression of marginalised communities in society). We have also been exploring ways that the role of a MAC-UK trustee can be more accessible to a young person from one of our projects so that they can engage in a way that fits with their age, experience and strengths.

Reflection is also based on ongoing evaluation. Evaluations ideally need to assess change on an individual, peer, community and national level to capture the changes occurring as a result of an intervention. Applied ethnography can also capture some of these changes and can involve community members. There are also examples within the community psychology literature of more hard-hitting ways of demonstrating outcomes to stakeholders. For example, the authors of this chapter have worked with young people to attend meetings with funders, organise youth-led conferences, create and share documentaries, and curate their art and music productions in exhibitions (Durcan *et al.* 2017). Most effective for real evaluation is having members of the community alongside any presentations to funders, policy-makers or commissioners, or when delivering any training. They can explain, using their own language, the impact of community projects. Certainly, the young people who have co-produced MAC-UK projects have been honest and forthright in what does and doesn't work throughout the life of the projects; as co-producers they feel invested to continually develop projects.

Participatory action research can also be an effective approach to understanding how services can be more responsive to people's needs. Bostock and Freeman (2003) worked alongside a group of young people to research their views on NHS service delivery. Young people indicated a preference for informal support over counselling and also suggested that professionals' attitudes towards them could be improved.

Researchers conducting evaluations of services can also design their approach so that it is reflective of the community they are working with. For example, at MAC-UK after sharing that some of the more popular and standardised self-report questionnaires were difficult to understand and not relevant to them, young people co-created a self-report questionnaire that was understood and meaningful for their cohort. We would argue that this has a different type of 'validity' to the standardised questionnaires. Finally, we have used the evaluation to try and change mental health, criminal justice and employment policy at a local and national level to become more aware of the social determinants of young people's mental health. Our reflections are that if we are not communicating our research with the wider stakeholders and policy-makers, we are not doing enough to create change.

The box below highlights what factors commissioners and other stakeholders may want to consider when deciding how to evaluate community interventions.

What does 'good' look like in psychological services for children and young people in which a community psychological approach is utilised?

- A service which at its core is driven by the values of social justice and transformational change using evidence-based and practice-based research.

- A service that proactively addresses the multiple levels that impact on the mental health of children and young people in its design, delivery and evaluation, from the individual through to the community and wider social context.

- A service that works with local communities, and particularly those from excluded groups, to define challenges and needs and co-produce solutions.

- A service in which practitioners and community members are empowered to create transformational social change to prevent future distress and exclusion; this may require developing learning practices and governance that enable this.

- A service that build alliances and networks to share learning and approaches.

- A service which works to have a positive impact on the most vulnerable and marginalised young people in society.

(Casale *et al.* 2015, p.84)

Community working in practice

The case study below aims to bring to life some of the content of this chapter and is based on the work that MAC-UK has engaged in. To protect identities, it is a combination of several real-life events. At MAC-UK, as a result of ongoing data collection, learning and reflection, we have developed a set of principles that guide the practice of the organisation, known as INTEGRATE principles. Some of these principles are inserted into the case study, in italics, to highlight how current services might apply them.

A case study to show the INTEGRATE principles in practice

Create services that are psychologically informed – psychological understanding of excluded young people is considered key to effective interventions.

MAC-UK set up a project in partnership with local statutory services. The project aimed to enable young people to reach their individual potential, improve service provision locally, change the way that they were perceived in their community, and engage in opportunities alongside young people to influence national policy and practice. The initial goal was to engage local young people and ask them for help to develop a project.

As part of their induction, staff in the project and from partner services attended introductory training in psychological approaches, particularly Adaptive Mentalisation-Based Integrative Therapy (AMBIT), attachment theory, systemic theory and community psychology. AMBIT applies mentalisation-based theory to face-to-face work, team working, professional networks and service learning (Bevington *et al.* 2017). To ensure these ideas became an embedded part of practice, formulation sessions, group reflective spaces and supervision were built into the project standard timetable and had a direct impact on the activities of the project.

Create services that are co-produced with young people and partners – these experts by experience and partner organisations will have skills to co-produce all aspects of service design and delivery.

After eight months of working with local young people, the team was introduced to David. David was a young man known to the local police and community safety team and considered to be on a path to a long-term stay in prison. There had been a gradual increase in his offending since the age of 15 years old, both in frequency and severity. David had been excluded from school and spent his time hanging out on his local estate with older friends. He started drug running and committing burglaries in response to pressure from older peers. He became involved in the local 'gang', partly just to keep himself safe but also because it afforded otherwise unavailable opportunities to feel successful, connected and powerful.

A friend from his estate called Mo had a job working at the project, and told David that this was a project where people listened and did activities based on what local people said they wanted or needed.

Create services that focus on and build resources and resiliencies – communities, young people and agencies contain resources and resiliencies that services can map, harness and then build on.

After sharing his frustrations at the lack of fitness activities locally, Mo had set up a weekly gym session which was popular, and he was considering becoming a personal trainer. He had been introduced to some local personal trainers who worked at the gym; as they knew of his reputation they were initially wary, but quickly decided to mentor him based on his enthusiasm and engagement in the project.

Create services that go to young people – understand physical and psychological barriers to access of services by listening to experts by experience and overcome them through taking services to young people, for example proactively hanging out in community areas and taking peer referrals.

David's friend knew he was into music and told him about the music production activity that two other young people had started. David agreed to go with him to record some lyrics.

Create services that are flexible and responsive – engage with and understand what experts by experience actually want from services and be flexible and responsive to this and led by them, for example if young people tell you there is a need for more local support with them developing their own businesses, start here and build services from there, wrapping other support around these sessions.

He met some staff there who seemed friendly. At first, they just sat in the room with him and others asking about the lyrics or music and listening to his tunes. During one of the sessions he overheard a peer talking about getting help with his court case from staff. He asked a staff member he had been speaking to about lyrics if they would write a character reference for his next court appearance for cannabis possession and they said they would.

Over the next few weeks the staff member contacted David several times, texting, calling and asking for his input into the reference. During these conversations about the character reference, David shared information about himself. This information was then shared in a formulation meeting with the team so that they could try to understand his context and support him to plan for the future.

David lived with his mother and three siblings in a community known to be deprived. His mother worked long hours to pay their rent and provide for the children. He was smoking skunk (a specific and potent strain of cannabis) every day. Sometimes the police would raid the home, suspicious that he was running drugs. In response to implementation dispersal orders (Joseph Rowntree Foundation 2007), he and his friends were regularly 'moved on' from their own housing estate, while having no local youth services to go to. They therefore often met on the streets. There David was repeatedly stopped and searched by police in his local community; he had once been strip searched. David was found with drugs in his pockets during one of these and although his white friends received cautions, he was charged. (This information reflected the national statistic where young black men are searched on average six times more than white peers locally and 56 per cent of white people receive cautions rather than charges for drug offences, compared with only 22 per cent of black people (Lammy 2017)).

David had witnessed a serious stabbing of a friend and was under threat himself. He had been offered various courses by council officers and youth workers but had not engaged. Several years earlier David had regularly met with a member of the local youth offending team. In these meetings, he had been invited to think about ways he could manage his anger and what he could do differently. While some of the ideas sounded okay, he did not remember to use them when outside the meetings.

Create services that work at multiple levels – they can intervene at an individual, organisational, community and national level with and for excluded young people.

As a result of the conversations during the formulation meeting, staff started to gently talk with David about the stress of court and how he would manage this. They started talking about skunk as an available and widely used way of managing mood among his peer group. Staff explored the conditions which might have contributed to his stress and coping behaviour, given his context. They applied ideas from community psychology, narrative and systemic practice during these conversations. This included normalising the stress and thoughts he had, exploring beliefs behind how others in his network managed stress, sharing national statistics relating his behaviour to wider inequalities, exploring what expectations and choices he had, and finding exceptions to his usual coping strategies.

After the court case, David asked for help to find a job. He completed several job applications with staff. He missed the first interview he was offered. Staff spoke with him about why this might have happened, and as a result supported him to go to a charity which provided clothes for interviews. On the way to this, David talked about what he was interested in doing and staff noticed his ambivalence towards working. They normalised this, using their understanding of why this might be. Using a mentalisation-based approach, staff spoke to each other in front of David about their experiences of discovering their interests, of volunteering to gain experience and of the enjoyment they gained from their work.

David was regularly asked for his help with the music activities and he arranged a trip to a studio for him and peers with staff. During the planning sessions for this activity, staff gradually asked him about his hopes for the future and used motivational interviewing, an evidence-based therapeutic technique used for behaviour change, to explore change with him. He spoke about feeling low and worrying all the time. Sometimes he had nightmares. Staff explored possible trauma issues and his low mood. They learned that all of his other relationships with services felt tense and that some of his friends were now in prison. He missed them and hadn't heard from them. He worried about his mother and felt there was nothing there to help his family. David's clinical needs were discussed again in a team meeting and on the basis of this, staff shared some of their understanding and supported him with his hopeless beliefs and provided strategies for his low mood using narrative and ACT techniques. They also spoke about what help might support his mother.

 As a result, David and staff decided to meet with representatives from the local council about the experience of local single parents.

Create services that build meaningful partnerships – including developing shared agency understandings together of what is needed in services for excluded young people.

Thinking about how to effect change in the systems around David, staff liaised with his probation worker, the police, the council and a drugs worker about David's positive work with the project. With David's explicit permission they shared their clinical understanding of him and spoke about 'what worked' with David. Staff also gained a deeper understanding of David through the other professionals' ideas. They also discussed with David the different professionals' roles and understanding of his needs.

Create services that harness experts by experience – generate opportunities and employment for those with lived experience to shape the development of new services for those groups.

A few months later, after attending trips and becoming employed as a 'youth leader', David and a friend again got into the idea of making music videos, so staff went with David and his friend to look into courses that might help them. They both enrolled with a reference from the staff. At first, project staff went and woke David up to go to college while continuing to explore motivation with him, as this went up and down over time. Staff reflected back to him the enormity of his transition back into education and, using a solutions-focused technique, asked how he had managed it and kept his motivation going.

Create services that address people in context – excluded young people often live in contexts of deprivation and economic hardship, as well as other contextual difficulties, and services should address these issues, for example through encouraging young people to become agents of social change.

David was then employed to go with the MAC-UK chief executive officer to a government roundtable on gang violence and gave his opinion on the strategy and the lack of resources in his community, explaining that his friendship connections and activities provided him with financial security and personal safety. They also gave a consultation to a parliamentary select committee.

Create services that apply evidence-based working and evaluation in relevant ways – enabling innovation and positive risk-taking and producing new practice-based evidence to inform service design as well as creating an opportunity for continual learning, evolution and evaluation of tried and tested clinical interventions, applied in new settings.

Knowing that the project had to regularly evaluate its impact, David and some of his friends decided to write lyrics describing their journey at the project, to be shared with potential evaluators, funders and other services. He was supported to do this by staff and by a local musician who had heard of the work of the project and had offered some of their time.

Conclusion

Research suggests that children benefit most from mental health services when the context of both the individual child *and* the child's environment are taken into account as per the ecological systems theory (Bronfenbrenner 1979). Despite this, there is a tendency to 'individualize wellness: the problematic site is the individual who is unwell, not the conditions surrounding her' (Prilleltensky 2012, p.18) and services are often designed accordingly.

The primary focus of this chapter is on understanding and working with people in their wider social context, as opposed to understanding them as isolated individuals. Community working is nationally recognised and encouraged. The NICE Guidelines for Community Engagement (2016) provide recommendations about how to reach communities, highlighting that co-production and asset-based approaches are key. However, current service provision is largely based on ameliorative approaches in which people help individuals make changes, while not addressing the social problems that exist. This chapter has outlined a more transformative community psychology approach, where practitioners seek to directly address the social, political and economic inequalities that exist in society and work to make changes to these. It goes beyond 'individualism' inherent in traditional psychological approaches, working with people in the context of their communities and with whole communities (Kagan *et al.* 2011). This approach also provides room for beneficial individual psychological change for young people and the people in their communities, providing potential for a more integrated view of society and an increased sense of agency, interdependency and connectedness.

Acknowledgements

We would like to thank all the young people, current and previous staff, partners and stakeholders of MAC-UK. The INTEGRATE approach we outline in our chapter has been built on the experience and assets of all these people and relationships and certainly does not belong to us as authors.

Chapter 9

Visions for the future

JULIA FAULCONBRIDGE, KATIE HUNT,
AMANDA LAFFAN AND DUNCAN LAW

Introduction

If the evidence presented in this book from both research and practice
is taken seriously, it alters the perspective we take around child mental
health. If instead of asking how we can help children with problems
to overcome them, we first ask how we can support communities and
families to bring up the next generation by minimising risk factors
and promoting positive psychological development, then new answers
start to emerge. Even using a term like 'primary prevention' – helping
to prevent problems – skews the direction of thought when compared
with a term like 'promoting psychological wellbeing'.

We will never achieve a society where every child is free from
psychological problems, so there will always be a need for services
to help them and their families. However, it is worth considering
the well-used analogy for health systems under pressure due to high
demand as being like 'overflowing sinks' (Trowell and Burkitt 1981).
In this metaphor, ill health is the water cascading out of a full sink
onto the floor. Our energy and resources go into trying to mop the
floor more effectively but the water still keeps pouring in. Over recent
years the emphasis in the children and young people's mental health
system has been on strategies to improve this 'mopping' by increasing
efficiency, effectiveness and availability of therapy. While valuable in
itself, this will not change the rate of flow of difficulties experienced
by children and young people; a flow which represents high levels
of distress and suffering with long-term consequences for them and
for our society. Indeed, the rate of flow has been increasing, in part
because there is a greater recognition of childhood distress in our
society and a greater will to do something about it. Ultimately, more
effective solutions come when the system works at preventing these

212 Improving the Psychological Wellbeing of Children and Young People

problems starting in the first place – by adopting strategies that aim to 'turn off the taps'.

The key roles of national and local government

Throughout this book there is discussion of ecological models of child development, stressing the importance of the roles played by society and culture at global, national and local levels, as setting the conditions in which all other factors impact on the child and their family. While people in local areas can achieve a great deal to improve what is available, ultimately addressing the major risk factors like poverty, social inequality, housing, employment practices and discrimination requires sustained government action. Creating the social changes that will start to reduce the occurrence of these risk factors is essentially a political and economic activity, and the roles of national and local governments are therefore key. Faulconbridge *et al.* (2016) discuss some of the ways that this could be done, including:

- government recognition of the long-term damage on individuals and, ultimately, on our society, created by poverty and social inequality, with the development of policies designed to reduce them and support families

- robust assessments of how any new policies impact on the wellbeing of children and families carried out at all levels of government

- leaders on health, education, social care, housing, police and so on working together to support their communities and ensure that localities promote psychological wellbeing

- all services and systems for children and young people planned to nurture good psychological health.

National policies and funding for health, education and social care are another key area that place constraints on what it is possible to achieve. There needs to be integrated and collaborative thinking across ministries and departments to facilitate good psychological health in children and young people which reflects the different spheres that children, young people and families operate in. The current fragmented models of service within health care and between health care and other bodies, with their potential for narrow policy development and consequent budgetary protectionism, are barriers to progress. The various components of the systems around children and families need to be integrated and cooperative and this will require new models of funding and shared resources. The system must support and facilitate implementation of a more active, preventative approach to psychological health, and ensure an effective and benign use of power to facilitate the change needed.

Investing in children

Achieving an improvement in the psychological wellbeing of our children would carry very significant economic benefits as well as the alleviation of suffering. In addition to the costs of providing health and social care, the long-term impact of poor childhood mental health is believed to be costing the UK a total of £550 billion in lost earnings (Centre for Longitudinal Studies 2015).

Investing in children would mean, for example:

- concerted efforts to reduce radically the incidence of poverty by supporting families, especially those where parents may be struggling to find work that pays sufficiently or at all

- addressing the housing crisis so that children are no longer living in unsafe, unsanitary conditions on insecure tenancies

- investing in 'greening' local neighbourhoods and making them safe places for children to play and for teenagers to spend time in

- tackling discrimination and racism and building increased community cohesion

- establishing (or re-establishing) more children's centres in accessible locations to act as one-stop shops for all families

- providing schools with the resources to develop a wide range of creative, sporting and other non-academic activities with and for the children and the local community

- resourcing social care to support families as soon as there are problems rather than most funding being spent on taking children into care

- listening to children and young people and ensuring their voices are heard and influence the development of the society around them.

Building better systems

The importance of the ecological approach, considering a child's development in their social and cultural context, has been discussed throughout this book with the recognition that a focus on the individual child is the least effective way of producing positive change. Building resilience in communities, in schools and in families is essential if we wish to nurture young people's psychological wellbeing and prevent the distress described by the chapter authors who work in settings where those children, young people and families are seen on a daily basis. The authors' practical experience, taken with the psychological evidence, shows how things can be done differently, but most policy making and commissioning still proceeds by applying models of individualised therapeutic work once problems have developed. Commissioning of services also tends to consider elements of provision in isolation, and the lack of integration leaves gaps in provision. Children with developmental and mental health difficulties are a classic example. Despite being some of the children in the greatest need of services, they can end up without any provision, or find themselves in the youth justice system where their needs are inadequately met and their vulnerabilities further increased (Taylor 2016).

We need to look more widely than individual services and really begin to take a whole-system approach to psychological health and wellbeing. We need a system that sees psychological health woven through every part of children's lives.

Building from the community up

The power and potential of community psychology approaches are described in Chapter 8. Community psychology has its origins in, and primary focus on, working with disadvantaged populations with social justice at its core (Orford 1992). It is action oriented, working in partnership with communities, and focused on preventive and community-led change (Casale, Zlotowitz and Moloney 2015).

These principles could be used more widely but seeing how this could be achieved requires thought. One of the problems with developing a community psychology model across all areas is the variability in what would constitute a community across the UK. The nature of the work undertaken by MAC-UK (see Chapter 8) is, to a large extent, dependent on a sufficiently small and coherent geographically based community to build the relationships with. It is easy to see how this could be translated into similar projects in inner cities but it would be more of a challenge in suburban or small town settings, let alone the large parts of the UK that are rural or semi-rural.

There are examples of communities coming together to create change themselves. Aditya Chakrabortty wrote in *The Guardian* newspaper in February 2018 about how the people living in the Granby area of Liverpool had taken control and successfully regenerated the inner-city community after decades of destruction and neglect. Although this has not been evaluated in terms of its impact on health, it would be very surprising if a renewed community spirit, improved local environment and increased employment did not result in greater psychological wellbeing.

Another project, mainly focused on the elderly population, has also demonstrated the value of community-based approaches (Brown 2018). Frome in Somerset has developed a 'compassionate community scheme' aimed at tackling the connection between loneliness and ill health, which has led to a 17 per cent reduction in emergency hospital admissions compared with an increase in the rest of the county of 29 per cent. Health Connections Mendip, the community development service at Frome Medical Practice, was set up in 2014. It compiled a service directory of care providers and volunteers from health centres, local charities and other groups to give support to people with poor health, ranging from attending to someone's physical and emotional needs to assisting with the shopping, walking the dog or helping someone attend a confidence-boosting activity such as the local choir. The people most needing support were identified and supported on a one-to-one basis, their needs matched to services, and new services were created to fill any gaps. GP services are now able integrate the links with the community they serve in their daily work, and are able to reconnect people into the community in which they live. It is not hard to see how such a model could be developed with a focus on families and children.

Developing a local infrastructure in which services can be developed in conjunction with people living there is an essential component to creating change. There are settings like schools or GP practices that can develop as bases for wider wellbeing services and these are discussed in the sections below. However, children's centres, as have been available in the UK in recent years operating as Sure Start centres, proved to be a very valuable model, especially for families with young children. They can provide play and nursery care for children, a wide range of support for parents and can be a site where other forms of community development can start. One very interesting model has provision for older people on the same site, with benefits to all (Hedd Jones 2017).

Community spaces for teenagers are sadly lacking in much of the UK, with few places they can go to be with friends outside school, acquire new skills and interests and receive help and advice when they need it. Again, establishing such centres provides a setting where more community development can be built with the young people. They can also provide mental health promotion and early intervention for young people and their families who are having difficulties, and safe havens for those whose needs at a particular time could otherwise lead them into A&E departments. Safe havens have been established in adult mental health for some time and are increasingly being explored for young people – for example, those provided in Surrey (http://surreyheathccg.nhs.uk/mental-health/safe-haven-aldershot).

Addressing discrimination and embracing diversity

As discussed throughout this book, the response of psychological and mental health services cannot focus simply on the impact of discrimination and racism on individual children and families, but must also acknowledge and act to influence the wider systems around them and the dominant socio-political discourse. Essentially, services must address the ways in which they are delivered (Fatimilehin and Hassan 2013; Fernando and Keating 2009) and the levels at which they are delivered. Prevention and early intervention are key components of responsive and effective mental health services. However, in many child and adolescent mental health services in the UK, there are inherent Eurocentric and middle-class biases in the theoretical and practice models of psychological intervention that are used, and the routes of access to services. These barriers to engagement, effectiveness and accessibility of services for children and families from minority ethnic backgrounds must be eliminated in order to begin to address the impact of discrimination.

Making sure that staff in all services are culturally competent and able to deliver appropriate assessments and intervention work is essential. As examples see Fatimilehin and Hunt's (2013) article on psychometric assessment across cultures, and Fatimilehin and Hassan's (2013) discussion of CBT with black and minority ethnic children and families.

However, there will still be the need to develop some services tailored specifically to the needs of particular groups in order to make them accessible and appropriate. A good example of this is the Building Bridges project in Liverpool (Fatimilehin 2007).

For further reading in this area, see the publications list on the Just Psychology website (www.justpsychology.co.uk/publications).

Integrated psychological services in primary care and community child health

In the past, in the UK, there have been many examples of psychologists and other mental health professions working in GP surgeries and in community child health, and also of mental health services being co-located with primary care services. The possibilities and challenges of this are discussed in detail in Chapter 4.

Primary care can provide the setting in which to develop integrated services for those who need interventions at an early stage in their difficulties. Around 33 per cent of people visiting their GP in the UK will be doing so with psychological or mental health problems (Mind 2016) and the psychological aspects of primarily physical illnesses like cancer are another major area of GP work. Some mental health practitioners, like clinical psychologists, are trained to work across the lifespan and are thus in a position to lead and deliver integrated family-based psychological services in general practice. The lifespan perspective is particularly important as it confers experience of working with developmental, behavioural and mental health challenges at different life stages. There are pilot projects in various places around the UK. One example is in Shropshire (L. Fisk 2017, personal communication) where 20 per cent of the first 1000 patients seen were under 25 years old and parents were seen in relation to parenting or child difficulties on over 200 occasions.

GPs may see different members of the same family, and so be aware of factors, including parental mental health difficulties and caring responsibilities, that are known to impact on a child's wellbeing. They are also in a position to understand many of the factors in their local communities that are impacting on their patients' health. This knowledge can enable proactive thinking about a family's or locality's needs and the development of both individual and community prevention initiatives with the psychologists.

Primary care is also the ideal setting for developing perinatal and early years support as described in Chapters 2 and 3, and for integrating physical and mental health provision as discussed in Chapter 6.

In the US, there has been significant development work undertaken to create and evaluate integrated family care in primary care settings. Susan McDaniel has been a leading proponent of this model and has written extensively on the topic with her team, as well as developing services and training courses. In this model, physical and psychological problems are all seen in the family service, as are all members of the family (McDaniel and deGruy 2014; McDaniel, Doherty and Hepworth 2014).

Creating such services would lead to significant improvement in a number of key areas, as outlined below.

Supporting families, health promotion, primary prevention

- Locally based parenting support across the age range.

- Building relationships with the voluntary sector to develop initiatives to improve wellbeing in the locality, for example reducing social isolation and youth provision.

- Linking physical and mental health provision for children and families.

Early intervention

- Accessible services in local communities.

- Specialist assessment and early intervention therapeutic work at the beginning of difficulties.

- Work with families and with parts of families, for example if a parent is depressed, supporting them in their own difficulties and in caring for their children.

- Minimising the problems associated with transition from child to adult services.

Developing psychological knowledge

- Co-working with other members of the primary care team, such as health visitors.

- Co-working with other services in the locality, including the voluntary sector.

- Providing training and consultation to all those working with children and young people in the area.

Joining community child health and primary care

- Specialist psychological provision to support multidisciplinary local assessment, for example for neurodevelopmental difficulties such as autism.

- Providing local psychological work with families where a child is physically ill, in conjunction with hospital-based paediatrics.

Integrating schools and colleges into the systems

The importance of schools as a setting in which to develop psychological wellbeing and to deliver help early is described in Chapter 5. Schools have the potential to become key drivers for the changes we are looking for, but there are many barriers in the way, such as educational pressures and policies, employment practices in education, financial pressures, and the fragmentation of the education system as the establishment of academies and free schools has reduced local authority involvement.

Schools are vital to the healthy development of children's minds. If all schools, along with youth clubs, sports academies and spiritual centres, were truly psychologically informed environments, there would likely be a great positive impact on the wellbeing, learning and development of all children and young people who attend them. Simply locating services within schools and giving or encouraging responsibility for mental health within school is far from being what is required; genuinely joined-up cross-services thinking and working, properly resourced, with the child and family at the centre is key, along with properly resourced interventions delivered by staff appropriately trained in both the assessment and delivery of mental health interventions.

Schools need to be joined into their local networks because, as a rule, they do not have expertise in commissioning mental health support, and even when they do commission, they may not do so in a joined-up way. A school may, for example, buy in support for students who self-harm, but fail to link this in to other pastoral provision in the school, because they see students who self-harm as a distinct group. Schools also generally lack the expertise to tease out what is evidenced-based practice and as a result can buy in packages that may sound effective but are untested and may be, at worst, harmful; there are many examples of this. Being truly linked in to local networks is crucial so that we avoid situations where some schools in some areas are commissioning a service and other schools are not, leading to catchment area/postcode lotteries in terms of what is available to the most vulnerable children and young people, and a potential lack of sustainable provision.

There are examples of innovative ways of commissioning services, such as public health funding for the Lancashire Emotional Health in Schools Service, jointly funded across local authority public health and the NHS to provide a service free to schools to deliver training, advice and support on mental health issues to school staff. These initiatives are, however, few and far between but may be a way forward to enable services to truly hold the whole child at the centre of thinking and commissioning.

The importance of a focus on those most in need

While we argue for services and systems that support the psychological wellbeing of *all* children and young people, it is important to recognise that in order for all young people to be equally supported, those most in need will likely require more help and greater allocation of resources. As discussed in Chapter 1, young people who experience a greater number of risk factors (such as living in poverty, facing discrimination or bullying, and having physical health or neurodevelopmental difficulties) are more likely to experience emotional and social difficulties.

Children with physical health or neurodevelopmental difficulties

In Chapter 6, there is detailed discussion of how children and young people with physical health conditions may be more likely to experience psychological difficulties than their healthy peers, as may young people with neurodevelopmental conditions. In order to ensure these children and their families have the best chances of thriving within potentially very distressing circumstances, health services need to be 'psychologically minded', with the emotional health and bio-psychosocial wellbeing of patients being given adequate attention alongside the children's physical needs. This means that physical health practitioners (doctors, nurses, allied health professionals and administrative staff) need appropriate training and support to help nurture the resilience and coping skills of their patients.

Having mental health specialists who are trained in psychological wellbeing across the lifespan and fully integrated into physical health services (from primary care through to specialist tertiary and quaternary services) will help to ensure that expert knowledge and supervision is accessible to all staff members. Similarly, should young people or their families require more specialist support due to the psychological impact of ill health or disability, these mental health practitioners would be ideally placed to provide this, without necessarily needing onward referral to mental health services. These will not have the same understanding of the young person's condition and treatment, and may be perceived as stigmatising by the young person and family.

Supporting the most vulnerable

In order to reduce the likelihood of risk factors and adverse experiences leading to significant psychological difficulties, measures need to be put in place to:

• identify those at risk as early as possible

- provide the right level of support in the right locations – usually drawing on the child and caregivers' own strengths and resources

- ensure all agencies involved with the child and family are truly working together to provide joined-up, effective care that holds the child and family at the centre

- have clear pathways so that the child and family can access different levels of support as necessary

- have suitable means of evaluating interventions provided, including working with children and families to ensure their voices are heard in evaluation

- actively involve young people and families in the design of services and interventions, both regarding their own care, and for the benefit of future families.

There are sets of parents who will struggle to care sufficiently for their children without significant support so that their children have higher likelihoods of being taken into care and/or becoming involved in crime and, consequently, the youth justice system, leading to costly and potentially damaging interventions. Attitudes to these families are often categorised as either following child protection (which has a narrative of 'rescuing' children) or family support models. We would advocate the serious resourcing of a family support model to reduce the numbers of children being taken into care, using the strategies and programmes discussed in all chapters but particularly Chapters 2, 3, 7 and 8.

The importance of working with families and caregivers

When direct therapeutic work is indicated, we need to consider how this is best delivered. It may be appropriate for teenagers to be seen individually, but it is rarely going to be the case that working with a younger child separate from their family and wider context is going to be an effective approach. This is, however, the approach that is often used and often proposed – for example, interventions delivered in schools 'to' young children in the absence of involvement with parents, or without consideration of how the environment of the school might best be changed for the psychological good of all its students. Throughout this book, the theme of the centrality of families in both understanding the difficulties children experience and finding ways to improve them becomes clear.

There have been many examples in the literature of parents being explicitly blamed for their child's difficulties, for example Kanner's theory of autism (Kanner and Eisenberg 1956) being caused by 'refrigerator mothers', and it is a common explanation found in the popular press. Parents think and fear that they are 'to blame' for a child's difficulties and that this is a personal failing. They are therefore often very anxious about seeing professionals and their anxiety can be a real barrier to engagement. We must avoid 'parent-blaming' when identifying the role of parents in a child's difficulties. We must ensure that services hold a positive narrative that recognises the complexity of the relationships and the difficulties parents themselves may be experiencing as a result of their own childhoods or current circumstances. By listening to parents, we better understand the unique context and factors that underlie any childhood difficulties and we can collaboratively determine the best ways to support parents in bringing up their children in ways that maximise their children's emotional health and wellbeing. A useful discussion on the sensitivities of this, and working with parents in ways that do not make them feel blamed, can be found in Dallos (2015).

Recognising these issues and working to find ways that enable compassionate relationships to be built with families is essential to being able to deliver the family-based approaches that are needed. This is key to most work with children, young people and families; see also Gilbert (2009) for more discussion of compassion-focused therapy with adults. In the same way that we must avoid unhelpful 'parent-blaming', we must also avoid the patronisation of parents who are seen to need professional help. Once we recognise that *all* parents have expertise, the role of the professional is to work in collaboration with parents in a shared-expertise model that promotes the best interests of the child.

Psychological health and wellbeing services and the role of specialist services

This model for achieving integrated provision across localities with a primary focus on building wellbeing, preventing mental health problems and intervening as soon as possible when problems arise is proposed in the article 'What good could look like in integrated psychological services for children, young people and their families: preliminary guidance and examples of practice' (Faulconbridge *et al.* 2016).

Psychological health and wellbeing services (PHWBS) require joint working, integrated pathways and cross-service training and consultation, with the primary aim being to support families and promote healthy psychological development rather than a narrower focus on managing or treating problems. In developing such whole-system change, it is crucial that families, young people and others living in the local community are integral to the design and evaluation of the model. PHWBS should be built from the community up, with integrated primary care and community child health provision and schools as the bedrock. Most provision would be provided in the local communities and built on relationships within those localities.

Specialist mental health services (like CAMHS) are a key element of PHWBS. Their role would include multidisciplinary delivery of high-quality assessment and therapeutic care to those children, young people and families who need it due to the severity or complexity of their difficulties. However, the specialist staff would also be key to supporting the work of all other parts of the system through the provision of training, consultation and supervision and co-working so that their knowledge and experience strengthen all parts of the system. CAMHS provisions would therefore be fully integrated into the local services, not separate from them.

The model also requires a specialist psychological workforce which is not based in CAMHS but is integral to the range of community provisions, 'front-loading' expertise rather than it only being available in secondary or tertiary settings.

This will actually enable a range of additional people to become part of the developments by making training, supervision and consultation readily available across all settings and:

- increasing the psychological knowledge and skills of the current workforce in universal and targeted services like early years and youth services

- enhancing the capabilities of staff already working with children and young people with complex difficulties, for example in residential homes and secure settings

- empowering young people and families to help others. A well-established example would be Home Start, a group of 18,500 volunteers working with families with young children across the UK. Chapter 8 describes the ways that MAC-UK brings the young people it works with into the organisation so they become part of the work. More examples can be found in Faulconbridge *et al.* (2016).

In order to achieve the positive and scaled-up change needed, services need to be integrated so that there is:

- a highly unified, holistic system where services link

- the removal of duplication and overlap

- commissioning based on 'people' rather than 'problems'

- shared vision and values across the organisations

- close partnership working with shared resources and infrastructure.

This will include services currently in:

- health (both physical and mental)

- local authority and community (including housing)

- education (including early years)

- voluntary sector and local communities

- children's and youth services

- police and youth justice.

Psychological health everywhere

This book calls for a whole new vision of how we achieve psychological health and wellbeing. It calls for a wider perspective on how we understand mental health and wellbeing, its causes and its consequences. It calls for a new understanding of how we view psychological interventions that go way beyond the individual to the family, community and society as the unit of intervention. In short, it is a call to action for a new understanding and a new vision of psychological health for everyone, everywhere.

List of contributors

Sally Benson is a consultant clinical psychologist and Head of the Paediatric Clinical Psychology and Counselling Service in Cambridge. She was Clinical Director of the University of East London Clinical Psychology Doctoral Training Programme. Sally currently represents the British Psychological Society on the Paediatric Mental Health Association.

Ruth Butterworth is a consultant clinical psychologist in the Cheshire and Mersey Specialist Perinatal Service. She is passionate about developing a whole family approach to mental health that puts responsive relationships – between family members, and within the services that surround them – at its heart.

Laura Casale is a clinical and community psychologist with experience across the NHS, local authority and the third sector. She is Co-Clinical Director at MAC-UK and works as part of the REACH team in Barnet Children's Services. She is committed to addressing national and local issues of inequality and lack of opportunity when working with and for those in underprivileged and marginalised communities.

Mark Moubarak Chentite is a co-founder of MAC-UK. He has contributed to the development of the work of MAC-UK and led a psychologically informed project for young people at risk. He is committed to supporting young people and communities alongside written and spoken work to promote change at a national level.

Jaime Craig is a consultant clinical psychologist with many years' experience working in specialist child and adult mental health services (CAMHS), including leading an early intervention and prevention service. Previously Chair of the Faculty for Children, Young People and their Families (BPS), he works independently with families including as an expert witness in the Family Courts.

Iyabo Fatimilehin is a consultant clinical psychologist and Director of Just Psychology CIC, a social enterprise she founded in 2011 to address the psychological and mental health needs of children and families with a particular emphasis on cultural diversity, cultural competence and social justice. She worked in the NHS for over 20 years and was service lead for an award-winning specialist CAMH service for black and minority ethnic children and families.

Julia Faulconbridge is a consultant clinical psychologist who, before retirement from the NHS, led a community-based clinical psychology and counselling service in Nottingham. She is Chair of the Division of Clinical Psychology at the British Psychological Society and a past Chair of the Faculty for Children, Young People and their Families.

Michael Galbraith is a clinical psychologist and systemic psychotherapist. He jointly set up and is the clinical lead for the Liverpool Parent Infant Partnership service. Michael's passion for early years work was fuelled by his experience of working in Sure Start centres and he holds on to the fourth objective of the Sure Start local programmes which was/is to 'strengthen families and strengthen communities'.

Joe Hickey is a clinical psychologist in Islington CAMHS, a module lead and practice tutor at the Anna Freud National Centre for Children and Families, and an associate clinical tutor on UCL's Doctorate in Clinical Psychology. He has worked in schools since 2013 and is an accredited practitioner of interpersonal psychotherapy with adolescents (IPT-A).

Katie Hunt is a consultant clinical psychologist and paediatric clinical neuropsychologist with over 20 years' experience working mainly with children with complex special needs, neurodevelopmental difficulties and brain injury in NHS and independent sector settings. She has worked for the last nine years in independent practice, working with families, schools, and as an expert witness, and is currently interim chair of the BPS Faculty for Children, Young People and their Families.

Amanda Laffan is a clinical psychologist in the Specialist Paediatric Chronic Fatigue Syndrome (CFS/ME) Service at the Royal United Hospitals Bath NHSFT. She has a particular interest in supporting the psychological needs of young people living with health conditions.

Duncan Law is a consultant clinical psychologist with 25 years' experience across NHS, local authority and third sectors. He is a consultant clinical associate at the Anna Freud National Centre for Children & Families, honorary senior lecturer at UCL, a trustee of MAC-UK, board director of CORC and former chair of the Faculty for Children, Young People and their Families. He has a particular interest in improving services through co-production and collaborative practice.

Sara O'Curry is Assistant Head of the Paediatric Psychology and Counselling Service in Cambridge. She was formerly the Lead for Psychosocial, Family and Play Services in Cardiology and Critical Care at Great Ormond Street Hospital and worked in paediatric liaison and CAMHS in Huntingdon before that. She is past Chair of the Paediatric Psychology Network as well as Physical Health Representative on the BPS Faculty for Children, Young People and their Families.

Ruth O'Shaughnessy is a clinical psychologist based at Fresh CAMHS, Alder Hey Children's NHSFT, Liverpool. Ruth provides clinical and strategic oversight for infant and early years mental health within CAMHS. Her interests include the clinical applications of attachment theory and the impact of parental mental illness on child development and mental health outcomes.

Waveney Patel is a consultant clinical psychologist in City and Hackney CAMHS and has focused her work in the area of schools for the last 14 years. She is passionate about supporting children and young people to gain access to high-quality mental health services in schools and in collaboratively building capacity in schools alongside committed colleagues from education.

Anna Picciotto is a consultant clinical psychologist who works in Community CAMH services in London. She has a long-standing commitment to early intervention and preventative work in child mental health and to delivering collaborative CAMH services in community settings, particularly schools. Over the last ten years she has worked to establish Islington's universal CAMHS in schools.

Natalie Seymour is a clinical psychologist and works for MAC-UK. She has a particular interest in psychological wellbeing in adolescence and creating opportunities and circumstances for change alongside young people. She is also a world-class hockey player and triathlete.

Lisa Shostak is a clinical psychologist who is passionate about supporting organisations to use STAIRS approaches to embed psychological formulation, systemic thinking and a truly collaborative process of creating change into all they do. She currently works across a variety of social care and third sector/community settings.

Jenny Taylor is a consultant clinical psychologist who has worked in children's social care and youth offending for nearly 20 years, and has been key in developing policy around how psychologists work during her two terms as Chair of the Clinical Division of the BPS.

Caroline White is a consultant clinical psychologist and Head of the Children and Parents' Service (CAPS), a city wide, multi-agency early intervention service for over 20 years; for Manchester University NHS Foundation Trust. Caroline is an accredited Incredible Years Trainer and chairs the European Incredible Years Network.

Sally Zlotowitz is a clinical and community psychologist and Co-Clinical Director at MAC-UK. Sally is currently Chair of the BPS Community Psychology Section and co-founder of Psychologists for Social Change. She is passionate about changing psychological practice to better recognise and intervene in the structural inequalities and ecological damage that Western societies generate.

References

Chapter 1

Alleyne, A. (2009) 'Working Therapeutically with Hidden Dimensions of Racism.' In S. Fernando and F. Keating (eds) *Mental Health in a Multi-Ethnic Society: A Multidisciplinary Handbook* (2nd ed.). London: Routledge.

Anda, R.F., Butchart, A., Felitti, V.J. and Brown, D.W (2010) 'Building a framework for global surveillance of the public health implications of adverse childhood experiences.' *American Journal of Preventive Medicine, 39,* 1, 93–98.

Anderson, V., Catroppa, C., Morse, S., Haritou, F. and Rosenfeld, J. (2005) 'Functional plasticity or vulnerability after early brain injury?' *Pediatrics, 115,* 6, 1374–1382.

Arseneault, L., Bowes, L. and Shakoor, S. (2010) 'Bullying victimization in youths and mental health problems: "Much ado about nothing"?' *Psychological Medicine, 40,* 5, 717–729.

Asher, S.R., Hymel, S. and Renshaw, P.D. (1984) 'Loneliness in children.' *Child Development, 55,* 1456–1464.

Ayre, D. (2016) *Poor Mental Health: The Links Between Child Poverty and Mental Health Problems.* London: The Children's Society.

Beardslee, W.R., Gladstone, T.R.G., Wright, E.J. and Cooper, A.B. (2003) 'A family-based approach to the prevention of depressive symptoms in children at risk: evidence of parental and child change.' *Pediatrics, 112,* 2, e119–e131.

Barlow, J., Schrader-McMillan, A., Axford, N., Wrigley, Z. *et al.* (2016) 'Review: attachment and attachment-related outcomes in preschool children – a review of recent evidence.' *Child & Adolescent Mental Health, 21,* 11–20.

Becares, L. and Atatoa-Carr, P. (2016) 'The association between maternal and partner experienced racial discrimination and prenatal perceived stress, prenatal and postnatal depression: findings from the growing up in New Zealand cohort study.' *International Journal for Equity in Health, 15,* 1, 155.

Bellini, S. (2004) 'Social skill deficits and anxiety in high-functioning adolescents with autism spectrum disorder.' *Focus on Autism and Other Developmental Disabilities, 19,* 78–86.

Bick, J. and Nelson, C.A. (2016) 'Early adverse experiences and the developing brain.' *Neuropsychopharmacology, 41,* 177–196.

Bishop, D. and Rutter, M. (2004) 'Neurodevelopmental Disorders: Conceptual Issues'. In M. Rutter, D.V.M. Bishop, D.S. Pine, S. Scott *et al.* (eds) *Rutter's Child and Adolescent Psychiatry* (5th ed.). Chichester: Wiley.

Bowlby, J. (1969) *Attachment and Loss, Vol. 1: Attachment.* New York, NY: Basic Books.

Bowlby, J. (1973) *Attachment and Loss, Vol. 2: Separation.* New York, NY: Basic Books.

Bowlby, J. (1980) *Attachment and Loss, Vol. 3: Loss, Sadness and Depression.* New York, NY: Basic Books.

Bradlow, J., Bartram, F., Guasp, A. and Jadva, V. (2017) School Report: *The experiences of lesbian, gay, bi and trans young people in Britain's schools in 2017.* Available at https://www.stonewall.org.uk/sites/default/files/the_school_report_2017.pdf

Bronfenbrenner, U. (1979) *The Ecology of Human Development.* Cambridge, MA: Harvard University Press.

Bronfenbrenner, U. (1994) 'Ecological Models of Human Development'. In T. Husen and T.N. Postlethwaite (eds) *The International Encyclopedia of Education, Vol. 3* (2nd ed.). New York, NY: Elsevier Science.

Carter, R.T. (2007) 'Racism and psychological and emotional injury: recognizing and assessing race-based traumatic stress.' *The Counseling Psychologist, 35,* 1, 13–105.

Centre for Longitudinal Studies (2015) *Counting the True Cost of Childhood Psychological Problems in Adult Life.* Available at: www.cls.ioe.ac.uk/news. aspx?itemid=3223&itemTitle=Counting+the+true+cost+of+childhood+ psychological+problems+in+adult+life&sitesectionid=27&sitesectiontitle=News.

Children's Commissioner (2017) *On Measuring the Number of Vulnerable Children in England.* London: Children's Commissioner for England.

Cicchetti, D. (1989) 'Developmental psychopathology: some thoughts on its evolution.' *Development and Psychopathology, 1,* 1, 1–4.

Colman, I., Kingsbury, M., Garad, Y. *et al.* (2016) 'Consistency in adult reporting of adverse childhood experiences.' *Psychological Medicine, 46,* 3, 543–549.

Commodari, E. (2013) 'Preschool teacher attachment and attention skills.' *SpringerPlus, 2,* 673.

Crenshaw, K. (1989) 'Demarginalizing the intersection of race and sex: a black feminist critique of antidiscrimination doctrine, feminist theory and antiracist politics.' *University of Chicago Legal Forum: Vol. 1989,* Article 8.

Crenshaw, K. and Dobson, A. (2014) 'The urgency of intersectionality.' Available at: www. ted.com/talks/kimberle_crenshaw_the_urgency_of_intersectionality.

Cromby, J., Harper, D. and Reavey, P. (2013) *Psychology, Mental Health and Distress.* London: Palgrave Macmillan.

Crooks, C.V., Scott, K.L., Wolfe, D.A., Chiodo, D. and Killip, S. (2007) 'Understanding the link between childhood maltreatment and violent delinquency: what do schools have to add?' *Child Maltreatment, 12,* 3, 269–280.

de Bruin, E.I., Ferdinand, R.F., Sifra Meester, P.F. and de Nijs, F.N. (2007) 'High rates of psychiatric co-morbidity in PDD-NOS.' *Journal of Autism and Developmental Disorders, 37,* 5, 877–886.

Department for Education and Skills (DfES) (2006) *Ethnicity and Education: The Evidence on Minority Ethnic Pupils Aged 5–16.* Research topic paper: 2006 edition.

Department of Health (1999) *Saving Lives: Our Healthier Nation.* London: DOH.

Department for Work and Pensions (2015) *Households Below Average Income: An Analysis of UK Income Distribution 1994/95–2013/14.* London: DWP: National Statistics

Duckworth, A.L., Peterson, C., Matthews, M.D. and Kelly, D.R. (2007) 'Grit: perseverance and passion for long-term goals.' *Journal of Personality and Social Psychology, 92,* 6, 1087.

Durcan, G., Zlotowitz, S. and Stubbs, J. (2017) *Meeting Us Where We're At: Learning from INTEGRATE's Work with Excluded Young People.* London: Centre for Mental Health.

Elklit, A. (2002) 'Victimization and PTSD in a Danish national youth probability sample.' *Journal of the American Academy of Child & Adolescent Psychiatry, 41,* 2, 174–181.

Emerson, E. and Hatton, C. (2007) *The Mental Health of Children and Adolescents with Learning Disabilities in Britain.* Lancaster: Lancaster University/Foundation for People with Learning Disabilities.

Equality Act (2010) London: HMSO.

Equality and Human Rights Commission (EHRC) (2016) *Healing a Divided Britain: The Need for a Comprehensive Race Equality Strategy.*

Fatimilehin, I.A. (1999) 'Of jewel heritage: racial socialization and racial identity attitudes amongst adolescents of mixed African–Caribbean/White parentage.' *Journal of Adolescence, 22,* 3, 303–318.

Felitti, V.J. (2009) 'Adverse childhood experiences and adult health.' *Academic Pediatrics, 9,* 3, 131–132.

Felitti, V.J., Anda, R.F., Nordenberg, D., Williamson, D.F. *et al.* (1998) 'Relationship of childhood abuse and household dysfunction to many of the leading causes of death in adults. The Adverse Childhood Experiences (ACE) Study.' *American Journal of Preventive Medicine May 14,* 4, 245–258.

Fives, A., Pursell, L., Heary, C., Nic Gabhainn, S. and Canavan, J. (2014) *Parenting Support for Every Parent: A Population-Level Evaluation of Triple P in Longford Westmeath. Summary Report.* Athlone: Longford Westmeath Parenting Partnership (LWPP).

Fonagy, P., Cottrell, D., Phillips, J., Bevington, D., Glaser, D. and Allison, E. (2015) *What Works for Whom? A Critical Review of Treatments for Children and Adolescents* (2nd ed.). New York, NY: Guilford Publications.

Fox, S.E., Levitt, P. and Nelson III, C.A. (2010) 'How the timing and quality of early experiences influence the development of brain architecture.' *Child Development, 81,* 28–40.

Franke, H.A. (2014) 'Toxic stress: effects, prevention and treatment.' S. Acra (ed.) *Children, 1,* 3, 390–402.

Friedli, L. and Carlin, M. (2009) *Resilient Relationships in the North West: What Can the Public Sector Contribute?* Manchester: NHS Northwest and the Department of Health.

Fryer, D. (1998) 'Mental health consequences of economic insecurity, relative poverty and social exclusion.' *Journal of Community and Applied Social Psychology, 8,* 75–80.

Garmezy, N. (1971) 'Vulnerability research and the issue of primary prevention.' *American Journal of Orthopsychiatry, 41,* 1, 101–116.

Garmezy, N. (1985) 'Stress-resistant children: the search for protective factors.' *Recent Research in Developmental Psychopathology, 4,* 213–233.

Geddes, H. (2006) *Attachment in the Classroom.* London: Worth Publishing.

Gerhardt, S. (2004) *Why Love Matters.* Hove: Routledge.

Gershoff, E.T., Aber, J.L. and Raver, C.C. (2003) 'Child Poverty in the United States: An Evidence-Based Conceptual Framework for Programs and Policies.' In F. Jacobs, D. Wertlieb and R.M. Lerner (eds) *Handbook of Applied Developmental Science: Promoting Positive Child, Adolescent, and Family Development through Research, Policies, and Programs. Vol. 2.* Thousand Oaks, CA: Sage.

Gershoff, E.T., Aber, J.L., Raver, C.C. and Lennon, M.C. (2007) 'Income is not enough: incorporating material hardship into models of income associations with parenting and child development.' *Child Development, 78,* 70–95.

Goodman, R. (1997) 'The Strengths and Difficulties Questionnaire: a research note.' *Journal of Child Psychology and Psychiatry, 38,* 5, 581–586.

Grant, K.E., Compas, B.E., Thurm, A.E., McMahon, S.D. *et al.* (2006) 'Stressors and child and adolescent psychopathology: evidence of moderating and mediating effects.' *Clinical Psychology Review, 26,* 3, 257–283.

Green, H., McGinnity, A., Meltzer, H. *et al.* (2005) *Mental Health of Children and Young People in Great Britain, 2004.* London: ONS.

Gutman, L., Joshi, H., Parsonage, M. and Schoon, I. (2015) *Children of the New Century: Mental Health Findings from the Millennium Cohort Study.* London: Institute of Education, UCL and Centre for Mental Health.

Hagel, A. and Maughan, B. (2017) 'Epidemiology: Are Mental Health Problems in Children and Young People a Big Issue?' In N. Midgley, J. Hayes and M. Cooper (eds) *Essential Research Findings in Children and Adolescent Counselling and Psychotherapy.* London: Sage.

Harold, G., Acquah, D., Sellers, R. and Chowdry, H. (2016) *What Works to Enhance Inter-Parental Relationships and Improve Outcomes for Children.* London: Early Intervention Foundation.

Hart, A., Gagnon, E., Eryigit-Madzwamuse, S., Cameron, J. *et al.* (2016) 'Uniting resilience research and practice with a health inequalities approach.' *SAGE Open, 6,* 4, 1–15.

Humphreys, K.L. and Zeanah, C.H. (2015) 'Deviations from the expectable environment in early childhood and emerging psychopathology.' *Neuropsychopharmacology, 40,* 1, 154–170.

Kelly, Y., Becares, L. and Nazroo, J. (2012) 'Associations between maternal experiences of racism and early child health and development: findings from the UK Millennium Cohort Study.' *Journal of Epidemiology and Community Health, 67,* 35–41.

Kim, S.Y., Schwartz, S.J., Perreira, K.M. and Juang, L.P. (2018) 'Culture's influence on stressors, parental socialization, and developmental processes in the mental health of children of immigrants.' *Annual Review of Clinical Psychology, 14,* 1.

Kim, Y.S. and Leventhal, B. (2008) 'Bullying and suicide. A review.' *International Journal of Adolescent Medicine and Health, 20,* 2, 133–154.

Klasen, F., Otto, C., Kriston, L., Patalay, P., Schlack, R. and Ravens-Sieberer, U. (2015) 'BELLA study group.' *European Child and Adolescent Psychiatry, 24,* 6, 695–703.

Lasher, S. and Baker, C. (2015) *Bullying: Evidence from the Longitudinal Study of Young People in England 2, Wave 2 Research Brief.* London: Department for Education.

Lee, E., Larkin, H. and Esaki, N. (2017) 'Exposure to community violence as a new adverse childhood experience category: promising results and future considerations.' *Families in Society: The Journal of Contemporary Social Services, 98,* 1, 69–78.

Lereya, S.T., Copeland, W.E., Costello, E.J. and Wolke, D. (2015) 'Adult mental health consequences of peer bullying and maltreatment in childhood: two cohorts in two countries.' *The Lancet Psychiatry, 2,* 6.

Lundequist, A., Bohm, B. and Smedler, A. (2013) 'Individual neuropsychological profiles at age 5½ years in children born preterm in relation to medical risk factors.' *Child Neuropsychology, 19,* 3, 313–331.

MacPherson, W. (1999) *The Stephen Lawrence Inquiry: Report of an Inquiry.* London: The Stationary Office.

Malek, M. (2004) 'Understanding Ethnicity and Children's Mental Health.' In M. Malek and C. Joughin (eds) *Mental Health Services for Minority Ethnic Children and Adolescents.* London: Jessica Kingsley Publishers.

Marlow, N., Rose, A.S., Rands, C.E. *et al.* (2005) 'Neuropsychological and educational problems at school age associated with neonatal encephalopathy.' *Archives of Disease in Childhood. Fetal and Neonatal Edition, 90,* 5: F380–F387.

Marmot, M. (2001) 'From Black to Acheson: two decades of concern with inequalities in health. A celebration of the 90th birthday of Professor Jerry Morris.' *International Journal of Epidemiology, 30,* 5, 1165–1171.

Marmot Review (2010) *Fair Society, Healthy Lives: Strategic Review of Health Inequalities in England Post 2010.* London: Institute of Health Equity.

Masten, A.S. (2015) *Ordinary Magic: Resilience in Development.* New York, NY: Guilford Press.

Masten, A. and Cicchetti, D. (2010) 'Developmental cascades.' *Development and Psychopathology, 22,* 3, 491–495.

McCracken, K., Priest, S., FitzSimons, A., Bracewell, K., Torchia, K. and Parry, W. (2017) *Children's Social Care Innovation Programme Evaluation, Report 49.* London: Department for Education.

McCrory, E.J., Puetz, V., Maguire, E.A., Mechelli, A. *et al.* (2017) 'Autobiographical memory: a candidate latent vulnerability mechanism for psychiatric disorder following childhood maltreatment.' *The British Journal of Psychiatry, 58,* 4, 338–357.

McLaughlin, K.A., Sheridan, M.A. and Lambert, H.K. (2014) 'Childhood adversity and neural development: deprivation and threat as distinct dimensions of early experience.' *Neuroscience & Biobehavioral Reviews, 47,* 578–585.

Middlebrooks, J.S. and Audage, N.C. (2008) *The Effects of Childhood Stress on Health Across the Lifespan.* Atlanta, GA: Centers for Disease Control and Prevention, National Center for Injury Prevention and Control.

Ministry of Justice (2013) *Statistics on Race and the Criminal Justice System 2012.* London: Ministry of Justice.

Ministry of Justice (2015) *Statistics on Race and the Criminal Justice System 2014.* A Ministry of Justice publication under Section 95 of the Criminal Justice Act 1991. London: Ministry of Justice.

Murphy, M. and Fonagy, P. (2012) 'Mental health problems in children and young people.' *Annual Report of the Chief Medical Officer 2012.* London: Department of Health.

Music, G. (2011) *Nurturing Natures: Attachment and Children's Emotional, Sociocultural and Brain Development.* Hove: Psychology Press.

Nielsen, M.B., Tangen, T., Idsoe, T., Matthiesen, S.B. and Magerøy, N. (2015) 'Post-traumatic stress disorder as a consequence of bullying at work and at school. A literature review and meta-analysis.' *Aggression and Violent Behavior, 21,* 17–24.

Organisation for Economic Co-operation and Development (OECD) (2017) *Child Well-Being Data Portal Country Factsheet.* Available at: www.oecd.org/els/family/CWBDP_Factsheet_GBR.pdf.

Patalay, P. and Fitzsimons, E. (2016) 'Correlates of mental illness and wellbeing in children: are they the same? Results from the UK Millennium Cohort Study.' *Journal of the American Academy of Child & Adolescent Psychiatry, 55,* 9, 771–783.

Patel, N. and Fatimilehin, I. (1999) 'Racism and Mental Health.' In G. Holmes, C. Newnes and C. Dunn (eds) *This is Madness: A Critical Look at Psychiatry and the Future of Mental Health Services.* Monmouth: PCCS Books.

Pei, J., Kennedy, D., Hughes, J. and Rasmusen, C. (2011) 'Mental health issues in foetal alcohol spectrum disorder.' *Journal of Mental Health, 20,* 5, 473–483.

Pennington, B. (2009) *Diagnosing Learning Disorders.* New York, NY: Guilford Press.

Priest, N., Paradies, Y., Trenerry, B., Truong, M., Karlsen, S. and Kelly, Y. (2013) 'A systematic review of studies examining the relationship between reported racism and health and wellbeing for children and young people.' *Social Science & Medicine, 95,* 115–127.

Priest, N., Perry, R., Ferdinand, A., Paradies, Y. and Kelaher, M. (2014) 'Experiences of racism, racial/ethnic attitudes, motivated fairness and mental health outcomes among primary and secondary school students.' *Journal of Youth and Adolescence, 43,* 10, 1672–1687.

Reuben, A., Moffitt, T.E., Caspi, A. *et al.* (2016) 'Lest we forget: comparing retrospective and prospective assessments of adverse childhood experiences in the prediction of adult health.' *Journal of Child Psychology and Psychiatry, and Allied Disciplines, 57,* 10, 1103–1112.

Rutter, M. (1987) 'Psychosocial resilience and protective mechanisms.' *American Journal of Orthopsychiatry, 57,* 3, 316–331.

Rutter, M. (2006) 'Implications of resilience concepts for scientific understanding.' *Annals of the New York Academy of Sciences, 1094,* 1–12.

Rutter, M. (2012) 'Resilience as a dynamic concept.' *Development and Psychopathology, 24,* 02, 335–344.

Rutter, M. (2013a) 'Annual research review: resilience – clinical implications.' *Journal of Child Psychology and Psychiatry, 54,* 474–487.

Rutter, M. (2013b) 'Developmental psychopathology: a paradigm shift or just a relabeling?' *Development and Psychopathology, 25,* 4pt2, 1201–1213.

Rutter, M., O'Connor, T.G. and English and Romanian Adoptees (ERA) Study Team (2004) 'Are there biological programming effects for psychological development? Findings from a study of Romanian adoptees.' *Developmental Psychology, 40,* 1, 81–94.

Rutter, M., Tizard, J., Yule, W., Graham, P. and Whitmore, K. (1976) 'Isle of Wight Studies, 1964–1974.' *Psychological Medicine, 6,* 2, 313–332.

Sanders, M.R., Ralph, A., Sofronoff, K., Gardiner, P. *et al.* (2008) 'Every family: a population approach to reducing behavioral and emotional problems in children making the transition to school.' *Journal of Primary Prevention, 29,* 197–222.

Sanders, M.R., Turner, K.M.T. and Markie-Dadds, C. (2002) 'The development and dissemination of the Triple P—Positive Parenting Program: a multilevel, evidence-based system of parenting and family support.' *Prevention Science, 3,* 173.

Shonkoff, J.P., Garner, A.S., Siegel, B.S., Dobbins, M.I. *et al.* (2012) 'The lifelong effects of early childhood adversity and toxic stress.' *Pediatrics, 129,* e232–e246.

Smail, D. (1994) 'Community psychology and politics.' *Journal of Community and Applied Social Psychology, 4,* 3–10.

Smail, D. (2005) *Power, Interest and Psychology – Elements of a Social Materialist Understanding of Distress.* Monmouth: PCCS Books.

Stikkelbroek, Y., Bodden, D.H.M., Reitz, E., Vollebergh, W.A.M. and van Baar, A.L. (2015) 'Mental health of adolescents before and after the death of a parent or sibling.' *European Child & Adolescent Psychiatry, 25,* 49–59.

Strand, S. (2014a) 'Ethnicity, gender, social class and achievement gaps at age 16: intersectionality and "getting it" for the white working class.' *Research Papers in Education, 29,* 2, 131–171.

Strand, S. (2014b) 'School effects and ethnic, gender and socio-economic gaps in educational achievement at age 11.' *Oxford Review of Education, 40,* 2, 223–245.

Streissguth, A.P., Bookstein, F.L., Barr, H., Sampson, P.D., O'Malley, K., Young, J.K. (2004) 'Risk factors for adverse life outcomes in fetal alcohol syndrome and fetal alcohol effects.' *Journal of Developmental & Behavioral Pediatrics, 25,* 4, 228–238.

Sunak, R. and Rajeswaran, S. (2014) *A Portrait of Modern Britain.* London: Policy Exchange.

Svanberg, P.O. (1998) 'Attachment, resilience and prevention.' *Journal of Mental Health, 7,* 6, 543–578.

The Children's Society (2008) *Happy and They Know It – Developing a Well-Being Framework Based on Young People Consultation.* London: The Children's Society.

The Children's Society (2014) *At What Cost? Exposing the Impact of Poverty on School Life.* Report from the Children's Commission on Poverty. London: The Children's Society

The Children's Society (2017) *The Good Childhood Report 2017.* London: The Children's Society.

The Varkey Foundation (2017) *What the World's Young People Think and Feel: Generation Z: Global Citizenship Survey.* London: The Varkey Foundation.

Thompson, C. (2013) *Mental Health Bulletin: Annual Report from MHMDS Returns – England 2011–12, Initial National Figures.* Leeds: Health and Social Care Information Centre.

Thornberry, T.P., Henry, K.L., Ireland, T.O. and Smith, C.A. (2010) 'The causal impact of childhood-limited maltreatment and adolescent maltreatment on early adult adjustment.' *Journal of Adolescent Health, 46,* 4, 359–365.

Townsend, P. (1979) *Poverty in the United Kingdom.* London: Allen Lane and Penguin Books.

Ungar, M. (2011) 'The social ecology of resilience: addressing contextual and cultural ambiguity of a nascent construct.' *American Journal of Orthopsychiatry, 81,* 1, 1–17.

Van Dam, D.S., Van Der Ven, E., Velthorst, E., Selten, J.P., Morgan, C. and De Haan, L. (2012) 'Childhood bullying and the association with psychosis in non-clinical and clinical samples: a review and meta-analysis.' *Psychological Medicine, 42,* 12, 2463–2474.

Verschueren, K. and Koomen, H.M.Y. (2012) 'Teacher-child relationships from an attachment perspective.' *Attachment and Human Development, 14,* 3, 205–211.

Walsh, D., McCartney, G., Collins, C., Taulbut, M. and Batty, G.D. (2016) *History, Politics and Vulnerability: Explaining Excess Mortality in Scotland and Glasgow.* A report by the Glasgow Centre for Population Health, NHS Health Scotland, the University of the West of Scotland and University College London.

Weiss, M.J.S. and Wagner, S.H. (1998) 'What explains the negative consequences of adverse childhood experiences on adult health: insights from cognitive and neuroscience research.' *American Journal of Preventive Medicine, 14,* 4, 356–360.

Wille, N., Bettge, S., Ravens-Sieberer, U. *et al.* (2008) 'Risk and protective factors for children's and adolescents' mental health: results of the BELLA study.' *European Child and Adolescent Psychiatry, 17,* Suppl. 1, 133–147.

Windle, G. (2011) 'What is resilience? A review and concept analysis.' *Reviews in Clinical Gerontology, 21,* 2, 152–169.

World Health Organization (WHO) (2005) *Child and Adolescent Mental Health Policies and Plans, Mental Health Policy and Service Guidance Package.* Geneva: World Health Organization.

World Health Organization (WHO) (2012) *Risks to Mental Health: An Overview of Vulnerabilities and Risk Factors.* Geneva: World Health Organization.

Yates, T.M. and Masten, A.S. (2004) 'Fostering the Future: Resilience Theory and the Practice of Positive Psychology.' In P.A. Linley and S. Joseph (eds) *Positive Psychology in Practice.* Hoboken, NJ: Wiley.

Zayed, Y. and Harker, R. (2015) *Children in Care in England: Statistics.* London: House of Commons Library.

Zimmerman, M.A., Stoddard, S.A., Eisman, A.B., Caldwell, C.H., Aiyer, S.M. and Miller, A. (2013) 'Adolescent resilience: promotive factors that inform prevention.' *Child Development Perspectives, 7,* 215–220.

Chapter 2

Ainsworth, M.D.S., Bell, S.M. and Stayton, D. (1974) 'Infant-Mother Attachment and Social Development.' In M.P. Richards (ed.) *The Introduction of the Child into a Social World.* Cambridge: Cambridge University Press.

Aston, M. (2008) 'Public health nurses as social mediators navigating discourses with new mothers.' *Nursing Inquiry 15,* 280–288.

Ayers, S. (2014) 'Fear of childbirth, postnatal post traumatic stress disorder and midwifery care.' *Midwifery, 30,* 145–148.

Balbernie, R. (2008) *An Infant Mental Health Service: The Importance of the Early Years and Evidence-Based Practice.* London: Child Psychotherapy Trust.

Barnes, J., Ball, M., Meadows P., Howden, B. *et al.* (2011) *The Family Nurse Partnership Programme in England: Wave 1 Implementation in Toddlerhood and a Comparison between Waves 1 and 2a Implementation in Pregnancy and Infancy.* London: Department of Health.

Bauer, A., Parsonage, M., Knapp, M., Lemmi, V. and Adelaja, B. (2014) *The Costs of Perinatal Mental Health Problems.* London: Centre for Mental Health and London School of Economics.

Bernier, A. and Dozier, M. (2003) 'Bridging the attachment transmission gap: the role of maternal mind-mindedness.' *International Journal of Behavioral Development, 27,* 4, 355–365.

Bowlby, J. (1969) *Attachment and Loss, Vol. 1: Attachment.* New York, NY: Basic Books.

Bowlby, J. (1973) *Attachment and Loss, Vol. 2: Separation.* New York, NY: Basic Books.

Bowlby, J. (1980) *Attachment and Loss, Vol. 3: Loss, Sadness and Depression.* New York, NY: Basic Books.

Brink, S. (2013) *The Fourth Trimester: Understanding, Protecting, and Nurturing an Infant through the First Three Months.* Berkeley, CA: University of California Press.

Bronfenbrenner. U. (1994). 'Ecological Models of Human Development.' In T. Husen and T.N. Posttlethwaite (eds) *The International Encyclopaedia of Education, Vol. 3,* (2nd ed.) Oxford: Elsevier.

Browne, J., Martinez, D. and Talmi, A. (2016) 'Infant mental health (IMH) in the intensive care unit: considerations for the infant, the family and the staff.' *Newborn and Infant Nursing Reviews, 16,* 274–280.

Cassidy, J., Woodhouse, S., Sherman, L., Stupica, B. and Lejuez, C. (2011) 'Enhancing infant attachment security: an examination of treatment efficacy and differential susceptibility.' *Journal of Development and Psychopathology, 23,* 131–148.

Chitty, A. (2015) 'Infant mental health: health visitors as key partners.' *Community Practitioner, 88,* 10, 29–30.

Cohen, N.J., Muir, E., Lojkasek, M., Muir, R. *et al.* (1999) 'Watch, wait, and wonder: testing the effectiveness of a new approach to mother–infant psychotherapy.' *Infant Mental Health Journal, 20(4),* 429–451.

Coster, D., Brookes, H. and Sanger, C. (2015) *Evaluation of the Baby Steps Programme: Pre- and Post-Measures Study.* London: NSPCC.

Daws, D. and de Rementeria, A. (2015) *Finding Your Way with Your Baby: The Emotional Life of Parents and their Babies.* London: Routledge.

Diggins, A. (2011) *Think Child, Think Parent, Think Family: A Guide to Parental Mental Health and Child Welfare. Families' and Children's Services Guide 30.* London: Social Care Institute for Excellence.

Douglas, H. (2016) 'The Solihull Approach Antenatal Parenting Group: understanding pregnancy, labour, birth and your baby.' *International Journal of Birth and Parent Education, V4,* 29–31.

Ellis, A., Butterworth, R. and Law, G. (2017) 'How parents experience building a relationship with their baby on neonatal intensive care.' University of Birmingham unpublished thesis.

Etheridge, J. and Slade, P. (2017) '"Nothing's actually happened to me": the experiences of fathers who found childbirth traumatic.' *BMC Pregnancy and Childbirth, 17,* 80.

Evangelou, M. and Sylva, K. (2003) *The Effects of the Peers Early Educational Partnership (PEEP) on Children's Developmental Progress.* Oxford: University of Oxford.

Felitti, V.J., Anda, R.F. and Nordenberg, D. (1998) 'Relationship of childhood abuse and household dysfunction to many of the leading causes of death in adults: the Adverse Childhood Experiences (ACE) Study.' *American Journal of Preventive Medicine, 14,* 245–258.

Field, T., Diego, M. and Hernandez-Reif, M. (2006) 'Prenatal depression effects on the fetus and newborn: a review.' *Infant Behavior and Development, 293,* 3, 445–455.

Fonagy, P., Steele, M., Moran, G.S. and Higgitt, A. (1991a) 'The capacity for understanding mental states: the reflective self in parent and child and its significance for security of attachment.' *Infant Mental Health Journal, 12,* 201–218.

Fonagy, P., Steele, H., and Steele, M. (1991b) 'Maternal representations of attachment during pregnancy predict the organisation of infant-mother attachment at one year of age.' *Child Development, 62,* 5, 891–905.

Fraiberg, S., Adelson, E. and Shapiro, V. (1975) 'Ghosts in the nursery: a psychoanalytic approach to the problems of impaired infant-mother relationships.' *Journal of the American Academy of Child and Adolescent Psychiatry, 14,* 3, 387–421.

Gergely, G. and Watson, J.S. (1996) 'The social biofeedback theory of parental affect-mirroring: the development of emotional self-awareness and self-control.' *International Journal of Psycho-Analysis, 77,* 1181–1212.

Gluckman, P.D., Hanson, M.A. and Mitchell, M.D. (2010) 'Developmental origins of health and disease: reducing the burden of chronic disease in the next generation.' *Genome Medicine, 2010, 2,* 14.

Goodlin, R. and Schmidt, W. (1972) 'Human fetal arousal levels as indicated by heart rate recordings.' *American Journal of Obstetrics and Gynecology, 114,* 5, 613–621.

Hogg, S. (2013) *All Babies Count: Spotlight on Perinatal Mental Health – Prevention in Mind.* London: NSPCC.

Hosking, G. and Kelly, P. (2014) 'Reducing child maltreatment in pioneer communities: a preventive approach to creating a large scale step reduction in levels of child abuse, neglect and children witnessing domestic violence.' Paper presented at the National Children and Adult Services Conference, 30 October 2014.

Jones, A. (2010) 'Working with complex child protection cases.' Paper presented at the Association for Infant Mental Health UK (AIMH UK) National Conference, September 2010.

Kennedy, H., Ball, K. and Barlow, J. (2017) 'How does video interaction guidance contribute to infant and parental mental health and well-being?' *Clinical Child Psychology and Psychiatry, 22,* 3, 500–517.

Kenny, M., Conroy, S., Pariante, C., Seneviratne, G. and Pawlby, S. (2013) 'Mother-infant interaction in mother and baby unit patients: before and after treatment.' *Journal of Psychiatric Research, 47,* 1192–1198.

Knight, M., Tuffnell, D., Kenyon, S., Shakespeare, J., Gray, R. and Kurinczuk, J.J. (eds) on behalf of MBRRACE-UK (2015) *Saving Lives, Improving Mothers' Care. Surveillance of maternal deaths in the UK 2011–13 and lessons learned to inform maternity care from the UK and Ireland Confidential Enquiries into Maternal Deaths and Morbidity 2009–13.* Oxford: National Perinatal Epidemiology Unit, University of Oxford.

Leadsom, A., Field, F., Burstow, P. and Lucas, C. (2013) *The 1001 Critical Days: The Importance of the Conception to Age Two Period: A Cross-Party Manifesto.* London: Department of Health.

McAlister, A. and Peterson, C.C. (2007) 'Mental playmates: siblings, executive functioning and theory of mind.' *Cognitive Development, 22,* 2, 258–270.

McKenzie-McHarg, K., Crockett, M., Olander, E.K. and Ayers, S. (2015) 'Think pink! A sticker alert system for psychological distress or vulnerability during pregnancy.' *British Journal of Midwifery, 22,* 8, 495–501.

Meins, E. (2004) 'Infants' minds, mothers' minds, and other minds: how individual differences in caregivers affect the co-construction of mind.' *Behavioral and Brain Science, 27,* 1, 116.

Meins, E., Fernyhough, C., Wainwright, R., Das Gupta, M., Fradley, E. and Tuckey, M. (2002) 'Maternal mind-mindedness and attachment security as predictors of theory of mind understanding.' *Child Development, 73,* 1715–1726.

Music, G. (2011) *Nurturing Natures: Attachment and Children's Emotional, Sociocultural and Brain Development.* Hove: Psychology Press.

National Childbirth Trust (2015) 'Dads in distress: Many new fathers are worried about their mental health.' Available at https://www.nct.org.uk/press-release/dads-distress-many-new-fathers-are-worried-about-their-mental-health.

National Institute for Clinical Excellence (2014) *Antenatal and Postnatal Mental Health: Clinical Management and Service Guidance: Clinical Guideline 192.* London: National Institute for Clinical Excellence.

Nelson, F. and Mann, T. (2011) 'Opportunities in public policy to support infant and early childhood mental health: the role of psychologists and policymakers.' *American Psychologist, 66,* 2, February–March, 129–139.

Newman, L., Judd, F., Olsson, C.A., Castle, D. *et al.* (2016) 'Early origins of mental disorder: risk factors in the perinatal and infant period.' *BMC Psychiatry, 16,* 27.

NHS England (2016) *Perinatal Mental Health Community Services Development Fund: Application Guidance.* London: NHS England.

Noonan, M., Galvin, R., Doody, O. and Jomeen, J. (2017) 'A qualitative meta-synthesis: public health nurses' role in the identification and management of perinatal mental health problems.' *Journal of Advanced Nursing 73,* 3, 545–557.

Paulson, J.F. and Bazemore, S.D. (2010) 'Prenatal and postpartum depression in fathers and its association with maternal depression: a meta-analysis.' *JAMA, 303,* 19, 1961–1969.

Public Health England (2017) *Better Mental Health: JSNA Toolkit (Perinatal Mental Health).* London: Public Health England.

Puckering, C. (2013) 'Mellow Bumps: an attachment-based programme for pregnancy.' *International Journal of Birth and Parenting Education, 1,* 2, 29–33.

Puckering, C., McIntosh, E., Hickey, A. and Longford, J. (2010) 'Mellow Babies: a group intervention for infants and mothers experiencing postnatal depression.' *Counselling Psychology Review, 25,* 1.

Purra, K., Davis, H., Mantymaa, M., Tamminen, T. and Roberts, R. (2005) 'The outcome of the European Early Promotion Project. Mother-child interaction.' *The International Journal of Mental Health Promotion, 7,* 1, 82–94.

Sallenbach, W.B. (1993) 'The Intelligent Prenate: Paradigms in Prenatal Learning and Bonding.' In T. Blum (ed.) *Prenatal Perception, Learning and Bonding: Learning and Bonding.* Hong Kong: Leonardo.

Schore, A.N. (1994) *Affect Regulation and the Origin of the Self: The Neurobiology of Emotional Development.* Hillsdale, NJ: Lawrence Erlbaum Associates.

Seng, J. and Taylor, J. (2015) *Trauma Informed Care in the Perinatal Period (Protecting Children and Young People).* London: Dunedin Academic Press.

Siegel, D.J. (1999) *The Developing Mind: Toward a Neurobiology of Interpersonal Experience.* New York, NY: Guilford Press.

Sroufe, A., Egeland, B., Carlson, E. and Collins, A. (2005) *The Development of the Person: The Minnesota Study of Risk and Adaptation from Birth to Adulthood.* New York, NY: Guilford Press.

Steele, H. and Steele, M. (2005) 'Understanding and Resolving Emotional Conflict.' In K. Grossman, K. Grossman and E. Waters (eds) *Attachment from Infancy to Adulthood: The Major Longitudinal Studies.* New York, NY: Guilford Press.

Tronick, E., Adamson, L.B., Als, H. and Brazelton, T.B. (1975, April) 'Infant emotions in normal and pertubated interactions.' Paper presented at the biennial meeting of the Society for Research in Child Development, Denver, CO.

Tronick, E. and Brazelton, T. (1980) 'Preverbal Communication Between Mothers and Infants.' In D.R. Olson (ed.) *The Social Foundations of Language and Thought.* New York, NY: Norton.

University of Warwick (2013) *Infant Mental Health Pathway.* Coventry: Warwick Infant and Family Wellbeing Unit.

Ventevogel, P., Jordans, M.J.D., Eggerman, M., van Mierlo, B. and Panter-Brick, C. (2013) 'Child Mental Health, Psychosocial Well-Being and Resilience in Afghanistan: A Review and Future Directions.' In C. Fenando and M. Ferrari (eds) *Handbook of Resilience in Children of War.* New York, NY: Springer.

Wave Trust (2015) *Building Great Britons: Perinatal Inquiry – Evidence Session on First 1001 Days.* London: All Party Parliamentary Group for Conception to Age 2.

Wenger, E. (1998) *Communities of Practice.* Cambridge: Cambridge University Press.

Winnicott, D.W. (1965) *The Maturational Processes and the Facilitating Environment.* London: Karnac Books.

Chapter 3

Abidin, R.R. (1995) *Parenting Stress Index.* Odessa, FL: Psychological Assessment Resources.

Allen, G. (2011a) *Early Intervention: Smart Investment, Massive Savings.* London: Independent Report to HM Government.

Allen, G. (2011b) *Early Intervention: The Next Steps.* London: Independent Report to HM Government.

Allen, G. and Duncan-Smith, I. (2008) *Early Intervention: Good Parents, Great Kids, Better Citizens.* Cross-party paper. London: Centre for Social Justice and Smith Institute.

Asmussen, K., Feinstein, L., Martin, J. and Chowdry, H. (2016) *Foundations for Life: What Works to Support Parent Child Interaction.* London: Early Intervention Foundation.

Axford, N., Sonthalia, S., Wrigley, Z., Goodwin, A. *et al.* (2015) *The Best Start at Home.* London: Early Intervention Foundation.

Beck, A.T., Ward, C.H., Mendelson, M., Mock, J. and Erbaugh, J. (1961) 'An inventory for measuring depression.' *Archives of General Psychiatry, 4,* 561–571.

Brestan, E.V. and Eyberg, S.M. (1998) 'Effective psychosocial treatments of conduct-disordered children and adolescents: 29 years, 82 studies and 5,272 kids.' *Journal of Clinical Psychology, 27,* 180–189.

Broidy, L.M., Nagin, D.S., Tremblay, R.E., Bates, J.E. *et al.* (2003) 'Developmental trajectories of childhood disruptive behaviours and adolescent delinquency: a six site, cross-national study.' *Developmental Psychology, 39,* 222–245.

Bywater, T., Hutchings, J., Daley, D., Whitaker, C. *et al.* (2009) 'Long-term effectiveness of parenting intervention for children at risk of developing conduct disorder.' *The British Journal of Psychiatry, 195,* 318–324.

Department for Education (2011) *Supporting Families in the Foundation Years.* Public Reform Paper. London: DfE.

Eyberg, S.M. and Ross, A.W. (1978) 'Assessment of child behaviour problems: the validation of a new inventory.' *Journal of Clinical Child Psychology, 7,* 113–116.

Fergusson, D., Horwood, L. and Riddler, E. (2005) 'Show me the child at seven: the consequences of conduct problems in childhood for psychosocial functioning in adulthood.' *Journal of Child Psychology and Psychiatry, 46,* 837–849.

Field, F. (2010) *The Foundation Years: Preventing Poor Children Becoming Poor Adults.* Independent Review. London: HM Government.

Fixsen, D.L., Naoom, S.F., Blase, K.A., Friedman, R.M. and Wallace, F. (2005) *Implementation Research: A Synthesis of the Literature.* Tampa, FL: Louis de la Parte Florida Mental Health Institute.

Furlong, M., McGilloway, S., Bywater, T., Hutchings, J., Smith, S.M. and Donnelly, M. (2012) 'Behavioural and cognitive-behavioural group-based parenting programmes for early-onset conduct problems in children aged 3–12 years.' *Cochrane Database of Systematic Reviews.*

Gardner, F., Montgomery, P. and Knerr, W. (2015) 'Transporting evidence-based parenting programs for child problem behaviour (age 3-10) between countries: systematic review and meta-analysis.' *Journal of Clinical Child and Adolescent Psychology 0*, 0, 1–14.

Greater Manchester Combined Authority (2016) *Start Well: Early Years Strategy.* Manchester: GMCA.

Leadsom, A., Field, F., Burstow, P. and Lucas, C. (2014) *The 1001 Critical Days: The Importance of the Conception to Age Two Period: A Cross-Party Manifesto.* London: Department of Health.

Marmot, M. (2010) *The Marmot Review: Fair Society, Healthy Lives.* Independent Review. London: Department of Health.

McGilloway, S., NiMhaille, G., Bywater, T., Leckey, Y. *et al.* (2014) 'Reducing child conduct disordered behaviour and improving parent mental health in disadvantaged families: a 12-month follow-up and cost analysis of a parenting intervention.' *European Child and Adolescent Psychiatry, 23,* 783–794.

Møerch, W., Clifford, G., Larsson, B., Rypdal, P. *et al.* (2004) *The Incredible Years: The Norwegian Webster-Stratton Programme 1998–2004.* Trømso: University of Trømso.

National Institute for Health and Care Excellence (2012) *Social and Emotional Wellbeing: Early Years PH40.* London: National Institute for Health and Care Excellence.

National Institute for Health and Care Excellence (2013) *Antisocial Behaviour and Conduct Disorders in Children and Young People: Recognition and Management CG158.* London: National Institute for Health and Care Excellence.

National Institute for Health and Care Excellence (2018) *Attention Deficit Hyperactivity Disorder: Diagnosis and Management NG87.* London: National Institute for Health and Care Excellence.

NHS England (2015) *Future in Mind: Promoting, Protecting and Improving our Children and Young People's Mental Health and Wellbeing.* London: Department of Health.

Scott, S., Knapp, M., Henderson, J. and Maughan, B. (2001a) 'Financial cost of social exclusion: follow up study of antisocial children into adulthood.' *British Medical Journal, 323,* 191.

Scott, S., Spender, Q., Doolan, M., Jacobs, B. and Aspland, H. (2001b) 'Multicentre controlled trial of parenting groups for child antisocial behaviour in clinical practice.' *British Medical Journal, 323,* 28, 1–5.

Tickell, C. (2011) *The Early Years: Foundations for Life, Health and Learning.* Independent Review. London: HM Government.

Timimi, S. (2015) 'Children and Young People's Improving Access to Psychological Therapies: inspiring innovation or more of the same?' *British Journal of Psychiatry Bulletin, 39,* 57–60.

Webster-Stratton, C. (1990) 'Long-term follow-up of families with young conduct problem children: from preschool to grade school.' *Journal of Clinical Child Psychology 19,* 2, 144–149.

Webster-Stratton, C. (1997) 'Treating children with early-onset conduct problems: a comparison of child and parent training interventions.' *Journal of Consulting and Clinical Psychology, 65*, 1, 93–109.

Webster-Stratton, C. (1998) 'Preventing conduct problems in head start children: strengthening parenting competencies.' *Journal of Consulting and Clinical Psychology, 66*, 715–730.

Webster-Stratton, C. (2000) *The Incredible Years Training Series. Office of Juvenile Justice Delinquency Prevention Bulletin, 1–23.* United States: Department of Justice.

Webster-Stratton, C. (2004) *Quality Training, Supervision, Ongoing Monitoring and Agency Support: Key Ingredients to Implementing the Incredible Years Programs with Fidelity.* Seattle, WA: University of Washington.

Webster-Stratton, C. (2016) 'The Incredible Years Parent Programs: Methods and Principles that Support Program Fidelity.' In J.J. Ponzetti (ed.) *Evidence-Based Parenting Education: A Global Perspective.* New York, NY: Routledge.

Webster-Stratton, C. and Reid, M.J. (2012) 'The Incredible Years: Evidence-Based Parenting and Child Programs for Families in the Child Welfare System.' In A. Rubin (ed.) *Programs and Interventions for Maltreated Children and Families at Risk.* Hoboken, NJ: John Wiley & Sons.

Wolpert, M., Jacob, J., Napoleone, E., Whale, A., Calderon, A. and Edbrooke-Childs, J. (2017) *Child- and Parent–Reported Outcomes and Experience from Child and Young People's Mental Health Services 2011–2015.* London: CAMHS Press.

Chapter 4

Abrahams, S. and Udwin, O. (2002) 'An evaluation of a primary care-based child clinical psychology service.' *Child and Adolescent Mental Health, 7*, 3, 107–113.

Acri, M., Bornheimer, L.A., Jessell, L., Flaherty, H.B. *et al.* (2016) 'The impact of caregiver treatment satisfaction upon child and parent outcomes.' *Child and Adolescent Mental Health, 21*, 4, 201–208.

Barlett, H. (2015) 'Can school nurses identify mental health needs early and provide effective advice and support?' *British Journal of School Nursing, 10*, 3.

Benson, P. and Turk, T. (1988) 'Group therapy in a general practice setting for frequent attenders: a controlled study of mothers with pre-school children.' *Journal of the Royal College of General Practice, 38*, 317, 539–541.

Berger, M. (1996) 'Divided we stand! Issues for clinical psychology services for children and young people: a personal view.' *Clinical Psychology Forum*, February, 40–46.

Bishop, P., Gilroy, V. and Stirling, L. (2015) *A National Framework for Continuing Professional Development for Health Visitors – Standards to Support Professional Practice.* London: Institute of Health Visiting, Department of Health.

Bower, P., Garralda, E., Kramer, T., Harrington, R. and Sibbald, B. (2001) 'The treatment of child and adolescent mental health problems in primary care: a systematic review.' *Family Practice, 18*, 4, 373–382.

Bradley, S., Hickey, N., Kramer, T. and Elena Garralda, M. (2009) 'What makes a good CAMHS primary mental health worker?' *Child and Adolescent Mental Health, 14*, 1, 15–19.

Brett, D., Warnell, F., McConachie, H. and Parr, J.R. (2016) 'Factors affecting age at ASD diagnosis in UK: no evidence that diagnosis age has decreased between 2004 and 2014.' *Journal of Autism and Developmental Disorders, 46*, 6, 1974–1984.

Clarke, M., Coombs, C. and Walton, L. (2003) 'School based early identification and intervention service for adolescents: a psychology and school nurse partnership model.' *Child and Adolescent Mental Health, 8,* 1, 34–39.

Cockburn, K. and Bernard, P. (2004) 'Child and adolescent mental health within primary care: a study of general practitioners' perceptions.' *Child and Adolescent Mental Health, 9,* 21–24.

Cooper, M., Evans, Y. and Pybis, J. (2016) 'Interagency collaboration in children and young people's mental health: a systematic review of outcomes, facilitating factors and inhibiting factors.' *Child: Care, Health and Development, 42,* 3, 325–342.

Cousins, J. (2013) 'Assessing and responding to infant mental health needs.' *Community Practitioner, 86,* 9, 33–37.

Craig, J. and Power, C. (2010) 'Service innovation "on the cheap": the development of a health visitor/tier 2 CAMHS partnership.' *Clinical Psychology Forum, 205,* 1, 42–45.

Crane, L., Chester, J.W., Goddard, L., Henry, L.A. and Hill, E. (2016) 'Experiences of autism diagnosis: a survey of over 1000 parents in the United Kingdom.' *Autism, 20,* 2, 153–162.

Creswell, C., Hentges, F., Parkinson, M., Sheffield, P., Willetts, L. and Cooper, P. (2010) 'Feasibility of guided cognitive behaviour therapy (CBT) self-help for childhood anxiety disorders in primary care.' *Mental Health in Family Medicine, 7,* 1, 49.

Davie, M. (2015) 'Doing more for mental health.' *Archives of Disease in Childhood – Education and Practice 101,* 77–81.

Department of Children, Schools and Families (2010) *Early Intervention: Securing Good Outcomes for All Children and Young People.* London: Department of Children, Schools and Families. Contract No. DSCF-00349-2010.

Department of Health (2004) *National Service Framework: Children, Young People and Maternity Services.* London: Department of Health.

Department of Health (2011) *Health Visitor Implementation Plan 2011–15: A Call to Action.* London: Department of Health.

Department of Health (2012) *Getting it Right for Young People and Families Public Health Contribution of Nurses and Midwives: Guidance.* London: Department of Health.

Department of Health and NHS England (2015) *Future in Mind: Promoting, Protecting and Improving Our Children and Young People's Mental Health and Wellbeing.* London: Department of Health and NHS England.

Early Intervention Foundation (2017) *Early Intervention Foundation Guidebook.* Available at: http://guidebook.eif.org.uk.

Finney, J.W., Riley, A.W. and Cataldo, M.F. (1991) 'Psychology in primary health care: effects of brief targeted therapy on children's medical care utilization.' *Journal of Pediatric Psychology, 16,* 4, 447–461.

Galbraith, L. and Hewitt, K.E. (1993) 'Behavioural treatment for sleep disturbance.' *Health Visitor, 66,* 5, 169–171.

Gale, F. (2003) 'When tiers are not enough: the developing role of the primary child mental health worker.' *Child & Adolescent Mental Health in Primary Care, 1,* 1, 5–8.

Gillberg, C. (2010) 'The ESSENCE in child psychiatry: early symptomatic syndromes eliciting neurodevelopment.' *Research in Developmental Disabilities, 31,* 1543–1551.

Gowers, S., Thomas, S. and Deeley, S. (2004) 'Can primary schools contribute effectively to tier I child mental health services?' *Clinical Child Psychology and Psychiatry, 9,* 3, 419–425.

Hewitt, K. (1991) 'Parent education in preventing behaviour problems.' *Health Visitor, 64,* 12, 415–417.

Hinrichs, S., Owens, M., Dunn, V. and Goodyer, I. (2012) 'General practitioner experience and perception of Child and Adolescent Mental Health Services (CAMHS) care pathways: a multimethod research study.' *BMJ Open 2012, 2*:e001573.

Hunt, K. and Craig, J. (2015) 'Delivering psychological services for children and young people with neurodevelopmental difficulties and their families.' *The Child & Family Clinical Psychology Review, 3,* 141–152.

Hutchings, J., Bywater, T., Daley, D., Gardner, F. *et al.* (2007) 'Parenting intervention in Sure Start services for children at risk of developing conduct disorder: pragmatic randomised controlled trial.' *British Medical Journal, 334,* 7595, 678.

Hutchings, J. and Elen Williams, M. (2014) 'Joined-up thinking, joined-up services, exploring coalface challenges for making services work for families with complex needs.' *Journal of Children's Services, 9,* 1, 31–41.

Jacobs, C.O. and Loades, M.E. (2016) 'An investigation into GPs' perceptions of children's mental health problems.' *Child and Adolescent Mental Health, 21,* 2, 90–95.

Kearney, P., Levin, E. and Rosen, G. (2003) *SCIE Report 2: Alcohol, Drug and Mental Health Problems: Working with Families. Social Care Institute for Excellence (SCIE).* London: Social Care Institute for Excellence.

Le Couteur, A. (2003) *National Autism Plan for Children.* London: National Autistic Society, Royal College of Psychiatrists, Royal College of Paediatrics and Child Health, and the All Party Parliamentary Group on Autism.

Leighton, S., Worraker, A. and Nolan, P. (2003) 'School nurses and mental health. [Parts 1 & 2].' *Mental Health Practice, 7,* 4, 14–16.

Lundstrom, S., Reichenberg, A., Melke, J., Rastam, M. *et al.* (2015) 'Autism spectrum disorders and co-existing disorders in a nationwide Swedish twin study.' *Journal of Child Psychology and Psychiatry, 56,* 6, 702–710.

Martinez, R., Reynolds, S. and Howe, A. (2006) 'Factors that influence the detection of psychological problems in adolescents attending general practices.' *British Journal of General Practice, 56,* 529, 594–599.

McDougall, T. (2011) 'Mental health problems in childhood and adolescence.' *Nursing Standard, 26,* 14, 48–56.

Meltzer, H., Bebbington, P., Brugha, T., Farrell, M., Jenkins, R. and Lewis, G. (2003) 'The reluctance to seek treatment for neurotic disorders.' *International Review of Psychiatry, 15,* 1–2, 123–128.

Mercer, S.W. and Reynolds, W.J. (2002) 'Empathy and quality of care.' *British Journal of General Practice, 52:* S9–12.

MindEd (n.d.) Available at: www.e-lfh.org.uk/programmes/minded, accessed on 27 September 2017.

Montamedi, M. (2017) '"Best placed?" School nursing services' role in providing early mental health interventions.' *British Journal of School Nursing, 11,* 510–514.

Morrell, C.J., Slade, P., Warner, R., Paley, G. *et al.* (2009) 'Clinical effectiveness of health visitor training in psychologically informed approaches for depression in postnatal women: pragmatic cluster randomised trial in primary care.' *British Medical Journal, 338,* a3045.

National Institute for Health and Clinical Excellence (2015) *Attachment in Children and Young People Who Are Adopted from Care, in Care or Have a High Risk of Going into Care.* London: National Institute for Health and Clinical Excellence.

Neira-Munoz, E. and Ward, D. (1998) 'Side by side.' *Health Service Journal, 108,* 26–27.

O'Reilly, M., Vostanis, P., Taylor, H., Day, C., Street, C. and Wolpert, M. (2013) 'Service user perspectives of multiagency working: a qualitative study with children with educational and mental health difficulties and their parents.' *Child and Adolescent Mental Health, 18,* 4, 202–209.

Palmer, E., Ketteridge, C., Parr, J.R., Baird, G. and Le Couteur, A. (2011) 'Autism spectrum disorder diagnostic assessments: improvements since publication of the National Autism Plan for Children.' *Archives of Disease in Childhood,* archdischild172825.

Pettitt, B. (2003) *Effective Joint Working Between Child and Adolescent Mental Health Services (CAMHS) and Schools' Mental Health Foundation.* Brief No. 412. Nottingham: DfES Publications.

Pryjmachuk, S., Graham, T., Haddad, M. and Tylee, A. (2012) 'School nurses' perspectives on managing mental health problems in children and young people.' *Journal of Clinical Nursing, 21,* 5–6, 850–859.

Read, N. and Schofield, A. (2010) 'Autism: are mental health services failing children and parents?' *The Journal of Family Health Care, 20,* 4, 120–124.

Roberts, J.H. and Bernard, P.M. (2012) '"Can he have the test for bipolar, doctor? His dad's got it": exploring the potential of general practitioners to work with children and young people presenting in primary care with common mental health problems – a clinical initiative.' *Mental Health in Family Medicine, 9,* 2, 115–123.

Robling, M., Bekkers, M.J., Bell, K., Butler, C.C. *et al.* (2016) 'Effectiveness of a nurse-led intensive home-visitation programme for first-time teenage mothers (Building Blocks): a pragmatic randomised controlled trial.' *The Lancet, 387,* 10014, 146–155.

Robson, J. and Gingell, K. (2012) 'Improving care for families where children and parents have concurrent mental health problems.' *Child and Adolescent Mental Health, 17,* 3, 166–172.

Royal College of Paediatrics and Child Health (2017) *Covering All Bases – Community Child Health: A Paediatric Workforce Guide.* London: Royal College of Paediatrics and Child Health.

Royal College of Paediatrics and Child Health, Royal College of Nursing, and Royal College of General Practitioners (2015) *Facing the Future: Together for Child Health.* London: Royal College of Paediatrics and Child Health.

Sayal, K. and Taylor, E. (2004) 'Detection of child mental health disorders by general practitioners.' *British Journal of General Practice, 54,* 502, 348–352.

Social Care Institute for Excellence (SCIE) (2015, first published 2009) *Think Child, Think Parent, Think Family: A Guide to Parental Mental Health and Child Welfare.* London: SCIE.

Taylor, H. (2017) 'The Wirral Primary Mental Health Team Transformation.' Paper presented at the British Psychological Society Children and Young People Faculty Conference, September 2017.

Terry, J. (2006) 'Emotional health work with schools by primary mental health workers in Wales.' *Primary Care Mental Health, 4,* 4, 273–283.

Vallerand, I.A., Kalenchuk, A.L. and McLennan, J.D. (2014) 'Behavioural treatment recommendations in clinical practice guidelines for attention-deficit/hyperactivity disorder: a scoping review.' *Child and Adolescent Mental Health, 19,* 4, 251–258.

Van Steensel, F.J.A., Bogels, S.M. and Perrin, S. (2011) 'Anxiety disorders in children and adolescents with autistic spectrum disorders: a meta-analysis.' *Clinical Child and Family Psychology Review, 14,* 3, 302–317.

Vostanis, P., Humphrey, N., Fitzgerald, N., Deighton, J. and Wolpert, M. (2013) 'How do schools promote emotional well-being among their pupils? Findings from a national scoping survey of mental health provision in English schools.' *Child and Adolescent Mental Health, 18,* 3, 151–157.

Whitley, J., Smith, J.D. and Vaillancourt, T. (2013) 'Promoting mental health literacy among educators: critical in school-based prevention and intervention.' *Canadian Journal of School Psychology, 28,* 1, 56–70.

Whitworth, D. and Ball, C. (2004) 'The impact of primary mental health workers on referrals to CAMHS.' *Child and Adolescent Mental Health, 9,* 4, 177–179.

Wiener, A. and Rodwell, H. (2006) 'Evaluation of a CAMHS in primary care service for general practice.' *Child and Adolescent Mental Health, 11,* 3, 150–155.

Zwaanswijk, M., Verhaak, P.F.M., Bensing, J.M., Van der Ende, J. and Verhulst, F.C. (2003) 'Help-seeking for emotional and behavioural problems in children and adolescents: a review of recent literature.' *European Child and Adolescent Psychiatry, 12,* 153–161.

Chapter 5

Adi, Y., Killoran, A., Janmohamed, K. and Stewart-Brown, S. (2007a) *Systematic Review of the Effectiveness of Interventions to Promotion Mental Well-Being in Primary Schools: Universal Approaches which Do Not Focus on Violence or Bullying.* London: National Institute for Health and Clinical Excellence.

Adi, Y., Schrader McMillan, A., Killoran, A. and Stewart-Brown, S. (2007b) *Systematic Review of the Effectiveness of Interventions to Promote Mental Well-Being in Primary Schools: Universal Approaches which Focus on Prevention of Violence and Bullying.* London: National Institute for Health and Clinical Excellence.

Anna Freud Centre (n.d.) CASCADE model. Available at: www.annafreud.org.

Augustine, J.M. and Crosnoe, R. (2010) 'Mothers' depression and educational attainment and their children's academic trajectories.' *Journal of Health and Social Behavior, 51,* 3, 274–290.

Banerjee, R., Weare, K. and Farr, W. (2014) 'Working with "Social and Emotional Aspects of Learning (SEAL)": associations with school ethos, pupil social experiences, attendance, and attainment.' *British Educational Research Journal, 40,* 718–742.

Barrett, P. and Turner, C. (2001) 'Prevention of anxiety symptoms in primary school children: preliminary results from a universal school-based trial.' *British Journal of Clinical Psychology, 40,* 4, 399–410.

Barry, M.M., Clarke, A.M. and Dowling, K. (2017) 'Promoting social and emotional well-being in schools.' *Health Education, 117,* 5, 434–451.

Bowes, L., Joinson, C., Wolke, D. and Glyn, L. (2015) 'Peer victimisation during adolescence and its impact on depression in early adulthood: prospective cohort study in the United Kingdom.' *British Medical Journal, 350,* h2469.

Bronfenbrenner, U. and Ceci, S.J. (1994) 'Nature-nurture reconceptualised: a bioecological model.' *Psychological Review, 101,* 4, 568–586.

Chafouleas, S.M., Johnson, A.H., Overstreet, S. and Santos, N.M. (2016) 'Toward a blueprint for trauma-informed service delivery in schools.' *School Mental Health, 8,* 1, 144–162.

Challen, A.R., Machin, S.J. and Gillham, J.E. (2014) 'The UK Resilience Programme: a school-based universal nonrandomized pragmatic controlled trial.' *Journal of Consulting and Clinical Psychology, 82,* 1, 75–89.

Clarke, A.M., Morreale, S., Field, C.A., Hussein, Y. and Barry, M.M. (2015) *What Works in Enhancing Social and Emotional Skills Development During Childhood and Adolescence? A Review of the Evidence on the Effectiveness of School-Based and Out-of-School Programmes in the UK.* A report produced by the World Health Organization Collaborating Centre for Health Promotion Research, National University of Ireland Galway.

Collie, R.J., Shapka, J.D. and Perry, N.E. (2012) 'School climate and social–emotional learning: predicting teacher stress, job satisfaction, and teaching efficacy.' *Journal of Educational Psychology, 104,* 4, 1189.

Cooper, M., Evans, Y. and Pybis, J. (2016) 'Interagency collaboration in children and young people's mental health: a systematic review of outcomes, facilitating factors and inhibiting factors.' *Child: Care, Health and Development, 42,* 3, 325–342.

Cooper, P. (2011) 'Educational and Psychological Interventions for Promoting Social Emotional Competence in School Students.' In R.H Shute, P.T. Slee, R. Murray-Harvey and K.L. Dix (eds) *Mental Health and Wellbeing: Educational Perspectives.* Adelaide: Shannon Research Press.

Corcoran, R.P., Cheung, A., Kim, E. and Xie, C. (2017) 'Effective universal school-based social and emotional learning programs for improving academic achievement: a systematic review and meta-analysis of 50 years of research.' *Educational Research Review.* Advance online publication. https://doi.org/10.1016/j.edurev.2017.12.001.

Day, C. and Sammons, P. (2014) *Successful School Leadership.* Reading: Education Development Trust.

Day, L., Blades, R., Spence, C. and Ronicle, J. (2017) *Mental Health Services and Schools Link Pilots: Evaluation Report.* London: Department for Education.

Department for Education (2014) *Preventing and Tackling Bullying: Advice for Headteachers, Staff and Governing Bodies.* London: Crown Copyright.

Department for Education (2016) *Mental Health and Behaviour in Schools: Departmental Advice for School Staff.* London: Crown Copyright.

Department for Education (2017) *Supporting Mental Health in Schools and Colleges.* London: Crown Copyright.

Department for Education and Skills (2005) *Excellence and Enjoyment: Social and Emotional Aspects of Learning.* Nottingham: DfES Publications.

Department for Education and Skills (2007) *Social and Emotional Aspects of Learning for Secondary Schools (SEAL).* Nottingham: DfES Publications.

Dorado, J.S., Martinez, M., McArthur, L.E. and Leibovitz, T. (2016) 'Healthy Environments and Response to Trauma in Schools (HEARTS): a whole-school, multi-level, prevention and intervention program for creating trauma-informed, safe and supportive schools.' *School Mental Health, 8,* 1, 163–176.

Douglas, H. and McGinty, M. (2001) 'The Solihull Approach: changes in health visiting practice.' *Community Practitioner, 74,* 6, 222–224.

Dowling, E., and Osborne, E. (eds) (2003) *The Family and the School: A Joint Systems Approach to Problems with Children.* London: Karnac Books.

Durlak, J.A., Weissberg, R.P., Dymnicki, A.B., Taylor, R.D. and Schellinger, K.B. (2011) 'The impact of enhancing students' social and emotional learning: a meta-analysis of school-based universal interventions.' *Child Development, 82,* 1, 405–432.

Elfrink, T.R., Goldberg, J.M., Schreurs, K.M.G., Bohlmeijer, E.T. and Clarke, A.M. (2017) 'Positive educative programme: a whole school approach to supporting children's well-being and creating a positive school climate: a pilot study.' *Health Education, 117,* 2, 215–230.

Flannery-Schroeder, E. and Kendall, P.C. (1996) *Cognitive-Behavioral Therapy for Anxious Children: Therapist Manual for Group Treatment.* Ardmore, PA: Workbook Publishing.

Ford, T., Parker, C., Salim, J., Goodman, R., Logan, S. and Henley, W. (2017) 'The relationship between exclusion from school and mental health: a secondary analysis of the British Child and Adolescent Mental Health Surveys 2004 and 2007.' *Psychological Medicine, 48,* 4, 629–641.

Franklin, C.G.S., Kim, J.S., Ryan, T.N., Kelly, M.S. and Montgomery, K.L. (2012) 'Teacher involvement in school mental health interventions: a systematic review.' *Children and Youth Services Review, 34,* 5, 973–982.

Fry, D., Fang, X., Elliott, S., Casey, T. *et al.* (2018) 'The relationships between violence in childhood and educational outcomes: a global systematic review and meta-analysis.' *Child Abuse and Neglect, 75,* 6–28.

Gondek, D. and Lereya, T. (2017) 'What are the challenges involved in the prevention of depression in schools?' *Contemporary School Psychology, 145,* 1, 63.

Hassett, A. (2015) 'Evaluation of the Solihull Approach in Kent: Drawing Conclusions from the Data.' Unpublished report.

Hetrick, S.E., Cox, G.R., Witt, K.G., Bir, J.J. and Merry, S.N. (2016) *Cognitive Behavioural Therapy (CBT), Third-Wave CBT and Interpersonal Therapy (IPT) Based Interventions for Preventing Depression in Children and Adolescents.* London: The Cochrane Library.

Humphrey, N., Lendrum, A. and Wigelsworth, M. (2010) *Secondary Social and Emotional Aspects of Learning (SEAL): National Evaluation.* Nottingham: Department for Education.

Humphrey, N., Lendrum, A. and Wigelsworth, M. (2013) 'Making the most out of school-based prevention: lessons from the social and emotional aspects of learning (SEAL) programme.' *Emotional and Behavioural Difficulties, 18,* 3, 248–260.

Johnston, D., Propper, C., Pudney, S. and Shields, M. (2014) 'Child mental health and educational attainment: multiple observers and the measurement error problem.' *Journal of Applied Econometrics, 29,* 6, 880–900.

Langford, R., Bonell, C.P., Jones, H.E., Pouliou, T. *et al.* (2014) 'The WHO Health Promoting School framework for improving the health and well-being of students and their academic achievement.' *Cochrane Database of Systematic Reviews, 8,* 6, 650.

Langford, R., Bonell, C., Komro, K., Murphy, S. *et al.* (2017) 'The health promoting schools framework: known unknowns and an agenda for future research.' *Health Education and Behavior, 44,* 3, 463–475.

Lereya, S.T., Copeland, W.E., Costello, E.J. and Wolke, D. (2015) 'Adult mental health consequences of peer bullying and maltreatment in childhood: two cohorts in two countries.' *The Lancet Psychiatry 2,* 6, 524–531.

Martin, J., McBride, T., Brims, L., Doubell, L., Pote, I. and Clarke, A. (2018) *Evaluating Early Intervention Programmes: Six Common Pitfalls, and How to Avoid Them.* London: Early Intervention Foundation.

Masten, A. (2001) 'Ordinary magic: resilience processes in development.' *American Psychologist, 56,* 3, 227–238.

Mattison, V. and Fredman, G. (2017) 'Principles and Practices for Getting Started with Consultation in Mental Health.' In G. Fredman, A. Papadapoulou and E. Worwood (eds) *Collaborative Consultation in Mental Health: Guidelines for the New Consultant.* London and New York: Routledge.

Menzies Lyth, I. (1960) 'The functioning of social systems as a defence against anxiety: a report on a study of the nursing hospital of a general hospital.' In *Containing Anxiety in Institutions: Selected Essays.* London: Free Association Books, 1988.

Moore, G.F., Audrey, S., Barker, M., Bond, L. *et al.* (2015) 'Process evaluation of complex interventions: Medical Research Council guidance.' *British Medical Journal, 350,* h1258.

Morrison, B. (2002) *Bullying and Victimisation in Schools: A Restorative Justice Approach.* Canberra: Australian Institute of Criminology.

National Society for the Prevention of Cruelty to Children (2018) *Child Protection in the UK.* Available at: www.nspcc.org.uk.

Neave, C. and Patel, W. (2014) 'The Clinical Psychology in Schools (CLiPS) Service: Report and evaluation of work undertaken, September 2013–July 2014.' Unpublished report.

Neil, A.L. and Christensen, H. (2009) 'Efficacy and effectiveness of school-based prevention and early intervention programs for anxiety.' *Clinical Psychology Review, 29*, 208–215.

Newman, T. (2002) *Promoting Resilience: A Review of Effective Strategies for Child Care Services.* Exeter: Centre for Evidence-Based Social Services, University of Exeter.

Oberle, E., Domitrovich, C.E., Meyers, D.C. and Weissberg, R.P. (2016) 'Establishing systemic social and emotional learning approaches in schools: a framework for schoolwide implementation.' *Cambridge Journal of Education, 46*, 3, 277–297.

Olweus, D. (1993) *Bullying at School: What We Know and What We Can Do.* Malden, MA: Blackwell Publishing.

Parsons, S. (2011) 'Long-term impact of childhood bereavement.' Preliminary analysis of the 1970 British Cohort Study (BCS70). Child Wellbeing Research Centre Working Paper.

Patalay, P., Giese, L., Stanković, M., Curtin, C., Moltrecht, B. and Gondek, D. (2016) 'Mental health provision in schools: priority, facilitators and barriers in 10 European countries.' *Child and Adolescent Mental Health, 21*, 3, 139–147.

Paulus, F.W., Ohmann, S. and Popow, C. (2016) 'Practitioner review: school-based interventions in child mental health.' *Journal of Child Psychology and Psychiatry, 57*, 12, 1337–1359.

Phifer, L.W. and Hull, R. (2016) 'Helping sudents heal: observations of trauma-informed practices in the schools.' *School Mental Health, 8*, 1, 201–205.

Picciotto, A. (2014) 'Islington CAMHS in Primary and Secondary Schools: Annual Report, September 2013–July 2014.' Unpublished report.

Public Health England (2014) *The Link Between Pupil Health and Wellbeing and Attainment.* London: Crown Copyright.

Public Health England (2015) *Promoting Children and Young People's Emotional Health and Wellbeing: A Whole School and College Approach.* London: Crown Copyright.

Public Health England (2016) *Mental Health of Children in England.* London: Crown Copyright.

Reid, J., Eddy, J., Fetrow, R. and Stoolmiller, M. (2000) 'Description and immediate impacts of a preventive intervention for conduct problems.' *American Journal of Community Psychology, 27*, 4, 483–517.

Rutter, M. (1987) 'Psychosocial resilience and protective mechanisms.' *American Journal of Orthopsychiatry, 57*, 3, 316.

Sharpe, H., Ford, T., Lereya, S.T., Owen, C., Viner, R.M. and Wolpert, M. (2016) 'Survey of schools' work with child and adolescent mental health across England: a system in need of support.' *Child and Adolescent Mental Health, 21*, 3, 148–153.

Snyder, S. (2013) 'The simple, the complicated, and the complex: educational reform through the lens of complexity theory.' OECD Education Working Papers, 96.

Stallard, P. (2013) 'School-based interventions for depression and anxiety in children and adolescents.' *Evidence-Based Mental Health, 16*, 3, 60–61.

Stallard, P., Simpson, N., Anderson, S., Carter, T., Osborn, C. and Bush, S. (2005) An evaluation of the FRIENDS programme: a cognitive behaviour therapy intervention to promote emotional resilience.' *Archives of Disease in Childhood, 90*, 10, 1016–1019.

Stallard, P., Skryabina, E., Taylor, G., Phillips, R. *et al.* (2014) 'Classroom-based cognitive behaviour therapy (FRIENDS): a cluster randomised controlled trial to Prevent Anxiety in Children through Education in Schools (PACES).' *The Lancet Psychiatry,* *1,* 3, 185–192.

Straw, S., Tattersall, J. and Sims, D. (2015) *Teacher Voice Omnibus Research Report.* London: National Foundation for Educational Research.

Substance Abuse and Mental Health Services Administration (2014) *SAMHSA's Concept of Trauma and Guidance for a Trauma-Informed Approach.* *HHS Publication No.* *(SMA)* 14–4884. Rockville, MD: Substance Abuse and Mental Health Services Administration.

Taylor, R.D., Oberle, E., Durlak, J.A. and Weissberg, R.P. (2017) 'Promoting positive youth development through school-based social and emotional learning interventions: a meta-analysis of follow-up effects.' *Child Development, 88,* 4, 1156–1171.

The Guardian Newspaper (2016) 'Nearly half of England's teachers plan to leave in next five years.' 22 March 2016.

Toda, Y. (2011) 'Bullying (ijime) and its prevention in Japan: a relationships focus.' *Mental Health and Wellbeing: Educational Perspectives,* 179–189.

Ttofi, M.M. and Farrington, D.P. (2011) 'Effectiveness of school-based programs to reduce bullying: a systematic and meta-analytic review.' *Journal of Experimental Criminology,* *7,* 1, 27–56.

Verschueren, K. and Koomen, H.M.Y. (2012) Teacher-child relationships from an attachment perspective.' *Attachment and Human Development, 14,* 3, 205–211.

Weare, K. (2015) *What Works in Promoting Social and Emotional Well-Being and Responding to Mental Health Problems in Schools?* London: National Children's Bureau.

Weare, K. and Nind, M. (2011) 'Mental health promotion and problem prevention in schools: what does the evidence say?' *Health Promotion International, 26,* S1, i29–69.

Werner-Seidler, A., Perry, Y., Calear, A.L., Newby, J.M. and Christensen, H. (2017) 'School-based depression and anxiety prevention programs for young people: a systematic review and meta-analysis.' *Clinical Psychology Review, 51,* 30–47.

Wolpert, M., Humphrey, N., Belsky, J. and Deighton, J. (2013) 'Embedding mental health support in schools: learning from the Targeted Mental Health in Schools (TaMHS) national evaluation.' *Emotional and Behavioural Difficulties, 18,* 3, 270–283.

World Health Organization (2017) *WHO Recommendations on Adolescent Health: Guidelines Approved by the WHO Guidelines Review Committee.* (WHO/MCA/17.08). Geneva: World Health Organization.

Young, J. F., Mufson, L. and Gallop, R. (2010) 'Preventing depression: A randomized trial of interpersonal psychotherapy-adolescent skills training.' *Depression and Anxiety, 27,* 5, 426–433.

Young, J.F., Benas, J.S., Schueler, C.M., Gallop, R., Gillham, J.E. and Mufson, L. (2016) 'A randomized depression prevention trial comparing interpersonal psychotherapy–adolescent skills training to group counseling in schools.' *Prevention Science, 17,* 3, 314–324.

Chapter 6

Adkins, J.W., Storch, E.A., Lewin, A.B., Willliams, L. *et al.* (2006) 'Home-based behavioural health intervention: use of a tele-health model to address poor adherence to Type 1 diabetes medical regimens.' *Telemedicine and e-Health 12,* 3, 370–372.

Archibald, S., Maidment, M. and Casey, S. (2017, June) 'Supporting young people living with chronic health conditions using the tree of life: Outcomes and feedback.' Poster presented at the Paediatric Psychology Network Annual Study Day, Oxford.

Bøe, T., Øverland, S., Lundervold, A.J. and Hysing, M. (2012) 'Socioeconomic status and children's mental health: results from the Bergen Child Study.' *Social Psychiatry and Psychiatric Epidemiology, 47,* 10, 1557–1566.

Braga, L., Da Paz, A.C. and Ylvisaker, M. (2010) 'Direct clinician-delivered versus indirect family-supported rehabilitation of children with traumatic brain injury: a randomized controlled trial.' *Brain Injury, 19,* 10, 819–831.

Butler, R.W., Copeland, D.R., Fairclough, D.L., Mulhern, R.K. *et al.* (2008) 'A multicenter, randomized clinical trial of a cognitive remediation program for childhood survivors of a pediatric malignancy.' *Journal of Consulting and Clinical Psychology, 76,* 3, 367–378.

Center for Pediatric Traumatic Stress (2005) *Medical Events and Traumatic Stress in Children and Families.* Available at: www.nctsn.org/what-is-child-trauma/trauma-types/medical-trauma/effects, accessed on 29 April 2018.

Cystic Fibrosis Trust (2011) *Standards for the Clinical Care of Children and Adults with Cystic Fibrosis in the UK.* London: Cystic Fibrosis Trust.

Department of Health (2010) *Getting it Right for Children and Young People: Overcoming Cultural Barriers in the NHS so as to Meet their Needs.* London: Department of Health.

Department of Health (2015) *Future in Mind: Promoting, Protecting and Improving our Children and Young People's Mental Health and Wellbeing.* London: Department of Health.

Derbyshire Healthcare NHS Foundation Trust (2018) *CAMHS RISE – Rapid Intervention, Support and Empowerment.* Available at: www.derbyshirehealthcareft.nhs.uk/services/childrens-services/camhs/camhs-rise, accessed on 7 February 2018.

Donnan, J., Wright, J., McCluskey, J., Smith, A. and McKenzie, K. (2016) 'The hospital passport coping kit: an evaluation of a novel resource to promote healthcare staff's use of psychological strategies for managing procedural distress in children.' *Division of Clinical Psychology – Scotland Review, Issue 14.*

Douglas, J. and Benson, S. (2014) 'Psychological consultation in a paediatric setting: a qualitative analysis of staff experiences of a psychosocial forum.' *Clinical Child Psychology and Psychiatry, 20,* 3, 1–14.

Doyle, C., Lennox, L. and Bell, D. (2013) 'A systematic review of evidence on the links between patient experience and clinical safety and effectiveness.' *British Medical Journal Open, 3,* e001570.

Early Intervention Foundation (2015) *The Immediate Fiscal Cost of Late Intervention for Children and Young People: A First Estimate for England and Wales.* London: Early Intervention Foundation.

Evans, T. (2017) 'Managing mental health in paediatric acute care.' Paper presented at the Perinatal Mental Health Society, Leicester.

Faulconbridge, J., Gravestock, F., Laffan, A., Law, D. *et al.* (2016) 'What good could look like in integrated services for children, young people and their families: preliminary guidance and examples of practice.' *Child and Family Clinical Psychology Review, 4.*

Glasgow Children's Hospital Charity (2016) *HospiChill.* Available at: www.hospichill.net/index.html, accessed on 7 February 2018.

Glazebrook, C., Hollis, C., Heussler, H., Goodman, R. and Coates, L. (2003) 'Detecting emotional and behavioural problems in paediatric clinics.' *Child: Care, Health and Development, 29,* 2, 141–149.

Hotopf, M., Mayou, R., Wadsworth, M. and Wessely, S. (1999) 'Childhood risk factors for adults with medically unexplained symptoms: results from a national birth cohort study.' *The American Journal of Psychiatry, 156,* 11, 1796–1800.

Janicke, D.M. and Hommel, K.A. (2016) 'Introduction to special section on the cost-effectiveness and economic impact of pediatric psychology interventions.' *Journal of Pediatric Psychology, 41,* 8, 831–834.

Kazak, A.E. (1997) 'A contextual family/systems approach to pediatric psychology: Introduction to the special issue.' *Journal of Pediatric Psychology, 22,* 2, 141–148.

Kazak, A.E. (2006) 'Pediatric Psychosocial Preventative Health Model (PPPHM): research, practice and collaboration in pediatric systems medicine.' *Families Systems & Health, 24,* 4, 381–395.

Kazak, A.E., Rourke, M.T. and Navsaria, N. (2009) 'Families and Other Systems in Pediatric Psychology.' In M.C. Roberts and R.G. Steele (eds) *Handbook of Pediatric Psychology.* New York, NY: Guilford Press.

Kazak, A.E., Schneider, S. Didonato, S. and Pail, A.L.H. (2015) 'Family psychosocial risk screening guided by the Pediatric Psychosocial Preventative Health Model (PPPHM) using the Psychosocial Assessment Tool (PAT).' *Acta Oncologica, 54,* 5, 574–580.

Kush, S. and Campo, J. (eds) (1998) *Handbook of Pediatric Psychology and Psychiatry.* Needham Heights, MA: Allyn & Bacon.

McCusker, C.G., Doherty, N.N., Molloy, B., Casey, F. *et al.* (2007) 'Determinants of neuro-psychological and behavioural outcomes in early childhood survivors of congenital heart disease.' *Archives of Disease in Childhood, 92,* 137–141.

Meltzer, H., Gatward, R., Goodman, R. and Ford, T. (2000) 'Mental health of children and adolescents in Great Britain.' *International Review of Psychiatry, 15,* 1–2.

National Institute for Health and Care Excellence (2014) *Cancer Services for Children and Young People.* London: National Institute for Health and Care Excellence.

Ncube, N. (2006) 'The tree of life project.' *International Journal of Narrative Therapy & Community Work, 1,* 3.

NHS England (2013) *Best Practice for Commissioning Diabetes Services: An Integrated Care Framework.* Available at: www.diabetes-resources-production.s3-eu-west-1. amazonaws.com/diabetes-storage/migration/pdf/best-practice-commissioning-diabetes-services-integrated-care-framework-0313.pdf, accessed on 7 February 2018.

NHS England (2014) *Improving Patient Experience of Children and Young People.* Available at: www.patientexperiencenetwork.org/wp-content/uploads/2013/11/PEN-Improving-PE-for-Children-Young-People-Report-FINAL-Electronic-file.pdf, accessed on 7 February 2018.

Paediatric Intensive Care Society (2015) *Quality Standards for the Care of Critically Ill Children.* London: Paediatric Intensive Care Society.

Palermo, T. (2014) 'Evidence-based interventions in pediatric psychology: progress over the decades.' *Journal of Pediatric Psychology, 39,* 8, 753–762.

Ramchandani, P.G., Stein, A., Hotopf, M. and Wiles, N.J. (2006) 'Early parental and child predictors of recurrent abdominal pain at school age: results of a large population-based study.' *Journal of the American Academy of Child & Adolescent Psychiatry, 45,* 6, 729–736.

The King's Fund (2016) *Bringing Together Physical and Mental Health: A New Frontier for Integrated Care.* London: Kings Fund.

Velleman, S., Stallard, P. and Richardson, T. (2010) 'A review and meta-analysis of computerised cognitive behaviour therapy for the treatment of pain in children and adolescents.' *Child: Care, Health and Development, 36,* 4, 465–472.

Chapter 7

Bloom, S.L. (2005) 'The sanctuary model of organizational change for children's residential treatment.' *Therapeutic Community: The International Journal for Therapeutic and Supportive Organizations, 26,* 1, 65–81

Bolger, L. and Turner, K. (2013) *Psychologically Informed Planned Environments: Model Description Document V1. 0.* London: National Offender Management Service & NHS England.

Bostock, L., Forrester, D., Patrizo, L., Godfrey, A., Bird, H. and Tinarwo, M. (2017) *Children's Social Care Innovation Programme Evaluation Report 45.* London: Department for Education.

Bronfenbrenner, U. (1977) 'Toward an experimental ecology of human development.' *American Psychologist, 32,* 513–531.

Bunn, A. (2013) *Signs of Safety in England.* An NSPCC commissioned report on the Signs of Safety model in child protection. London: National Society for the Prevention of Cruelty to Children.

Butler, S., Baruch, G., Hickey, N. and Fonagy, P. (2011) 'A randomized controlled trial of multisystemic therapy and a statutory therapeutic intervention for young offenders.' *Journal of the American Academy of Child & Adolescent Psychiatry, 50,* 12, 1220–1235.

Chitsabesan, P., Kroll, L., Bailey, S.U.E., Kenning, C., Sneider, S. *et al.* (2006) 'Mental health needs of young offenders in custody and in the community.' *The British Journal of Psychiatry, 188,* 6, 534–540.

Christofides, S. (2016) 'Evidence-Oriented Practice.' In L. Smith (ed) *Clinical Practice at the Edge of Care.* London: Palgrave Macmillan.

Early Intervention Foundation (2017) *Early Intervention Foundation Guidebook.* Available at: http://guidebook.eif.org.uk.

Feinberg, M.E. (2008) 'Establishing family foundations: intervention effects on coparenting, parent/infant well-being and parent-child relations.' *Journal of Family Psychology, 22,* 1–19.

Feinberg, M.E., Jones, D.E., Roettger, M.E., Hostettler, M. and Solmeyer, A. (2014) 'Long-term follow-up of a randomized trial of family foundations: effects on children's emotional, behavioral, and school adjustment.' *Journal of Family Psychology, 28,* 821–831.

Ford, T., Vostanis, P., Meltzer, H. and Goodman, R. (2007) 'Psychiatric disorder among British children looked after by local authorities: comparison with children living in private households.' *The British Journal of Psychiatry, 190,* 4, 319–325.

Haigh, R., Harrison, T., Johnson, R., Paget, S. and Williams, S. (2012) 'Psychologically informed environments and the "Enabling Environments" initiative.' *Housing, Care and Support, 15,* 1, 34–42

Haines, A., Goldson, B., Haycox, A., Houten, R. *et al.* (2012) *Evaluation of the Youth Justice Liaison and Diversion (YJLD): Pilot Scheme Final Report.* Liverpool: University of Liverpool.

Harold, G., Hampden-Thompson, G., Rodic, M. and Sellers, R. (2017) *An Evaluation of the Adopt Parenting Programme: Research Report.* Andrew and Virginia Rudd Centre for Adoption Research and Practice. School of Psychology/School of Education and Social Work, University of Sussex.

Harvey, J., Rogers, A. and Law, H. (eds) (2015) *Young People in Forensic Mental Health Settings: Psychological Thinking and Practice.* London: Springer.

Henggeler, S.W., Schoenwald, S.K., Borduin, C.M., Rowland, M.D. and Cunningham, P.B. (2009) *Multisystemic Therapy for Antisocial Behavior in Children and Adolescents.* New York, NY: Guilford Press.

Jackson, S. and Martin, P.Y. (1998) 'Surviving the care system: education and resilience.' *Journal of Adolescence, 21,* 569–583.

Johnson, R. and Haigh, R. (2011) 'Social psychiatry and social policy for the 21st century: new concepts for new needs – the "Enabling Environments" initiative.' *Mental Health and Social Inclusion, 15,* 1, 17–23.

Jolly, W., Froom, J. and Rosen, M.G. (1980). 'The genogram.' *The Journal of family practice 10,* 2, 251–255.

Kan, M. and Feinberg, M. (2014) 'Can a family-focused, transition-to-parenthood program prevent parent and partner aggression among couples with young children?' *Violence and Victims, 29,* 6, 967–980.

Kan, M. and Feinberg, M. (2015) 'Impacts of a coparenting-focused intervention on links between pre-birth intimate partner violence and observed parenting.' *Journal of Family Violence, 30,* 3, 363–372.

Knibbs, S., Mollidor, C. and Bierman, R. (2016) *KEEP Standard Evaluation Research Report, Children's Social Care Innovation Programme Evaluation Report 10.* Ipsos Mori.

McCracken, K., Priest, S., FitzSimons, A., Bracewell, K. *et al.* (2017) *Evaluation of Pause.* Department for Education (DFE) Opcit Research, University of Central Lancaster.

Minnis, H. and Devine, C. (2001) 'The effect of foster carer training on the emotional and behavioural functioning of looked-after children.' *Adoption & Fostering, 25,* 1, 44–54.

Newton, R., Litrownik, A. and Landsverk, J. (2000) 'Children and youth in foster care: disentangling the relationship between problem behaviours and number of placements.' *Child Abuse and Neglect, 24,* 10, 1363–1374.

NICE (2013) *Antisocial Behaviour and Conduct Disorders in Children and Young People: The NICE Guideline on Recognition, Intervention and Management (NICE Mental Health Guidelines).* National Collaborating Centre. RCPsych Publications.

Roberts, R., Glynn, G. and Waterman, C. (2016) '"We know it works but does it last?" The implementation of the KEEP foster and kinship carer training programme in England.' *Adoption & Fostering, 40,* 3, 247–263.

Rogers, A. and Budd, M. (2015) 'Developing Safe and Strong Foundations; The DART Framework.' In A. Rogers, J. Harvey and H. Law (eds) *Young People in Forensic Mental Health Settings: Psychological Thinking and Practice.* London: Palgrave.

Ryan, T. and Mitchell, P. (2011) 'A collaborative approach to meeting the needs of adolescent offenders with complex needs in custodial settings: an 18-month cohort study.' *Journal of Forensic Psychiatry and Psychology, 22,* 3, 437–454.

Saxe, G.N., Ellis, B.H. and Kaplow, J.B. (2007) *Collaborative Treatment of Traumatized Children and Teens: The Trauma Systems Therapy Approach.* New York, NY: Guilford Press.

Schofield, G., Ward, E., Biggart, L., Scaife, V. *et al.* (2012) *Looked After Children and Offending: Reducing Risk and Promoting Resilience.* Norwich: The Centre for Research on the Child and Family, University of East Anglia.

Sexton, T.L. and Alexander, J.F. (2003) 'Functional Family Therapy: A Mature Clinical Model for Working with At-Risk Adolescents and their Families'. In T.L. Sexton, G.R. Weeks and M.S. Robbins (eds) *Handbook of Family Therapy: The Science and Practice of Working with Families and Couples.* New York, NY: Brunner-Routledge.

Sexton, T. and Turner, C.W. (2010) 'The effectiveness of functional family therapy for youth with behavioral problems in a community practice setting.' *Journal of Family Psychology, 24,* 3, 339.

Smith, L. (ed.) (2016) *Clinical Practice at the Edge of Care.* London: Palgrave Macmillan.

Swenson, C.C., Schaeffer, C.M., Henggeler, S.W., Faldowski, R. and Mayhew, A. (2010) 'Multisystemic therapy for child abuse and neglect: a randomized effectiveness trial.' *Journal of Family Psychology, 24,* 497–507.

Taylor J., Shostak, L., Rogers, A. and Mitchell, P. (2018, forthcoming). *Rethinking mental health provision in the secure estate for Children and Young People: An introduction to a Framework for Integrated Care (SECURE STAIRS).*

Viner, R.M. and Taylor, B. (2005) 'Adult health and social outcomes of children who have been in public care: population-based study.' *Pediatrics, 115,* 4, 894–899.

Webster-Stratton, C., Jamila Reid, M. and Stoolmiller, M. (2008) 'Preventing conduct problems and improving school readiness: evaluation of the incredible years teacher and child training programs in high risk schools.' *Journal of Child Psychology and Psychiatry, 49,* 5, 471–488.

Chapter 8

Afuape, T. and Hughes, G. (eds) (2016) *Towards Emotional Well-Being Through Liberation Practices: A Dialogical Approach.* London: Routledge.

Amsden, J. and VanWynsberghe, R. (2005) 'Community mapping as a research tool with youth.' *Action Research, 3,* 4, 357–381.

Atkinson, M. (2012) 'Inequalities in health outcomes and how they might be addressed.' Children and Young People's Health Forum. The Office of the Children's Commissioner.

Barn, R. and Harman, V. (2005) 'A contested identity: an exploration of the competing social and political discourse concerning the identification and positioning of young people of inter-racial parentage.' *British Journal of Social Work, 36,* 8, 1309–1324.

Bevington, D., Fuggle, P., Cracknell, L. and Fonagy, P. (2017) *Adaptive Mentalization-Based Integrative Treatment: A Guide for Teams to Develop Systems of Care.* Oxford: Oxford University Press.

Bilson, A. and Martin, K.E. (2016) 'Referrals and child protection in England: one in five children referred to children's services and one in nineteen investigated before the age of five.' *British Journal of Social Work, 47,* 3, 793–811.

Bostock, J. and Freeman, J. (2003) 'No limits: doing participatory action research with young people in Northumberland.' *Journal of Community & Applied Social Psychology, 13,* 6, 464–474.

Bronfenbrenner, U. (1979) *The Ecology of Human Development.* Cambridge. MA: Harvard University Press.

Bywaters, P., Brady, G., Sparks, T. and Bos, E. (2016) 'Child welfare inequalities: new evidence, further questions.' *Child & Family Social Work, 21,* 3, 369–380.

Casale, L., Zlotowitz, S. and Moloney, O. (2015) 'Working with whole communities: delivering community psychology approaches with children, young people and families.' *The Child and Family Psychological Review, 3,* 84–94.

Christensen, L., Murphy, M., Allister, J., Atkinson, M. *et al.* (2012) *Improving Children and Young People's Mental Health Outcomes.* Report of the Children and Young People's Health Outcomes Forum, Mental Health Sub-Group. London: Department of Health.

Costello, E.J., Angold, A., Burns, B.J., Stangl, D.K. *et al.* (1996) 'The Great Smoky Mountains Study of Youth: goals, design, methods, and the prevalence of DSM-III-R disorders.' *Archives of General Psychiatry, 53,* 12, 1129–1136.

Courtney, M.E., Piliavin, I., Grogan-Kaylor, A. and Nesmith, A. (2001) 'Foster youth transitions to adulthood: a longitudinal view of youth leaving care.' *Child Welfare, 80,* 6, 685.

Department of Health, Department for Children, Schools and Families, Ministry of Justice, Home Office (2009) *Healthy Children, Safer Communities: A Strategy to Promote the Health and Well-Being of Children and Young People in Contact with the Youth Justice System.* London: HM Government.

Dixon, J. and Stein, M. (2005) *Leaving Care: Throughcare and Aftercare in Scotland.* London: Jessica Kingsley Publishers.

Durcan, G., Zlotowitz, S. and Stubbs, J. (2017) *Meeting Us Where We Are At: Learning from INTEGRATE's Work with Excluded Young People.* London: Centre for Mental Health.

Eamon, M. K. (2001) 'The effects of poverty on children's socioemotional development: an ecological systems analysis.' *Social Work, 46,* 3, 256–266.

Foot, J. (2012) *What Makes Us Healthy. The Asset Approach in Practice: Evidence, Action, Evaluation.* London: Asset Based Consulting.

Ford, T., Vostanis, P., Meltzer, H. and Goodman, R. (2007) 'Psychiatric disorder among British children looked after by local authorities: comparison with children living in private households.' *The British Journal of Psychiatry, 190,* 4, 319–325.

Freire, P. (1993) *Pedagogy of the Oppressed.* London: Burns & Oates.

Fryer, D., Duckett, P. and Pratt, R. (2004) 'Critical community psychology: what, why and how?' *Clinical Psychology Forum, 38,* 39–43.

Gillies, V. (2013) 'Personalising Poverty: Parental Determinism and the Big Society Agenda.' In W. Atkinson, S. Roberts and M. Savage (eds) *Class Inequality in Austerity Britain.* London: Palgrave Macmillan.

Glasgow Centre for Population Health (2011) *Concepts Series 9 – Asset Based Approaches for Health Improvement.* Glasgow: GCPH.

Hagell, A. (2002) *The Mental Health of Young Offenders: Bright Futures – Working with Vulnerable Young People.* London: Mental Health Foundation.

Harper, D. (2017) 'The promise (and potential pitfalls) of a public health approach in clinical psychology.' *Clinical Psychology Forum, 297,* 23–32.

Holland, S. (1992) 'From Social Abuse to Social Action: A Neighbourhood Psychotherapy and Social Action Therapy for Women.' In P. Nicholson and J. Ussher (eds) *Gender Issues in Clinical Psychology.* London: Routledge.

Home Office, HM Government (2011) *Ending Gang and Youth Violence: A Cross-Government Report Including Further Evidence and Good Practice Case Studies.* London: HM Government.

Hutchings, M. (2015) *Exam Factories? The Impact of Accountability Measures on Children and Young People.* London: National Union of Teachers.

Johnstone, L. and Boyle, M. with Cromby, J., Dillon, J. *et al.* (2018) *The Power Threat Meaning Framework: Overview.* Leicester: British Psychological Society.

Joseph Rowntree Foundation (2007) *The Use and Impact of Dispersal Orders.* London: Joseph Rowntree Foundation.

Kagan, C. (2008) 'Broadening the boundaries of psychology through community psychology.' *Psychology Teaching Review, 14,* 2, 28–31.

Kagan, C. and Burton, M. (2001) *Critical Community Psychological Praxis for the 21st Century.* Manchester: IOD Research Group, Manchester Metropolitan University.

Kagan, C., Burton, M., Duckett, P., Lawthom, R. and Siddiquee, A. (2011) *Critical Community Psychology*. Chichester: Wiley.

Kee, Y. and Nam, C. (2016) 'Does Sense of Community Matter in Community Well-Being?' In Y. Kee, S.J. Lee and R. Phillips (eds) *Social Factors and Community Well-Being*. Cham: Springer.

Kerka, S. (2003) *Intergenerational Learning and Social Capital*. Columbus, OH: ERIC Clearinghouse on Adult Career and Vocational Education.

Khan, L., Saini, G., Augustine, A., Palmer, K., Johnson, M. and Donald, R. (2017) *Against the Odds. Evaluation of the Mind Birmingham Up My Street Programme*. London: Centre for Mental Health

Kinderman, P. (2014) *A Prescription for Psychiatry: Why We Need a Whole New Approach to Mental Health and Wellbeing*. London: Palgrave Macmillan.

Kramer, S., Seedat, M., Lazarus, S. and Suffla, S. (2011) 'A critical review of instruments assessing characteristics of community.' *South African Journal of Psychology, 41,* 4, 503–516.

Lammy, D. (2017) *The Lammy Review: An Independent Review into the Treatment of, and Outcomes for, Black, Asian and Minority Ethnic Individuals in the Criminal Justice System*. London: Ministry of Justice.

Lazarus, S., Naidoo, A.V., May, B., Williams, L., Demas, G. and Filander, F.J. (2014) 'Lessons learnt from a community-based participatory research project in a South African rural context.' *South African Journal of Psychology, 44,* 2, 149–161.

Marmot, M., Ryff, C.D., Bumpass, L.L., Shipley, M. and Marks, N.F. (1997) 'Social inequalities in health: next questions and converging evidence.' *Social Science & Medicine, 44,* 6, 901–910.

Melzer, D., Fryers, T., and Jenkins, R. (eds) (2004) *Social Inequalities and the Distribution of the Common Mental Disorders*. Hove and New York, NY: Psychology Press.

Milner, A., Hjelmeland, H., Arensman, E. and De Leo, D. (2013) 'Social and environmental factors and suicide mortality: a narrative review of over 200 articles.' *Sociology Mind, 3,* 137–148.

Milner, A., McClure, R. and De Leo, D. (2012) 'Socio-economic determinants of suicide: an ecological analysis of 35 countries.' *Social Psychiatry and Psychiatric Epidemiology, 47,* 1, 19–27.

Ministry of Justice (2010, 2011, 2012) *Compendium of Reoffending Statistics and Analysis*. London: Ministry of Justice.

Morsillo, J. and Prilleltensky, I. (2007) 'Social action with youth: interventions, evaluation, and psychopolitical validity.' *Journal of Community Psychology, 35,* 6, 725–740.

MQ (2015) *UK Mental Health Research Funding*. London: MQ.

Murali, V. and Oyebode, F. (2004) 'Poverty, social inequality and mental health.' *Advances in Psychiatric Treatment, 10,* 3, 216–224.

National Institute for Clinical Excellence (2016) *Community Engagement: Improving Health and Wellbeing and Reducing Health Inequalities*. London: NICE.

Nelson, G. and Prilleltensky, I. (2005) 'The Project of Community Psychology: Issues, Values and Tools for Liberation and Well-Being.' In G. Nelson and I. Prilletensky (eds) *Community Psychology: In Pursuit of Liberation and Well-Being*. London: Palgrave Macmillan.

Patterson, C.J., Kupersmidt, J.B. and Vaden, N.A. (1990) 'Income level, gender, ethnicity, and household composition as predictors of children's school-based competence.' *Child Development, 61,* 2, 485–494.

Prilleltensky, I. (2010) 'Child wellness and social inclusion: values for action.' *American Journal of Community Psychology, 46,* 1–2, 238–249.

Prilleltensky, I. (2012) 'Wellness as fairness.' *American Journal of Community Psychology, 49,* 1–21.

Prilleltensky, I., Nelson, G. and Peirson, L. (2001) 'The role of power and control in children's lives: an ecological analysis of pathways toward wellness, resilience and problems.' *Journal of Community & Applied Social Psychology, 11,* 2, 143–158.

Purdie, N., Dudgeon, P. and Walker, R. (2010) *Working Together: Aboriginal and Torres Strait Islander Mental Health and Wellbeing Principles and Practice.* Canberra: ACT.

Rappaport, J. (1977) *Community Psychology: Values, Research, and Action.* New York, NY: Harcourt School.

Repper, J. and Carter, T. (2011) 'A review of the literature on peer support in mental health services.' *Journal of Mental Health, 20,* 4, 392–411.

Ryan, W. (1971) *Blaming the Victim.* New York, NY: Vintage.

Scottish Community Development Centre (2011) *Community Resilience and Co-production: Getting to Grips with the Language: A Briefing Paper.* Glasgow: Scottish Community Development Centre.

Smail, D. (1994) 'Community psychology and politics.' *Journal of Community & Applied Social Psychology, 4,* 1, 3–10.

Stein, M. (2006) 'Research review: young people leaving care.' *Child & Family Social Work, 11,* 3, 273–279.

Stoddard, S.A. and Pierce, J. (2015) 'Promoting positive future expectations during adolescence: the role of assets.' *American Journal of Community Psychology, 56,* 3–4, 332–341.

Tarren-Sweeney, M. (2008) 'Retrospective and concurrent predictors of the mental health of children in care.' *Children and Youth Services Review, 30,* 1, 1–25.

Thompson, K., Tribe, R. and Zlotowitz, S. (2018) *Guidance for Psychologists Working with Communities.* Leicester: British Psychological Society.

United Nations Human Rights Council (2010) *Report of the Special Rapporteur on the Right of Everyone to the Enjoyment of the Highest Attainable Standard of Physical and Mental Health, Addendum: Mission to India,* 15 April 2010, A/HRC/14/20/Add.2. Available at: www.refworld.org/docid/4c0367cf2.html.

Velez, C.N., Johnson, J.I.M. and Cohen, P. (1989) 'A longitudinal analysis of selected risk factors for childhood psychopathology.' *Journal of the American Academy of Child & Adolescent Psychiatry, 28,* 6, 861–864.

Wilkinson, R. and Pickett, K. (2010) *The Spirit Level: Why Equality is Better for Everyone.* London: Penguin.

Wiseman, J. and Brasher, K. (2008) 'Community wellbeing in an unwell world: trends, challenges, and possibilities.' *Journal of Public Health Policy, 29,* 3, 353–366.

World Health Organization and Calouste Gulbenkian Foundation (2014) *Social Determinants of Mental Health.* Geneva: World Health Organization.

Youth Justice Working Group (2012) *Rules of Engagement: Changing the Heart of Youth Justice.* London: Centre for Social Justice.

Zlotowitz, S., Barker, C., Moloney, O. and Howard, C. (2016) 'Service users as the key to service change? The development of an innovative intervention for excluded young people.' *Child and Adolescent Mental Health, 21,* 2, 102–108.

Chapter 9

Brown, M. (2018) 'Tackling loneliness and isolation reduces health bill.' *Resurgence and Ecologist, 37,* March/April. Available at: www.resurgence.org/magazine/article5039-compassionate-community-project.html.

Casale, L., Zlotowitz, S. and Moloney, O. (2015) 'Working with Whole Communities: Delivering Community Psychology Approaches with Children, Young People and Families.' In J. Faulconbridge, D. Law and A. Laffan (eds) *What Good Looks Like in Psychological Services for Children, Young People and their Families. Child & Family Clinical Psychology Review No 3.* Leicester: The British Psychological Society.

Centre for Longitudinal Studies (2015) *Counting the True Cost of Childhood Psychological Problems in Adult Life.* London: Centre for Longitudinal Studies.

Chakrabortty, A. (2018, February) 'How one community beat the system, and rebuilt their shattered streets.' *The Guardian.* Available at: www.theguardian.com/commentisfree/2018/feb/14/community-liverpool-residents-granby.

Dallos, R. (2015) 'Don't blame the parents: is it possible to develop non-blaming models of parental causation of distress?' In C. Newnes (ed.) *Children in Society: Politics, Policies and Interventions.* Monmouth: PCCS Books.

Fatimilehin, I. (2007) 'Building bridges in Liverpool: delivering CAMHS to black and minority ethnic children and their families.' *Journal of Integrated Care, 15,* 3, 7–16.

Fatimilehin, I. and Hassan, A. (2013) 'Working with Black and Minority Ethnic Children and their Families.' In P. Graham and S. Reynolds (eds) *Cognitive Behaviour Therapy for Children and Families.* Cambridge: Cambridge University Press.

Fatimilehin, I. and Hunt, K. (2013) 'Psychometric assessment across cultures.' *Assessment & Development Matters, 5,* 3, 21–23.

Faulconbridge, J., Gravestock, F., Laffan, A., Law, D. *et al.* (2016) 'What good could look like in integrated psychological services for children, young people and their families: preliminary guidance and examples of practice.' *Child & Family Clinical Psychology Review No 4.* Leicester: The British Psychological Society.

Fernando, S. and Keating, F. (eds) (2009) *Mental Health in a Multi-Ethnic Society: A Multidisciplinary Handbook* (2nd ed.). London: Routledge.

Gilbert, P. (2009) *The Compassionate Mind: A New Approach to the Challenges of Life.* London: Constable & Robinson.

Hedd Jones, C. (2017) 'Combining daycare for children and elderly people benefits all generations.' Available at: http://theconversation.com/combining-daycare-for-children-and-elderly-people-benefits-all-generations-70724.

Kanner, L. and Eisenberg, L. (1956) 'Early infantile autism 1943–1955.' *American Journal of Orthopsychiatry, 26,* 3, 556–566.

McDaniel, S.H. and deGruy, F.V. III (2014) 'An introduction to primary care and psychology.' *American Psychologist, 69,* 4, 325–331.

McDaniel, S.H., Doherty, W.J. and Hepworth, J. (2014) *Medical Family Therapy and Integrated Care* (2nd ed.). Washington, DC: American Psychological Society.

Mind (2016) *Mental Health in Primary Care: A Briefing for Clinical Commissioning Groups.* London: Mind.

Orford, J. (1992) *Community Psychology: Theory and Practice.* Chichester: Wiley & Sons.

Taylor, C. (2016) *Review of the Youth Justice System in England and Wales.* London: Ministry of Justice.

Trowell, H.C. and Burkitt, D.P. (eds) (1981) *Western Diseases: Their emergence and prevention.* London: Edward Arnold.

Subject index

Author index